THE
GREATEST
CRUSADE

ALSO BY RICHARD HOUGH

Edwina: Countess Mountbatten of Burma
The Great War at Sea, 1914–1918
Buller's Dreadnought
Mountbatten
Buller's Guns
Wings of Fictory
The Fight of the Few
Wings Against the Sky
Man O' War
The Last Voyage of Captain Cook
The Great Admirals
One Boy's War
Advice to My Granddaughter (ed.)
The Mountbattens
Captain Bligh and Mr. Christian
The Blind Horn's Fate
Fighting Ships
Admiral of the Fleet
The Long Pursuit
The Great Dreadnought
Dreadnought
Death of the Battleship
The Potemkin Mutiny
Admirals in Collision
The Fleet That Had to Die

THE
GREATEST
CRUSADE

Roosevelt, Churchill, and the Naval Wars

by
RICHARD HOUGH

William Morrow and Company, Inc.
New York

Library of Congress Cataloging-in-Publication Data

Hough, Richard Alexander, 1922–
The greatest crusade.

Bibliography: p.
Includes index.
1. World War, 1939–1945—Naval operations,
British. 2. World War, 1939–1945—Naval operations,
American. 3. Roosevelt, Franklin D. (Franklin Delano),
1882–1945. 4. Churchill, Winston, Sir, 1874–1965.
I. Title.
D771.H73   1986   940.54′5   85-15442
ISBN 0-688-04309-7

Printed in the United States of America

First Edition

1 2 3 4 5 6 7 8 9 10

BOOK DESIGN BY JAMES UDELL

Preface

"They were in a way, an odd couple," Arthur Schlesinger, Jr., has written; and has speculated, "Would the two men ever have been passionate friends had they not been President and Prime Minister? . . . They were indeed very different men." But they also had much in common, the same determination to smash the most evil tyranny of modern times, the same strength of political ambition, and the same deep-seated need to make their mark on history. Both men were ready to work together and to chip away cheerfully at any rough edges that obstructed the dovetailing in their personal compatability and the transatlantic bridge.

Mutual survival was at stake in the end, and that combined with a hatred of the enemy that glowed as brightly in the White House as in 10 Downing Street did the trick—was certain to do the trick from the moment Adolf Hitler sent his panzers rumbling into Poland and the military rulers of Japan gave their admirals the green light to attack American naval power.

It is easy enough today to recognize the inevitability of Allied victory in the Second World War, and Churchill for one had no doubt of the outcome from the moment he heard, through a faint alcoholic haze at the end of dinner, that Japanese planes were bombing Pearl Harbor. But there were many bleak and dangerous months ahead and there was acrimony at many levels of command before Churchill greeted once more a sick Roosevelt at Malta in February 1945. Then they flew off to talk with Stalin about the final phases of the war, the delicate subject of spheres of influence and occupation in postwar Europe, and the imminent atom bomb.

In no area of warfare was the going more difficult and dangerous than in the operations at sea, where for eighteen months after Pearl Harbor, and for every day and week before that day of salvation as well as infamy, the war seemed as if it could be lost by strangulation of supplies and trade.

As former naval persons, Roosevelt as Assistant Secretary of the Navy in the First World War and Churchill twice as First Lord of the Admiralty, the two war leaders enjoyed a special affection for and interest in their navies. The war at sea was a common base, a medium in which they spoke the same language and possessed a mutual understanding that would have seen them happily through even if they had not shared so much else, not least a similar patrician background.

This book, then, is an account of the lives in naval terms of two of the most remarkable and powerful men of this century who came together in a massive cause, which they tackled with zest and joyous authority. Their mutual affection and admiration were so evident that they were, in the eyes of those close to them, something to behold.

They may have been "indeed very different men." Their humor, their styles, their relations with their colleagues, their daily timetables of work, their attitudes to women, to the past, to drink, and much else—all these may have been as different as the time spans and histories of their countries, but their heartbeats were in tempo and so was their certain conviction that nothing could save Western civilization and Western democracy if the war at sea was lost.

This theme is one that I have discussed over many years with fellow naval historians and many officers who served at sea in the Second World War, and some in the First World War. Of them all I would like to single out for grateful acknowledgment Lieutenant Commander Peter Kemp, whose contribution and tangible help is evident throughout; Admiral Sir Guy Grantham, Captain John Litchfield, the late Captain Stephen Roskill, the late Professor Arthur Marder, Martin Gilbert, Sir Clifford Jarrett, and the late Sir John Lang, who have seen so much of the inside of the Admiralty; and many more of the "silent service." In America the Historical Department of the Department of the Navy and the archivists and staff of the Franklin D. Roosevelt Library at Hyde Park, New York, have been particularly helpful, and I am most grateful to them.

RICHARD HOUGH

CONTENTS

THE FISHING PARTY

On August 4, 1941, the battleship *Prince of Wales*, still carrying the scars of her recent fight with the German battleship *Bismarck*, steamed out of the bleak Orkney anchorage of Scapa Flow into the mist of the North Atlantic. Unlike her departure in May, her errand was a peaceful one. There were 14-inch and 5.5-inch shells in the ship's magazines, but there were also rare prime beef, grouse, caviar, champagne, and brandy in the galley's stores. There were other refinements for the satisfaction of the battleship's principal passenger, including a number of full-length feature films for showing after dinner in the wardroom. One of them was *That Hamilton Woman*, starring Laurence Olivier and his wife Vivien Leigh.

It was twenty-seven years to the day since this passenger, now the Prime Minister of Britain, had sent out the message to every ship of the Royal Navy: "Commence hostilities against Germany." As the Prime Minister signaled the President of the United States, reminding him of the anniversary, "We must make a good job of it this time. Twice ought to be enough."

And now this Second World War had been waged against the same adversary for almost two years, with Britain and the British Empire and Commonwealth, along with a few thousand men who had escaped from overrun European nations, fighting for much of the time alone against the fascist dictatorships of Germany and Italy.

The British people had been told nothing of this trip. A special train had steamed out of Marylebone Station in London at noon the previous day with the chiefs of staff and their staffs and many others of the hierarchy of government and the war machine on board. An hour later the train stopped briefly at a small station where the Prime Minister awaited it. Winston Churchill was wearing a blue suit and a yachting cap as if heading for Cowes regatta and he was, as always, smoking a large cigar. He smiled and waved to the crowd on the opposite platform, stepped into the train, and almost at once settled down to a substantial lunch of tomato soup, sirloin of beef, raspberry tart, and currant tart, washed down with champagne. He was in a jovial mood of youthful excitement for the adventure that lay ahead, an expedition that contained all the ingredients he relished—a secret journey, a historic first meeting at a secret rendezvous with Roosevelt, another man of supreme power and authority with whom he had struck up a close friendship by letter, telegram, and telephone. In addition, a sight at least of the North American continent, which he loved, and all this with a generous dose of danger.

And now, as the *Prince of Wales* rose and fell with ponderous dignity on the swell, Churchill emerged to take a turn on the quarterdeck, pausing to be introduced to two writers who were part of the Prime Minister's entourage, Howard Spring and H. V. Morton. "I hope we shall have an interesting and enjoyable voyage," he said with the faint lisp familiar to the whole civilized world through his recent broadcasts. Then after a brief pause and change of voice: "And one not entirely without profit."

The voyage was never without interest but was not always enjoyable, even for the Prime Minister, who evacuated himself from his admiral's quarters in the middle of a night storm and settled himself down in the admiral's sea cabin on the bridge instead. The destroyer escort could not maintain station in this storm and the battleship proceeded on its own high speed as the best defense against U-boat attack. But there were calmer days later. Churchill conducted his affairs of state, sent and received numerous messages, talked, read one of C. S. Forester's Hornblower books with great enjoyment, and attended a film show every night—his favorite form of relaxation.

The films were a mixed lot, Laurel and Hardy in the unfortunately titled *Saps at Sea* ("a gay but inconsequent entertainment" was the Prime Minister's comment), Paulette Goddard in *The Ghost Breakers,* and *That Hamilton Woman,* which he had already seen four times but which made him cry again when Nelson, dying, begged his old friend and captain, "Kiss me, Hardy." When the lights went up Churchill stood, turned, and addressed the audience in solemn tones. "I thought this would interest you, gentlemen," he said in reference to the *Bismarck* fight, "who have been recently engaged with the enemy in matters of equal importance. Good night!"

Another pastime for the Prime Minister was playing backgammon with Harry Hopkins. Hopkins, aide, close friend, and confidant of President Roosevelt, had been in London and subsequently in Moscow to discuss with Stalin how best the United States could help Russia with war matériel. Churchill had taken this frail-looking, shrewd, and kindly American to his heart. Hopkins had arrived by bomber from Russia in time to join the *Prince of Wales* for this crossing, and he provided welcome company for Churchill. H. V. Morton had first seen him "standing in the shadow of a gun turret, holding a soft felt hat on his head, a loose American overcoat of brown tweed blowing about him." He was, wrote Morton, "a thin man of extraordinary pallor and fragility. He looked as I have seen men look when they come out of a nursing home." Moscow had caused him to need a nursing home. "Harry returned dead-beat from Russia," Churchill signaled Roosevelt.

Hopkins fancied himself as a backgammon player and, it appears, usually beat Churchill. "The Prime Minister's backgammon game is not of the best," Hopkins wrote. "He likes to play what is known to all backgammon addicts as a 'back game.' As a matter of fact, he won two or three very exciting games from me by these tactics. He approaches the game with great zest, doubling and redoubling freely."

Destroyers from Iceland rendezvoused with the battleship on August 6 and provided a renewed escort for the remainder of the voyage, which offered no greater excitement than the showing of more films, *High Sierra* and *The Devil and Miss Jones,* which Alexander Cadogan from the Foreign Office described respectively as "bad" and "awful bunk." On the last day at sea there was a full-scale rehearsal of the reception for President Roosevelt, with Churchill in the leading role.

At dawn on August 9, a cold gray day with a calm sea, Churchill emerged onto the admiral's bridge, dressed in his siren suit, his first cigar of the day alight. Only a scattering of sailors on watch were up, besides the eager Morton, who was to report this occasion. Churchill was looking for the first sight of the American escort that was to lead them into their anchorage; "his sandy hair still ruffled from the pillow, he stood watching the sea that stretched to the New World."

The American destroyers came into sight at 7:30 A.M. and

Churchill, now in his uniform of warden of the Cinque Ports, stood at the salute as they passed by on either quarter, and then led the battleship, full war paint in striking contrast with the shining American men-of-war, towards land.

The anchorage chosen for this historic meeting was Placentia Bay, the southern of two deep bays that almost cut off the southeastern tip of Newfoundland. Placentia, the finest anchorage on the eastern coast of North America, is ninety miles deep and fifty-five miles wide at its entrance. "This is all an iron-bound coast—cliffs against which the ocean swells perpetually dash, and with many harbor openings," Samuel Eliot Morison has described it. "The scenery is very fine," Baedeker declares. Many of the *Prince of Wales*'s company compared it with the anchorage of Scapa Flow, which they had left the previous Sunday, but Placentia is grander in scale and the forests rising above the indented shoreline offer a softer scene than the shoreline of Hoy or South Ronaldsay. Lieutenant James Cook, soon to open up the Pacific Ocean, served part of his navigating apprenticeship along this southern shore of Newfoundland as master of the *Northumberland* in 1762. He moored this ship at the entrance for a week, and later his "Draughts and Observations," according to Rear Admiral Lord Colville, were proof of "Mr Cook's Genius and Capacity."

The battleship rounded the five-hundred-foot-high Cape St. Mary which John Cabot had first noted in 1497. Now, almost five hundred years later, "as the battleship steamed towards that wide inland sea perhaps no more eager voyagers have ever gazed towards the shores of Newfoundland than those who stood together on the morning of Saturday, August the ninth upon the bridge of the *Prince of Wales*." It was a sight to move the heart of anyone who witnessed it, this powerful detachment of peacetime warships of the New World. With flags flying and bands playing, they greeted this single great battleship, camouflaged and rust streaked from hawsepipe and bow flare, carrying the man who, more than any other, had defied the tyranny of Nazism.

One American has written, "As the sun burned through the morning fog, the mist broke, revealing a hill-rimmed harbor filled with United States ships of all sizes, their decks lined with seamen that were cheering and bands that were playing. Slowly and majestically the *Prince of Wales*, its band playing and a marine detachment standing at present arms, moved to its anchorage."

THE FISHING PARTY

The cable ran out on the *Prince of Wales*'s forecastle, the one note on the bugle—the G—rang out mournfully, the booms swung out, gangways went down, and the Union Jack was hoisted at the bows. Churchill and his party prepared to disembark. A message for King George VI was dispatched to London: "I have arrived safely and am visiting the President this morning."

During the summer of 1941, as the German armies marched into Russia on a massive front, it had become increasingly evident both in London and in Washington that the two Western leaders must meet. The exchange of messages between Roosevelt and Churchill, becoming ever longer and more frequent, as well as the exchange of officials and emissaries—Harry Hopkins was one of many—provided a stout link, and the flying-boat service across the Atlantic had led to a relatively swift passage for these officials. But Churchill especially was longing for the opportunity to talk personally with the President, and Roosevelt increasingly accepted the need for a long tête-à-tête. In the end, like a woman who proposes marriage, it was Roosevelt who suggested the meeting; and the ardent suitor leaped at the idea. Harry Hopkins put it more celestially: "You'd have thought," he wrote of Churchill during the voyage, "he was being carried up into the heavens to meet God."

Once the date and place of their meeting had been decided, it was agreed by both leaders that security must be total. For Roosevelt, it would have been politically damaging for the newspapers to learn beforehand that the President was off on a "war parley." United States neutrality was delicately poised, and any hint that the President was frog-marching the American people into another European war, however circuitously, must be highly damaging. As for Churchill, whose appreciation of the value of tight security went back to the First World War, he took every precaution to ensure that his whereabouts and his mission remained concealed for as long as possible, for safety rather than political reasons. The North Atlantic was thick with U-boats—a wall chart in the *Prince of Wales* daily noted the position, as far as it was known, of each one—and here was a torpedo's target like none other.

Security was tight, the mythmakers were busy, in Washington. The White House let it be known that the President would shortly embark on the little white presidential yacht, the 370-ton *Potomac,* for a summer fishing trip. *Time* magazine had it all pat for its readers:

> Franklin Roosevelt . . . glanced at his cluttered desk. There was the same old optimistic cast in his eye. It was still possible to hope, in spite of all, that the U.S. would not have to get into a shooting war. The President was still hopeful. . . . The heat was melting the tar on Massachusetts Avenue. Mr. Roosevelt patted his moist forehead. . . . Then he fled from the White House, fled from Washington. A week or ten days on the yacht *Potomac* out on salt water would be fine, and, so far as he could see, it was a good time to take a vacation.

Roosevelt embarked at New London, Connecticut, at 7 P.M. on August 2, one day before Churchill left London, to "cruise away from all newspapermen & photographers & I hope to be gone ten days," he told his mother. Among those he had with him were General Edwin M. "Pa" Watson, his military aide-de-camp; Ross McIntyre, his physician; and his naval aide-de-camp, Captain John R. Beardall. Out of sight of land off Martha's Vineyard, Roosevelt and his party transferred to the heavy cruiser *Augusta.* The *Potomac* then continued her shadow fishing trip, passing through the Cape Cod Canal with four figures impersonating Roosevelt and his party on the afterdeck, and later dispatching telegrams *en clair* reporting their catches—"Watson got the big fish today. . . ."

On August 6 the U.S. Navy Department made public a message: "Cruise ship proceeding slowly along coast with party fishing. Weather fair, sea smooth. Potomac River sailors responding to New England air after Washington summer."

The two leaders could not hope to stem all curiosity about their absence, and speculation began to grow rapidly. Why was Churchill not at the christening ceremony of his godson as expected? On August 7 the *Augusta*'s newspaper, the *Morning Press,* aroused amusement among the sailors with this report: "Mystery still surrounded the absence from London of Prime Minister Churchill as neither London nor Washington officials denied that he had left to fly across the Atlantic for a rendezvous with President Roosevelt."

THE FISHING PARTY

It may have been inspired guesswork, intelligent speculation, or the result of a leak. But even before the two men met, a midwestern American newspaper printed the story that the President and Prime Minister were about to meet somewhere at sea, a Swiss radio station broadcast the same message, and the Japanese ambassador in Washington cabled Tokyo that the meeting was about to take place. In London the Foreign Secretary, Anthony Eden, learned that the cat was out of the bag and suggested to John G. Winant, American ambassador, that a statement be made in Parliament, without mentioning time or place. Winant passed on the proposal to Roosevelt, who emphatically opposed any such thing. Later, Roosevelt learned that, contrary to the agreement that neither side should bring any members of the press, Churchill had brought two writers, Morton and Spring, masquerading as Ministry of Information officers. This was a misinterpretation of the role to be played by the two writers, whose function was purely historical, but the damage had been done. Fearing the outcry from American reporters, Morton and Spring were excluded from all U.S. men-of-war. All this did no lasting damage, and Roosevelt determined to make no reference to upset a meeting to which he was looking forward as keenly as Churchill, with whom he shared a fellow feeling for the great historic occasion.

Escorted by destroyers, the *Augusta* entered Placentia Bay on August 8 and anchored close to the battleship *Arkansas.* There was much naval activity in the anchorage unconnected with the imminent visit. At the small town of Argentia the U.S. Navy was swiftly building the facilities for a full-scale naval base on land recently granted to it by Britain.

The mist had cleared and the morning of August 9 was turning bright as Roosevelt came up on deck helped by his son Elliott, and waited under an awning rigged up midships. The President was wearing a tan Palm Beach suit, without hat, and for all his fine tall figure and familiar features might from a distance have been mistaken for a disabled and elderly tourist at that Florida resort. He watched the admiral's barge carrying the Prime Minister and his party swing away from the gangway of the battleship, which dwarfed all the American men-of-war, and cut through the calm water separating the two ships. The side of the *Augusta*'s hull

17

obstructed Roosevelt's view of Churchill momentarily, the marines' band striking up "God Save the King" indicating that the Prime Minister had stepped onto the gangway and was making his way up the steps. "The Star-Spangled Banner" followed the British anthem, the last notes died; Churchill stepped forward with a letter in his hand, bowed almost imperceptibly, smiled, and handed the taller man the sealed envelope. It was a letter from the King.*

The proceedings began with a small awkwardness that, like the security episode, irritated the President. Churchill remarked on how happy he was to meet at last the man with whom he had corresponded and talked on the transatlantic telephone so often. Roosevelt told him in reply that indeed they had met before, in the summer of 1918 on a day when he had also met the King's father, George V. It was at dinner at Gray's Inn and Roosevelt as Assistant Secretary of the Navy had made a speech that Churchill, as a member of the British War Cabinet, had listened to. Churchill covered up the gaffe skillfully but it was clear that he did not remember the occasion. Later, however, in his war memoirs he wrote warmly of Roosevelt at this first meeting at the close of another war, before Roosevelt was struck down with polio and Churchill had suffered his many years in the political wilderness. Roosevelt, for his part, it became clear later, made no reference to the 1918 meeting in his extensive diaries and letters at that time. It might never have happened.

Churchill was now taken on a brief tour of the American cruiser and rejoined Roosevelt and his party in the *Augusta*'s wardroom, where, thankfully, the U.S. Navy's alcohol prohibition was lifted for the preliminaries but not for the disappointing fork lunch that followed for all but the two chiefs. The British and American officials mingled and then paired off, American Undersecretary of State Sumner Welles with Cadogan; General George C. Marshall, Chief of Staff of the Army, with General Sir John Dill; Admiral Harold Stark, Chief of Naval Operations, with Admiral Sir Dudley Pound; and General Henry Arnold, Deputy Chief of Air Staff, with Air Chief Marshal Sir Wilfrid Freeman.

* See Appendix A.

THE FISHING PARTY

Roosevelt and Churchill had lunch (*not* dry), at which they spoke freely and easily, rapidly getting to know one another. W. Averell Harriman, Roosevelt's "special representative," wrote of Churchill being "in his best form"; and "the President liked him enormously." So all Churchill's anxieties, expressed earlier to Hopkins—"I wonder if he will like me"—were laid to rest.

While the staff talks continued, on subjects from high strategy to some of the more mundane aspects of waging a war in which only one partner was yet fighting, the Churchill-Roosevelt relationship rapidly flowered. Both men had guided their navies through difficult times, loved to talk naval history and naval affairs generally, and now discussed, like old shipmates, the present difficulties in the North Atlantic, where U-boats were again proving so destructive and the U.S. Navy was already becoming more deeply involved in the Battle of the Atlantic. And what more appropriately nautical venue could these two sailor-statesmen have than a fine eight-inch-gunned heavy cruiser and the battleship that had first damaged the mighty *Bismarck* before she was soon hounded down to her destruction?

Churchill returned to the *Augusta* to dine on that first evening together, a lengthy and bonhomous occasion, at which Prime Minister and President as well as the British chiefs of staff made speeches. They ate vegetable soup, broiled chicken, spinach omelet, lettuce and tomato salad, and chocolate ice cream. Later, conversation deviated from the war and high policy, and, according to Cadogan, who was sitting on his left, Roosevelt "conversed charmingly about his country estate at Hyde Park, where he hoped to grow Christmas trees for the market."

But Churchill did most of the informal talking and the rest of the company were content to listen. "Winston Churchill held every one of us that night—and was conscious every second of the time he was holding us," Elliott Roosevelt recalled later. "All that Father did was to throw in an occasional question—just drawing him on, drawing him out. . . . Churchill rared back in his chair, he slewed his cigar around from cheek to cheek and always at a jaunty angle, he hunched his shoulders forward like a bull, his hands slashed the air expressively, his eyes flashed. He held the floor that evening. . . ."

The emotional culmination of the Newfoundland meeting

was the combined service on Sunday, August 10, on the quarter-deck of the *Prince of Wales*. It was the sort of occasion that Churchill relished and for which he prepared with loving attention, including the choice of the hymns, "Onward, Christian Soldiers," "O God, Our Help in Ages Past," and the sailors' hymn, "Eternal Father, Strong to Save."

To transport the crippled President from the *Augusta* to the *Prince of Wales* with the least inconvenience required a complex process, with the destroyer *McDougal* coming alongside the cruiser's main deck on the same level as the destroyer's bow. The *McDougal* then steamed across to the *Prince of Wales* and made a Chinese landing—bow to stern—on the battleship, again on the same level. Morison described how "the British crew were drawn up at attention along the rail, Mr. Churchill alone being on the fantail to receive the President. A chief boatswain's mate of *McDougal* hailed the Premier with 'Hey! Will you take a line?' Mr. Churchill replied 'Certainly!' and not only caught the line but hauled it most of the way in before British tars came to his assistance."

Roosevelt arrived on board dressed in a dark suit with an ivory-handled stick, leaning heavily on the arm of his son Elliott, and took his seat next to Churchill facing the four 14-inch guns of Y turret. The congregation, half American and half British, mixed freely and were given only 250 hymnbooks for the 500 persons in attendance, so that all had to share.

The lesson was from the first chapter of Joshua: "There shall not any man be able to stand before thee all the days of thy life: as I was with Moses, so will I be with thee: I will not fail thee, nor forsake thee. Be strong and of a good courage. . . ." The first prayer was for the President: "O Lord, High and Mighty, Ruler of the Universe, look with favor, we beseech thee, upon the President of the United States of America and all others in authority. . . ." Prayers followed for the King and his ministers and admirals, generals, and air marshals; prayers for the invaded countries, the wounded, the prisoners, the sick and exiled, the homeless, the anxious, the bereaved; a prayer that "we may be preserved from hatred, bitterness, and all spirit of revenge."

No one was more moved than Churchill himself. "This service," he wrote, "was felt by us all to be a deeply moving expression of the unity of faith of our two peoples, and none who took part in it will forget the spectacle presented that sunlit morning on the crowded quarterdeck—the symbolism of the Union Jack and the Stars and Stripes draped side by side on the pulpit; the American and British chaplains sharing in the reading of the prayers . . .''

Roosevelt wanted to see as much as possible of the battleship and her company. He "was having a fine time," wrote Robert E. Sherwood, playwright and presidential speech writer, "and so was the Former Naval Person [the term used by Churchill in mock code to identify himself]. Here, on the decks of a mighty battleship, these two old seafaring men were on common ground."

The diplomatic culmination of this meeting lay in the signature of a joint Anglo-American declaration of principles. "President Roosevelt told me at one of our first conversations that he thought it would be well if we could draw up a joint declaration laying down certain broad principles which should guide our policies along the same road," Churchill wrote later. On the issue of United States entry into the war, it was evident from the first that Churchill would get nowhere, as he had been warned by Hopkins on the voyage over. But the joint signature of a document of the kind proposed by Roosevelt, powerfully worded for all the world to read, could clearly have an enormous moral effect and proclaim clearly how close were the two Western nations.

Churchill took on the task of drawing up "the substance and spirit" of what was to be called the Atlantic Charter;* and with encouraging ease and speed the two leaders, with a little compromise on both sides, agreed a draft to put up to their governments. It was, in essence, an idealistic proclamation of freedom and peace at a time when half the world was enslaved at war, committing the two nations to "seek no aggrandisement," and "no territorial changes" without the express wishes of the people; to respect the right of all to choose their own form of government; to strive to bring about greater equality of production in the world; and to seek a peace "which will cast down for ever the Nazi tyranny."

Roosevelt added two further clauses, committing the two nations to establish peace for all on the high seas and oceans, and to

* See Appendix B.

use every endeavor to further peace in the world and abandon the use of force.

This Atlantic Charter, it was agreed between Prime Minister and President, should be proclaimed simultaneously to the world on August 14, together with a statement that they had held conversations at sea, along with members of their respective staffs, who had worked out details of the aid to be granted under the Lend-Lease Act; but, striking a cautious political note for the sake of the Americans, there was no reference to naval or military commitments of any kind "other than as authorised by Act of Congress."

Churchill and Roosevelt left well satisfied with the meeting, both leaders feeling that future communication must benefit from the intimacy of their long talks. Just as Hopkins from his visit to Stalin had brought into focus the needs and plight of the Russians facing the onslaught of Germany from the west, so Churchill had succeeded in itemizing realistically and graphically the needs of Britain. For his part, Churchill recognized more clearly the political problems Roosevelt had to face while governing a nation that had unbounded sympathy and admiration for the British people but was still hard in its opposition to direct involvement.

American newsmen, who had been waiting at Swampscott, Massachusetts, for the return of the President from his fishing trip for almost two weeks, were furious at being misled and hoodwinked and upstaged by the British "newsmen" when they had been muzzled. They were advised to move to Rockland, Maine; and there, after two further days of waiting, they got their story. At Penobscot Bay, at 3 P.M. on August 15, 1941, the mist cleared and the blue-gray hull of the *Potomac* came into sight, escorted by a Coast Guard cutter. A few minutes later Roosevelt gave them the news of the meeting and the signature of the Atlantic Charter. He did not say where but *Time* magazine guessed correctly that it had been Placentia Bay. "President Roosevelt was back from the most momentous journey of all his 200,000 miles of White House travel." And *The New York Times,* recalling the German Deputy Führer's recent sensational flight to Britain, commented, "Franklin Roosevelt and Winston Churchill, no men to let a beetle-browed Nazi named Hess run off with the title of Mystery Man of

THE FISHING PARTY

World War Two, last week presented the world with the deepest, juiciest, most momentous mystery since the war began."

The *Prince of Wales* sailed out of Placentia Bay at 5 P.M. on August 12, the ship's company suddenly rich in the little luxuries that had for long been scarce or unobtainable in Britain—chocolate and razor blades, canned food, stockings for their wives and girls, glossy magazines. The presence of American destroyers as escort as far as Iceland—one of them with the President's son Franklin D. Roosevelt, Jr., serving on board—emphasized on the one hand the newly reinforced accord between the two nations, and the dangers that lay ahead on the return crossing of the Atlantic. They were back at war. This was reemphasized on the following morning when the voice of the battleship's captain, John Leach, blared out from every loudspeaker throughout the ship. The captain told the ship's company, and the passengers, that the historic meeting had become known in Germany, and that it was also known there that it had taken place off Newfoundland. U-boat attack, therefore, was likely, and there might also be attack from the air when nearer to Britain. "If ever there was a time when the utmost vigilance is required, it is upon this voyage," Captain Leach concluded.

The journey home was completed safely. But within fifteen weeks, the *Prince of Wales* had been sent to the bottom of the South China Sea. Captain Leach was drowned and some three hundred officers and men perished with him. When Churchill had been asked in the battleship's gun room if the Japanese were likely to come into the war, he had replied, "No, I don't think so." No loss at sea saddened Churchill more than this.

The U.S.S. *Augusta* had a longer war, escorting convoys to Murmansk and bombarding the D-Day beaches in June 1944. Churchill saw more of her proud silhouette when she escorted the *Queen Mary,* in which he was a passenger, to New York. And in her final exalted role the cruiser carried another President, Harry Truman, on a more extended "fishing trip" to and from the Potsdam Conference in 1945.

ONE

Kitchener
the Blackguard

The meeting at Placentia Bay in August 1941 marked the beginning of a relationship unlike any other in history between two great leaders. It was on the one hand a wartime collaboration with mutual aims and close military cooperation, on the other hand a friendship that was to oil the wheels of alliance, making it predominantly a cordial business. This in turn brought mutual friendliness into the proceedings of most of the chiefs of staff and their underlings in both wartime governments. And this led to a war-winning formula that could not fail.

Friendship was sustaining and bred efficiency, brought the war to an end sooner, and saved unnumbered lives. What more could be asked of allies fighting the greatest evil of modern times? And imagine what it would have been like if either Churchill or Roosevelt had been another Charles de Gaulle!

The first source of the cordiality these two men enjoyed stemmed from their patrician background and their inherited qualities of leadership. Then they also shared sparkling intelligence, political acumen, abiding ambition, a deep conviction in the justice of their cause, and the qualities of humor, tolerance, and judgment. They loved their work and shared the relish in fighting, at first with their backs to the wall, and then preparing and executing the offensives that brought victory.

THE GREATEST CRUSADE

The branch of war that they shared above all others was naval. Roosevelt and Churchill had given more of their political lives and experience to their navies than to the other services, Churchill from the age of thirty-seven as First Lord of the Admiralty, Roosevelt from the age of thirty-one as Assistant Secretary of the Navy. But the roads that had led them to high political naval responsibility were as widely separated as the British Home Fleet and the American Pacific Fleet, and their relationships and their political records with their navies were as different as their childhoods and early lives.

At the age of twenty-three and under fire for only the second time in his life, Churchill wrote to his mother that he was "more ambitious for a reputation for personal courage than for anything else in the world." And three weeks later he wrote to her again, as "a philosopher," that bullets were not worth considering. "Besides I am so conceited I do not believe the Gods would create so potent a being as myself for so prosaic an ending."

Churchill was approaching the high point of his military career—a young soldier destined later to impose as great an influence on the Royal Navy as any sailor, but at this age, glowing with the heat of limitless ambition, with no thought of war at sea. In the tradition of his great ancestor, the first duke of Marlborough (at Blenheim in 1704, then Ramillies, Oudenarde, and Malplaquet), it was the evolutions of great armies, the thunder of artillery, the rattle of musketry, and the pounding hooves of the cavalry that set the heart of this ardent lieutenant beating faster.

Fifteen years earlier, the young Winston had written from the ancestral home of Blenheim Palace to thank his mother for his eighth birthday present, "Soldiers and Flags and Castle they are so nice it was so kind of you . . ." The toy soldier army grew mightier at every Christmas and birthday until it numbered over fourteen hundred troops, just as the real-life Navy was to expand under his overall leadership when he grew up.

Churchill was fourteen when he joined the Army Class at Harrow, and from that time his education contained a strong element of the military to prepare him for Sandhurst. To the distress of his father, Lord Randolph, and mother he did not find it easy to qualify and "was relegated as a forlorn hope to a 'crammer.' "

At length all obstacles were overcome and he was accepted at the military college.

Winston's father, the second son of the seventh duke of Marlborough, was not a great credit to the noble family, for all his charm, spriteliness, and political courage when he was a young man. Profligate, like so many of his ancestors, he was also insensitive and utterly selfish. When he was twenty-four he met and instantly fell in love with an American woman, Jennie Jerome, at a royal reception and dance on board the frigate H.M.S. *Ariadne* at Cowes. Amongst the numerous beauties on this fashionable occasion, Jennie stood out as the ultimate beauty of them all. Lord Randolph Churchill, son of a great English duke: What more wonderful match could there be? "I must say I have been very happy all day," commented Mr. Leonard Jerome, her father, when he heard of the engagement. The duke was less certain and wanted the couple to wait for a year to consider "the unwisdom of your proceedings."

Jennie's father was a successful financier and stockbroker, a politician, a patron of the turf and of the arts. Jerome Park in New York City was built by him as a racetrack. He founded the American Jockey Club, suppported opera. His origins were Huguenot. Jennie was the second of four daughters by his wife, Clarissa. Randolph and Jennie were married in Paris on April 15, 1874. Their first child, a son, was born at Blenheim on November 30 in the same year, two months prematurely because the dashing Jennie refused to give up riding. He was christened Winston Leonard Spencer Churchill. Like many children of his social class and life style, Winston saw little of his mother and even less of his father, but he loved inordinately his beguiling, feckless, extravagant, and lively-minded mother and admired and loved equally his brilliant, intemperate, and undisciplined father.

In Parliament, Lord Randolph was regarded as one of the most promising young politicians of his day, "a great elemental force in British politics," but his career was as brief as the passage of a comet. With sensational speed he rose to be Chancellor of the Exchequer. His precipitateness led to a damaging social quarrel with the Prince of Wales, and politically to his resignation over the failure of the Army and the Navy to cut expenditure. The events surrounding the end of Lord Randolph's political career

touched on points of loyalty to a principle and what he judged
to be the disloyalty of his colleagues. His father's fall from grace
and office made a deep and lasting impression on his elder son. It
was, no less, the fall of his god. To Winston his father was right in
all things, good in all things, a brilliant orator, compassionate
towards the less privileged, at fault only in his failure to com-
prehend the wicked chicanery and treachery of his enemies.

The spur to right this great wrong, to rehabilitate the name of
Churchill in politics, to rise himself to the uttermost peaks, was
dug deep into the flanks of Winston's ambition when his father
died, a syphilitic wreck, in 1895. "There remained for me only to
pursue his aims and vindicate his memory," Churchill recalled
later. He was twenty years old; and on this January 24, seventy
years to the day before his own death, his military-political career
was released, like a long-distance runner at the starting line. It
was to be a dangerous and varied course that sometimes brought
him almost to his knees; but with his courage and ruthlessness, his
perceptive eye and judgment, the priceless combination of brains
and good luck, his sentimentality and patriotism, he could not fail
to become the greatest Briton of this century.

Churchill sailed for India with his regiment in the late summer of
1896. "Life out here is stupid dull & uninteresting," he complained to his mother, who appeared unwilling to use her influence to have him transferred to Egypt. There an expeditionary
force was being assembled to recover Khartoum and the Sudan
and avenge the death of General Charles Gordon at the hands of
the Dervishes and their leader, the Mahdi.

Churchill had been following this Egyptian river campaign
with envious fascination. In one letter to his mother (January 10,
1898) he wrote, "Oh how I wish I could work you up over Egypt!
I know you could do it with all your influence—and all the people
you know. It is a pushing age and we must shove with the
best. . . ."

In the event, Churchill succeeded in joining another punitive
expedition, to the North-West Frontier from which he sent back
dispatches to the *Daily Telegraph* in London describing skirmishes
with the tribesmen and his own brushes with death. Later he succeeded in finding a publisher for a book about the expedition.

KITCHENER THE BLACKGUARD

This was the first of his numerous books and he entitled it *The Story of the Malakand Field Force.*

The book attracted the attention of a number of people, including the Prime Minister, Lord Salisbury, who summoned him to his office when Churchill was on leave in London. The interview concluded with Salisbury making an offer: "If there is anything at any time that I can do which would be of assistance to you, pray do not fail to let me know." These were sweet words to Churchill's ears, and words that were soon acted upon.

"I am vy anxious to go to Egypt and to proceed to Khartoum with the Expedition . . ." Churchill wrote to Salisbury on July 18, 1898. Almost three years after he had visited the United States and observed the fighting in Cuba, his fortunes were about to change. From this time sword and pen together were to keep his name in the public eye, from which he never disappeared for long until a seat in Parliament launched him from battlefield to the cut-and-thrust of politics. On the way he was to acquire many admirers other than Lord Salisbury, and many enemies, none so damaging as one of the most famous soldiers of his day, General Sir Horatio Herbert Kitchener.

Years before Churchill's birth, Kitchener had been a fighting soldier about the world, most notably as a volunteer with the French against the Germans in the Franco-Prussian War. He later served in the Sudan campaign of 1882–85 and the expedition up the Nile intended to relieve the besieged General Gordon in Khartoum. Since 1892 he had been Commander in Chief ("Sirdar") of the Anglo-Egyptian Army and was now engaged in another long-drawn-out Sudan campaign. He was an austere, unmarried, devout man, unusually tall, with piercing eyes that did not invite debate, and a full moustache that was already becoming a national military insignia.

It was Churchill's faith in "shoving" as a boost to progress, his "scribbling" as a journalist and book writer, and his aristocratic lineage and the brash self-confidence this engendered, that led to the suspicion and distaste that the humbly born Kitchener felt for Churchill long before he met him.

Churchill was always quick to recognize an enemy and he knew that he had to overcome the opposition of this notable soldier before he could fulfill his immediate ambitions. . . . "Quite early in the process of making my arrangements to take part in the Sudan campaign, I became conscious of the unconcealed disapproval and hostility of the Sirdar of the Egyptian Army, Sir Herbert Kitchener," Churchill wrote of his early Army life. "My application to join that army, although favoured by the War Office, was refused, while several other officers of my service and rank were accepted. The enquiries which I made through various channels made it clear to me that the refusal came from the highest quarter."

But "shoving," together with the good luck that rarely forsook him, brought Churchill success nonetheless. A crack cavalry regiment, the 21st Lancers, was due to join Kitchener's expedition, and the death of a young officer created a vacancy that Churchill eagerly filled, making his own way to Alexandria, then up the Nile to Luxor. Before leaving England he had taken two important steps. The first, and more prosaic, was to secure a contract with the *Morning Post* to write dispatches; and second, he made a political speech at Bradford that was a brilliant success and attracted the interest and admiration of a number of influential politicians. As he had told Lord Salisbury, it was not his intention to make his career in the Army, and his political ambitions were now widely known.

These ambitions, and Churchill's intention of leaving the Army, were also known to Kitchener before he arrived, and were deplored. He was "only making a convenience of it," Kitchener commented bitterly. Churchill, for his part was now well aware of the hostility of the C in C. "Whatever his knowledge of war may be his acquaintance with truth is rudimentary," he wrote to his mother. "He may be a general—but never a gentleman."

In the last days of August 1898, Kitchener's Anglo-Egyptian Army of some twenty-six thousand mixed British, Egyptian, and Sudanese troops, supported by a vast supply train and numbers of Nile River gunboats, had arrived at a point twenty miles from Omdurman. They faced an army of sixty thousand well-armed and fanatical Dervishes, and an action, large in scale and decisive in its result, had become inevitable.

On his return from a reconnaissance, Churchill reported direct to Kitchener himself, the first meeting face to face between the twenty-three-year-old cavalry lieutenant and the famous forty-eight-year-old general. Churchill found Kitchener calm, prepared for any eventuality, indifferent as to whether Khalifa— the Mahdi's successor—attacked that day or the next. "The heavy moustaches, the queer rolling look of the eyes, the sunburnt and almost purple cheeks and jowl made a vivid manifestation upon the senses," Churchill wrote.

Another first meeting that Churchill was to remember for the rest of his life, and that was to lead later to a happier relationship, took place the day before the two armies clashed. Churchill and a brother officer were strolling in the heat beside the Nile awaiting the call to battle when they were hailed by a naval officer commanding one of the gunboats. "How are you off for drinks?" he asked. "We have got everything in the world on board here. Can you catch?"

A bottle of champagne was slung like a howitzer shell from the vessel, falling short of its target. Churchill waded in and retrieved it. The name of the benefactor, he learned, was David Beatty. Some forty-eight years later Churchill calculated that he had averaged half a bottle of champagne a day throughout his adult life. On this one day at least of campaigning in the desert, he was thus able to keep up his average.

The following day, September 2, 1898, the two great armies met, and the 21st Lancers were called upon to make a classic cavalry charge. Churchill relied on his Mauser pistol as his first weapon, and was thankful that he did so. "The charge . . . passed like a dream and some part I cannot quite recall," he wrote home to his mother. "The Dervishes showed no fear of cavalry and would not move unless you knocked them over with the horse. They tried to hamstring the horses, to cut the bridles—reins— slashed and stabbed in all directions and fired rifles at a few feet range. Nothing touched me. I destroyed those who molested me and so passed out without any disturbance of body or mind."

In spite of the reputation he was later to acquire as a belligerent man of war, Churchill learned during the few minutes of danger and exhilaration of this charge, and the aftermath of mourning for lost friends, "the shoddiness of war. . . . You cannot gild it," he told his mother. "The raw comes through." The blend of excitement and disgust that he experienced at Omdurman remained with him for long. A number more of his friends had been wounded. They were well cared for, unlike the Khalifa's wounded. Kitchener's orders to finish off the Dervish wounded as they lay on the desert disgusted Churchill and hardened his hatred of the general. "I shall merely say that the victory of Omdurman was disgraced by the inhuman slaughter of the wounded and that Kitchener was responsible for this," he wrote.

Churchill also spread the scandal of the desecration of the Mahdi's tomb and the treatment of his bones. As a gesture of vengeance for the Mahdi's murder of General Gordon in Khartoum, Kitchener entrusted Gordon's nephew, a major in his army, with the razing to the ground of the Mahdi's tomb and the casting into the river Nile of his bones. The fine large skull was, however, retained and presented to Kitchener as a trophy. This resulted in some rare ribaldry among Kitchener and his staff as they—including Kitchener himself—played with the skull and discussed what to do with it. Kitchener was reported to have unwisely suggested various uses for it, as his inkwell or drinking cup, or that it should be sent to the Royal College of Surgeons in London.

Churchill reported this first in his articles for the *Morning Post* and later and more damagingly in the book he wrote, *The River War*. "Being now free from military discipline, I was able to write what I thought about Lord Kitchener without fear, favour or affection," Churchill wrote of his second book. "And I certainly did so. I had been scandalized by his desecration of the Mahdi's tomb and the barbarous manner in which he had carried off the Mahdi's skull in a kerosene-can as a trophy."

In this book, which attracted a greal deal of attention, Churchill wrote of Kitchener that he "treated all men like machines—from the private soldiers whose salutes he disdained, to the superior officers he rigidly controlled. The comrade who had served with him and under him for many years in peace and peril was flung aside incontinently as soon as he ceased to be of use. . . . The stern and unpitying spirit of the commander was communicated to his troops, and the victories which marked the progress of the River War were accompanied by acts of barbarity not always justified even by the harsh customs of savage conflicts."

Churchill's next brush with Kitchener occurred in South Africa during the Boer War more than a year later. Churchill was now a war reporter for the *Daily Mail* in London after an initial failure to enter Parliament. He soon got on to the wrong side of the military hierarchy, including Field Marshal Lord Roberts, General Sir George White, and, of course, Kitchener himself. While Churchill became almost overnight a public hero for his capture, after displaying great gallantry, and his subsequent daring escape from the Boers, he was refused permission to rejoin the Army in order to see more of the fighting. He then made himself highly unpopular by writing in favor of treating the Boers generously after their rebellion had been put down.

In April 1902, now a Conservative member of Parliament, Churchill ensured Kitchener's enduring hatred, and the deep suspicions of his own party, by attacking the authorities for refusing to allow the editor of a South African newspaper to come to England for private reasons. This editor, A. P. Cartwright, had served a year in prison after being found guilty of seditious libel in publishing a statement that Kitchener had issued instructions to the troops not to take prisoners. Churchill accused the military authorities of incompetence for abusing their powers under military law, and the British government for violating the liberty of the subject.

Although Churchill did not come face to face with Kitchener again for more than ten years, his dislike of the general never cooled. "I always hated Kitchener," he told his friend Wilfrid Blunt in October 1910. "Kitchener behaved like a blackguard in that business [the Mahdi's head scandal]. He pretended to have sent the head back in a kerosene tin, but the tin may have contained anything, perhaps ham sandwiches. He kept the head, and has it still."* A year later, after Kitchener had been appointed as British agent, consul general, and minister plenipotentiary (euphemisms for ruler) to Egypt on July 16, 1911, by the Liberal government, Churchill wrote to Blunt, "I was glad to find from your letter . . . that my belonging to a government wicked enough to send Lord Kitchener to Egypt has not altered our relations."

To Churchill, Kitchener was war stripped of all honor and glory and the trappings of action, romance, and excitement, a denial of Churchill's strongly held conviction, "In war: resolution; in

* This was quite untrue.

33

defeat: defiance; in victory: magnanimity; in peace: goodwill."*

To Churchill, Kitchener was the unacceptable face of war making, an activity that dominated a great part of his life. War to Churchill was "a vile and wicked folly" that also sent his heart beating faster and found him, when it came, "interested, geared up & happy." Kitchener sullied the martial spirit and the figure of the soldier.

Kitchener remained like an unsponged stain, a beastly memory in the past, a threat for the future, as Churchill climbed the political ladder with consummate ease: Colonial Undersecretary in 1906, president of the Board of Trade in 1908, Home Secretary in 1910 . . .

During these years Churchill was to establish a relationship with another great service chief—an admiral of a strongly contrasting personality to Kitchener—who was to become a partner to Churchill in the great trial of strength that lay ahead. These three men, the politician, the soldier, and the sailor, were to figure in a trinity of mutual destruction.

In the year after Churchill became Home Secretary, a serious crisis developed with Germany, which appeared to be on the point of establishing a naval base on the Atlantic seaboard of Africa at Agadir. Later it was learned that the entire German High Seas Fleet had put to sea. And where was the British Fleet at this time when war might break out at any minute? It was scattered all over the place, and the First Sea Lord, the professional chief of the Navy, had gone shooting in Scotland. Churchill complained, "I cannot help feeling uncomfortable about the Admiralty. They are so cocksure, *insouciant* and apathetic." The result was that Churchill himself was appointed by the Prime Minister, Herbert Asquith, to replace the Minister responsible for the Navy, the First Lord of the Admiralty, Reginald McKenna. The stiff, arrogant McKenna was furious and never forgave Churchill, whom he suspected, with some justification, of plotting his downfall.

And so, with the engaging and youthful exuberance that the Prime Minister's daughter—and many others who knew him—

---

* "Moral of the Work," printed in Churchill's history of the Second World War.

found so attractive, Churchill sealed his career and ambition with the Royal Navy, a service that was to carry him to the heights of success and triumph and to the depths of failure.

The historian Arthur Marder has commented on Churchill at this time, "All the traits that were to win him global renown in World War II were clearly discernible before World War I: self-confidence, vivacity, inexhaustible vitality and power of work, courage, eloquence, temperament and a great brain.... He was aggressive and truculent in his official capacity, showing a disregard for the opinions and sensibilities of his opponents; but he was full of charm and tolerance and amiability in social intercourse."

Churchill's welcome at the Admiralty was not rapturous, nor was his appointment approved by the Conservative opposition in the House of Commons or the Conservative press. Many people thought he was brash, arrogant, unreliable, and a turncoat. His crossing of the floor from the Conservative to the Liberal side in the House of Commons was not forgotten after seven years, and was linked with his robust efforts to trim the naval estimates later. He was seen simplistically by many people as an unpatriotic small-navy man; and now here he was conning the dreadnoughts at a time of acute national danger.

The traditionalist admirals loathed him or at best were deeply suspicious of him. It was known to them all that he had been appointed to turn everything inside out and to create a naval war staff, towards which they were totally opposed. The *Spectator* considered it an appalling appointment. "He has not the loyalty, the dignity, the steadfastness, and the good sense which makes an efficient head of a great office. He must always be living in the limelight, and there is no fault more damning in an administrator."

Determined to be a "sailor's First Lord," contrary to the style of the deskbound McKenna, Churchill began cruising in the Admiralty yacht *Enchantress* soon after assuming office, steaming from one naval base to another on tours of inspection accompanied by his professional entourage and often with friends and relations on board.

The *Enchantress* was a graceful, single-funnel steam yacht of thirty-five hundred tons, a slightly scaled down version of the royal yacht, *Victoria and Albert,* and almost as luxuriously appointed. It was the exclusive prerogative of the First Lord and, with Admiralty House, one of the two greatest privileges of the appointment.

"These were great days," Churchill wrote. "From dawn to midnight, one's whole mind was absorbed by the fascination and novelty of the problems which came crowding forward. And all the time there was a sense of power to act, to form, to organize. . . . Saturdays, Sundays and any other spare day I spent always with the Fleets at Portsmouth or at Portland or Devonport. . . .

"The Admiralty yacht *Enchantress* was now to become largely my office, almost my home; and my work my sole occupation and amusement. In all, I spent eight months afloat in the three years before the war. . . ."

Arthur Balfour, the Conservative ex–Prime Minister, was blessed with a private secretary, J. S. Sandars, with a talent for hearing all the gossip and promptly passing it on to his master. Shortly after taking up office in the Admiralty, Churchill had dismissed the elderly, much respected First Sea Lord, Admiral Sir Arthur Wilson, in a particularly peremptory manner. Wilson's successor, chosen by Churchill for his apparent willingness to do exactly as he was told, Admiral Sir Francis Bridgeman, was soon passing to Sandars complaints about his civil chief. It had become so bad that not only Bridgeman but the entire Board of Admiralty were up in arms about what they regarded as Churchill's arrogant and ill-mannered behavior—so bad that it threatened to lead to their mass resignation, with all its shattering political consequences.

The trouble was exacerbated because Churchill had followed an acquiescent First Lord who had got on well with his admirals and had none of Churchill's eagerness for bustle, change, and reform. As Sandars reported to Balfour, all this outrage to official decorum at the Admiralty had led Bridgeman and the Second Sea Lord, Prince Louis of Battenberg (a cousin of King George V), to meet and discuss what to do about the situation. As a result Bridgeman "plainly told [Churchill] that he must mend his manners or his Board would have to take action . . . that as Winston could not give a single order outside the Admiralty building without the consent of the Board & that he was only *primus inter pares* the terms in which he had been addressing his colleagues was most improper."

Churchill at first bridled at this questioning of his powers. Bridgeman therefore said that the board would have to take the matter to the Prime Minister, "and ultimately to the King." At this Churchill appears to have suddenly broken down and, to the wonder and discomfiture of his First Sea Lord, burst into tears. "He has behaved better since," Bridgeman reported with satisfaction, suspecting wrongly that Churchill was suffering from ill health.

If Churchill was not rebuking his admirals he was frequently to be heard patronizing or instructing or correcting them in an insensitive manner. This continued unabated even after Bridgeman was dismissed as thoughtlessly as his predecessor, and Prince Louis of Battenberg installed in his place.

The only admiral for whom Churchill felt unqualified respect and admiration was Admiral of the Fleet Lord Fisher of Kilverstone. Jacky Fisher was a fiery reformer who had risen through the Royal Navy by following his self-description of being "ruthless, relentless and remorseless." All his life he had been loved or hated. Almost all women (but not Churchill's wife, Clementine) loved him. Queen Alexandra adored him; so did King Edward VII, who first introduced him to Churchill. He "invented" the dreadnought type of battleship and reformed—and divided—the Navy through his spectacular career. He had retired by the time Churchill came to the Admiralty, but he had taught Churchill almost all that the latter knew of the Royal Navy. Fisher was in his seventies, Churchill in his late thirties. Together, their minds sparkled like star shells on a dark night. Edward VII called them "the chatterers." His son, George V, distrusted Fisher; George was certainly not in what was called the fish pond.

As a prophet himself, Churchill would no doubt eventually have embraced the cause of the submarine and aviation without Fisher's volatile encouragement. But Fisher nudged him along with his persuasive arguments and demands in capital letters, double underlinings, exclamation marks, quotations from the Bible, psalmbook, and classics, and apt similes. Small cruisers, he insisted, "will all be gobbled up by an armoured cruiser, like the armadillo gobbles up the ants—puts out its tongue and licks them up one after another—and the bigger the ant the more placid the digestive smile." And on speed: "No armour for anything but the super-*Lion, and there restricted!* ... you'll make the Germans 'Squirm'! *You had better adopt 2 keels to 1! You have it now.* It will be safe; it will be popular; it will head off the approaching German naval increase. Above all remember Keble in *The Christian Year.* 'The dusky hues of glorious War!' "

Time and again Fisher also pressed upon Churchill the great power and brilliance of Admiral Sir John Jellicoe, "the coming Nelson" who would command at the second Trafalgar when war came. Jellicoe could do no wrong in Fisher's eyes, and for a long time Churchill accepted Fisher's judgment on this officer. Jellicoe was not an impressive figure, being short in stature with a big nose and "letter box" mouth and a style that was not at first impressive. His health was not robust. As a young officer he had been shot through a lung out in China. He was suffering from Malta fever when the *Victoria,* the flagship in which he was serving, was sunk rapidly in a collision and he endured severe rheumatism as a result. He was tortured by piles and bad teeth.

Jellicoe, however, had impressive powers of reasoning, and was a tidy administrator and a fine handler of a fleet. He was widely regarded as one of the Navy's few considerable brains, had sat with Prince Louis on the *Dreadnought* committee, and although greatly admired by Fisher was never regarded by Fisher's enemies as being in the fish pond.

Churchill's respect for Jellicoe was not reciprocated. Jellicoe thought Churchill had a baleful effect on the Navy. He considered him "quite ignorant of naval affairs. . . . His fatal error," Jellicoe thought, "was his entire inability to realize his own limitations as a civilian."

Another exception to Churchill's generally dismissive attitude towards Royal Navy admirals was Prince Louis and this was, at least in part, because of the importance of his palace connections. But he also recognized Prince Louis's powers of organization and administration, and although Churchill frequently exasperated the prince, there was mutual respect and never a cross word was exchanged.

*   *   *

KITCHENER THE BLACKGUARD

It would have been impossible for Churchill to have carried out all the reforms still vitally necessary after Fisher's time without causing antagonism, suspicion, and bitterness in a service that still lived in the afterglow of the nineteenth-century Pax Britannica and had not fought a serious battle since Trafalgar. Churchill rightly considered it necessary to establish a naval war staff (Agadir had shown that!), to improve pay and conditions and eliminate some of the savage nineteenth-century punishments, to begin the Navy's conversion from coal to oil, to lay down battleships that would make even the *Dreadnought* obsolete, to encourage promotion from the lower deck to officer status, to build up the nucleus of an aviation arm, and much, much more.

It was quite impossible to conduct all this business in less than the three years before war broke out without attracting hostility and suspicion. But he had no need to be so ill-mannered and peremptory with loyal, decent officers almost twice his age. His manner need not have been so brash or so disdainful of other opinions than his own. The feeling against him amongst almost all Royal Navy senior officers was "deeper than did ever plummet sound."

This was widely known in political circles, and Conservatives spread the word and used it to attack him personally and to attack the Liberal party. The Germans were well aware of it, too. On December 3, 1913, eight months before the outbreak of war, the German naval attaché in London reported home, "The sea-officers of the British Navy are often enraged against Mr. Churchill . . . for the youthful civilian Churchill, on his frequent visits to the fleet and dockyards, puts on the air of a military superior. Through his curt behaviour he offends the older officers in their feeling of rank and personal pride. And thus, according to many, through his lack of tact he injures discipline by his ambition for popularity with the lower ranks."

In January 1914, Fisher prepared a memorandum on the submarine, and this was sent to Asquith to be presented at a meeting of the Committee of Imperial Defence on May 14. "The coming of the submarine, " Fisher insisted, "means that the whole foundation of our traditional naval strategy, which served us so well in the past, has been broken down!" As far as commerce destruction was concerned, the elaborate international rules—putting a prize crew on board an enemy merchantman, convoying the vessel into harbor, and so on—could not be observed. The very nature of the submarine prohibited doing so.

Fisher then went on to predict in unerring detail the imminent unrestricted U-boat warfare conducted by the Germans, which came within a whisker of winning the war by starving out Britain and cutting off war supplies.

"There is nothing else the submarine can do except sink her capture, and it must therefore be admitted that (provided it is done, and however inhuman and barbarous it may appear) this submarine menace is a truly terrible one for British commerce and Great Britain. . . ."

Asquith was so shocked by the suggestion that an enemy could descend to such depths that he suppressed the paper. Fisher sent a copy to Churchill, who was equally outraged, and found it a "frankly unthinkable proposition. . . . I do not believe this would ever be done by a civilized power." On October 20 of that same year (1914), the German submarine *U-17* sank a British steamer off the Norwegian coast. The sinking was in accordance with international law. But by January 1915, when the German Naval Staff had been convinced of the true potential of their U-boat force, unrestricted submarine warfare was considered, and put into effect. From February 18 all merchant ships would be sunk within the waters of the British Isles "without it always being possible to avoid danger to the crews and passengers."

The airplane and seaplane had a much stronger appeal to Churchill than the submarine. He was always prepared to go down in a submarine and showed his usual interest in the mechanical workings, but his imagination and sense of romance and wonder were quite carried away by the flying machine. When Fisher was still First Sea Lord in January 1909 it had been decided to build an experimental airship for scouting purposes. The Germans were far ahead in lighter-than-air machines, and the British never got things quite right, with the result that the British airship program was dropped during Churchill's years of office.

Encouraged by Fisher ("You told me you would push *avia-tion*—you are right . . .") Churchill fought the Treasury for funds for aviation and eventually won.

KITCHENER THE BLACKGUARD

* * *

The Agadir Crisis of 1911, which had led to Churchill's arrival at the Admiralty and all that stemmed from this appointment, also led to much bitterness and increasing paranoia in Germany, and a resolve to build up the strength of the fleet to a point where such rebuffs and humiliations could not occur again. On his very first day in office, Churchill received a letter from the palace telling him that one of the King's relations in Germany, recently in Berlin, had informed the King of the mood there: "At the time when the Morocco [Agadir] crisis had reached its acute stage . . . Germany would have gone to war with England but her Fleet was not ready yet and would *not* be until 1915 when the Canal would be finished so that all the largest ships could pass through [between the Baltic and the North Sea], and by that time they would have enough Dreadnoughts launched to deal with any power. . . ."

Germany's determination was confirmed when a supplementary navy bill was secretly prepared authorizing the building of more battleships in order to achieve a 2 : 3 ratio with Britain. This provocative proposal, which soon reached Churchill's ears, did not immediately lead him to propose a counterstroke, only the promise in his first public speech as First Lord that there could certainly be a reduction in the Navy estimates if Germany made no increase to the existing program.

The picture of Churchill as a man of peace is not one that immediately comes to mind, least of all in Germany in 1911–12. But to Churchill, who had seen war at first hand, the idea of war with Germany was abhorrent. "I deeply deplore the situation," he wrote to his old friend Sir Ernest Cassel, "for as you know I have never had any but friendly feelings towards that great nation and her illustrious Sovereign & I regard the antagonism wh has developed as insensate. Anything in my power to terminate it, I wd gladly do. . . ." Again, at the Royal Academy banquet (May 4, 1912): "I believe that if any two great civilized and highly scientific nations go to war with one another, they will become heartily sick of it before they come to the end of it."

Right up to August 1914, Churchill kept the door open to a reduction in warship building, proposing from time to time what he called a "naval holiday" in which all construction should cease for a stated time. But it was like trying to halt a thirty-thousand-ton battleship in its slide down the slipway. Moreover, it infuriated the Germans, and Kaiser Wilhelm II, who regarded any-thing like it as meddling in Germany's internal affairs. As late as May 1914, Churchill, with the blessing of the Foreign Office, was trying to arrange through Cassel a meeting in Germany with Alfred von Tirpitz, the head of the German Navy, in order that he could demonstrate the genuineness of his proposals for a naval holiday.

Naval holiday? Britain could well talk about a year without any naval construction, was the orthodox German view, when her Navy was more powerful than any other two navies in the world. "It is absurd England always looking at Germany," complained the Kaiser to the British naval attaché in Berlin. But within weeks what had been dreaded by so many, and judged inevitable by others, had come to pass and Churchill had to switch his power from reform while searching for peace to conducting the Royal Navy in its greatest challenge since the days of Napoleon.

TWO
"The Salt Air and Bracing Climate"

F ranklin Roosevelt's first experience in the highest echelons of the United States Navy was of a more modest and less controversial, critical, and urgent nature than Churchill's. But it was equally important in forming the young "naval person" of the First World War and the United States Navy's Commander in Chief of the Second World War.

Winston Churchill was seven years old when Franklin Roosevelt was born on the family estate at Hyde Park overlooking the Hudson River north of New York City. The boy Churchill who rarely saw his mother or father and the infant son of James Roosevelt and Sara Delano had little in common except a long and distinguished ancestry. James Roosevelt was already past middle age when his son was born on January 30, 1882, an affluent, contented businessman-cum-country-gentleman, a loving family man who doted on his second wife (his first had died in 1876) and his two sons, one by each marriage.

The Roosevelts were secure and united, a family spread wide over a maturing nation, insulated from the hurly-burly of Wall Street and the clatter and squalor of the roaring expanding new industrial cities of the United States. Nothing disturbed the even tenor of life at Hyde Park. When they traveled, it was comfortably by sea or private coach on the train. Even the politics of the day—and James was a Democrat—lacked the bitterness of Whitehall and the English shires. It is easy to understand the contrast between the sense of security that governed the Roosevelts, and the insecurity that clung like a harsh burden to Churchill's back for all his life.

Franklin knew none of the unhappiness and loneliness suffered by young Churchill. The household reflected his own happiness and pleasurable childhood. He saw his father and mother constantly; the servants made much of him; by contrast with the long, miserable years at school experienced by Winston, Franklin was taught at home and had shared lessons later with a neighboring family. He did not see the inside of a school until he was fourteen.

The school was Groton, where Franklin was still carefully insulated from all classes of society outside his own and where he achieved success and was as happy and as close a subject of his parents' concern as Winston was miserable and neglected by his parents at Harrow. Franklin was still at school when Lieutenant Churchill was charging the Dervishes at Omdurman and a prisoner of the Boers in South Africa; and, to track back nearly twenty years, Winston had already possessed—"commanded," he would have claimed—a considerable lead-soldier army when Franklin was born. And here lay the most significant contrast between the two boys. For Franklin Roosevelt was as closely related to the sea and the Navy as was Churchill to the Army. There is at Hyde Park a small oil painting inscribed "Clipper Ship *Surprise* on which Sara Delano sailed from New York to Hong Kong. 1862." She was eight years old, and was nearly shipwrecked in a storm.

Sara's family was of Flemish origin, and she had known from her own earliest childhood of her ancestor Philippe De La Hoye, who had arrived in Plymouth in 1621, a hundred years before the death of the first duke of Marlborough. The prosperity of the Delanos stemmed from trading and seafaring through many generations. Her father, Warren, aroused in Franklin from his earliest years a fascination for the sea with tales of exploration and tropical oceans and Arctic storms. From Hyde Park the broad sweep of the Hudson River was like a signpost to the sea. At six years he was sailing his iceboat on the Hudson, and when his father bought a fifty-one-foot yacht his conversion to the sea life was complete. "Franklin was so fascinated he could hardly be lured ashore," wrote one biographer. "Photographs show him at the helm in choppy weather, his head scarcely coming above the wheel." When he was sixteen he was given his own boat and spent the summer navigating the coast of the Bay of Fundy, teaching himself the art of sailing through difficult tides and currents. His distant kinsman, actually his fifth cousin, Theodore Roosevelt, became Assistant Secretary of the Navy while Franklin was at Groton, himself planning a naval career with Annapolis as his next goal. "I've always liked the navy," he recalled later. "In fact I only missed by a week going to Annapolis. I would have done so only my parents objected." Later, at Harvard, he began a collection of books about the sea, which he eventually narrowed down to U.S. warships.

During his intense and wide reading about the sea and the Navy, Franklin fell under the spell of Captain Alfred Thayer Mahan, the finest thinker and naval historian of his day. Mahan combined exceptional intelligence with the ability to communicate the importance of sea power through his writings and speeches. Mahan was keenly read in Britain, too, a nation that already possessed the greatest Navy in the world and had the most reason for appreciating the value of the sea power that had asserted and maintained the Pax Britannica for almost a century. Mahan's life of Nelson and his *Influence of Sea Power upon History* (1890) were greatly admired by British historians, who presented him with honorary degrees at both Oxford and Cambridge—his first. More significantly, it was the theories of Mahan that led the Kaiser to determine that his country must become a maritime nation of the first magnitude, and led to the naval arms race with Britain and the First World War.

In the United States, which was a major naval power when Franklin Roosevelt was growing up, Mahan's teachings began to assert a wide and deep influence at a time when the country was emerging from a century-long period of relative isolation and parochial self-sufficiency. Under the presidency of William McKinley in 1898, while Teddy Roosevelt was Assistant Secretary of the Navy, war was waged against Spain. In the Caribbean, Cuba and Puerto Rico were occupied; in the Pacific, the Hawaiian Islands,

the Philippines, and Guam—evidence of the country's new imperial and outward-looking ambitions.

When Japan surprised the world by roundly defeating Russia
at sea as well as on land (1904–05), she was deprived of her expected gains at the peace conference by American pressure to sus-
tain the status quo in the Far East. The fever of the naval rivalry
between Britain and Germany swept across the Atlantic in the
early years of the twentieth century, and the hammering of rivets
and the thunder of the steel mills was soon echoing from American shipyards, from Cramps in South Carolina to Mare Island
near San Francisco. The U.S. Navy completed plans for a revolutionary all-big-gun battleship before any other navy, but was
beaten to completion by the British Navy's swifter construction of
the *Dreadnought.*

These were stirring years for a young American who loved the
Navy and the sea, and whose kinsman, now President, was intro-
ducing a new note of national consciousness. "Viewing the world
in the perspective of his adviser and friend, Alfred Thayer
Mahan," Nathan Miller has written, "[Teddy] Roosevelt believed
that the United States should have an influence in the world com-
mensurate with its wealth and strength. He was convinced that
the nation should follow a policy of expansion. . . . The capstone
of this imperialist structure was to be a strong navy." Teddy Roosevelt proclaimed to Congress, "The American people must either
build and maintain an adequate Navy, or else make up their
minds definitely to accept a secondary position in international
affairs."

On December 16, 1907, with a brilliantly orchestrated send-
off, Teddy Roosevelt dispatched the entire American battle fleet
on a voyage round the world—the Great White Fleet, it was
called—to proclaim the debut of a new naval power. During its
circumnavigation the U.S. Corps of Army Engineers was entrusted with the task of completing the Panama Canal, which by
1914 made America a two-ocean naval power, and also now the
third greatest in the world.

When the Great White Fleet was still on the other side of the
world, Franklin Roosevelt at twenty-five years of age was practic-
ing as a lawyer in New York City, married two years to Teddy
Roosevelt's niece Anna Eleanor, his maritime activities still re-

stricted to ocean liners and yachting, his political ambitions still dormant. But within three years a personal metamorphosis had taken place with the stirring of political and community ambitions. His son Elliott has written of this period, "F.D.R.'s entry into politics was as natural and unrestrained as his subsequent ascent of the political ladder." The example of "Uncle Ted," as Franklin now called him, was one factor of influence. Another was the arguments of his friends. But more important, according to his eldest son, were "the factors within himself. . . . The spirit of adventure and the thrill of answering a challenge were instinctive features of his character," not forgetting the strong streak of idealism with which he was born.

On November 8, 1910, Roosevelt was elected to the New York State Senate, and he and his family moved from New York City to a house in the state capital, Albany, on State Street. "He is thirty-two years of age," reported the *New York World,* "of spare figure and lean intellectual face, suggesting in appearance a student of divinity rather than a practical politician. Gold bowed spectacles loop his long thin nose, and a frock coat drapes his figure. He is wealthy . . . and is able and of pleasing personality."

Moving now to January 1913: Franklin Roosevelt has just won a second term of office as a New York State senator; Woodrow Wilson is the President-elect. Roosevelt has just received a not altogether unexpected telegram from Wilson's private secretary asking him to attend a conference. Matters of patronage are on the agenda. Young Roosevelt's naval ambitions are already widely known, and here is the opportunity to draw attention to them again. It is believed that Wilson is sympathetic. The new Secretary of the Navy is one Josephus Daniels—a curious choice, one might consider, for he is "a home-spun North Carolina editor," a Methodist prohibitionist, "a pacifist of puritanical mind," and a bit of an old woman, truth to tell; but a kind man, efficient, hardworking, honest to a fault for a politician. But Wilson recognized his usual qualities. "I know of no one I trust more entirely or affectionately," he wrote when offering Daniels his post.

It is the morning of Wilson's inauguration, and political excitement is intense. In the lobby of the Willard Hotel, Roosevelt by chance finds himself face to face with Daniels and at once congratulates him on his appointment. Daniels thanks the young man, twenty years his junior, and asks him, "How would you like to come to Washington as Assistant Secretary of the Navy?"

Roosevelt is reported as having beamed with pleasure. "How would I like it?" he replies. "I'd like it bully well. It would please me better than anything in the world. I'd be glad to be connected with the new administration. All my life I have loved ships and have been a student of the Navy, and the assistant secretary-ship is the one place, above all others, I would love to hold."

Daniels was later warned by a senator, "Whenever a Roosevelt rides, he wishes to ride in front." But Daniels felt no anxiety on that score, and, as he wrote later of their first meeting, "A lasting friendship was born, which has increased with the passing years, not broken even when we were in occasional disagreement." According to Daniels, Roosevelt at this time "possessed a spontaneity and gaiety, as well as good looks, fine bearing, and sterling qualities."

When Roosevelt had to undergo an operation, Daniels canceled his holiday. "It will be a pleasure for me to remain on deck," he told Roosevelt. "You will need the salt air and bracing climate," he added looking forward to Roosevelt's eventual convalescence in Maine. "For the present you need to rest and sleep, with your mother near you. Your friend will look for your early getting out and ready for play. With my love and happiness that you are coming on so finely," he ended his letter, "Sincerely your friend . . ."

On receiving a painting as a Christmas present from Roosevelt, Daniels replied, "Nothing could have given me more pleasure. I will keep it and transmit it to one of my sons and also transmit to all of them the affection and regard to you. When I came to Washington," he continued, "one of the anticipated pleasures was the close association with you . . . this association has been both helpful and delightful. I wish you to know my regard and appreciation of you as a man and as a fellow worker."

"Uncle Ted," now retired from politics, was delighted to hear of Franklin's appointment. A big-navy man if ever there was one, the elder Roosevelt wrote to him, "I was very much pleased that you were appointed. . . . It is interesting to see that you are in another place which I myself once held. I am sure you will enjoy yourself to the full and that you will do capital work." One of

"THE SALT AIR AND BRACING CLIMATE"

Roosevelt's friends, on the other hand, offered advice that fell on the deafest of ears: "I hope when you 'put this uniform on' you will not, like the Right Honorable Winston Churchill, First Lord of the Admiralty, be carried away by the zeal for a big navy. . . ."

Aside from the important qualification that he was not the supreme commander, the status of Assistant Secretary of the United States Navy in 1913 was comparable with that of First Lord of the Admiralty in Britain, and we read in a letter of July 29, 1913, to his wife of Roosevelt working on the United States Navy budgetary estimates on board the Navy yacht *Sylph* at the same time as Churchill was preparing for his own battle with the Treasury and the small-navy politicians for the British Navy estimates for 1914. In both posts there was wide flexibility in the range of duties to which one could appoint oneself, with custom tending to be adhered to more tenaciously in London than Washington. Custom had been followed quite closely by Churchill's predecessors, which made his own deviation more evident and therefore more open to controversy. The job of an American assistant secretary of the Navy was almost as wide and varied as he cared to make it, and after only a few weeks in office Roosevelt was sailing into waters uncharted by his predecessors, but navigating with such style and bravura that no one—least of all Josephus Daniels—bade him nay. Here was no American McKenna; more a transatlantic Churchill.

By tradition, the Assistant Secretary was responsible for all civilian labor employed by the U.S. Navy, including all those employed in government shipyards, the numbers varying from fifty thousand to one hundred thousand. Seven years later, Roosevelt was able to claim that throughout his period as Assistant Secretary "the Navy has not had a single strike or a single serious disagreement. . . . We have had happy Navy Yards, with a wholly satisfactory output of work." But the Assistant Secretary might be assigned any sort of activity by the Secretary, and Daniels took full advantage of this custom by piling wider and wider responsibilities on his young assistant as he worked his way into his post. Roosevelt grasped everything that came his way with wide-open arms, but still had plenty of room for more. Many years later, when Roosevelt was in the White House and Daniels was retired, he would be asked what his assistant of twenty years earlier had been most interested in. Daniels would answer by quoting Roosevelt himself: "I get my fingers into about everything," adding defiantly, "and there's no law against it." As early as 1916 when about to address a party of New York naval reservists, Roosevelt's toastmaster proclaimed amid loud cheers, "I know it would not hurt your feelings if the word 'Assistant' were crossed out of this man's title."

To the everlasting credit of Daniels, he made no attempt to curb Roosevelt's activities, while at the same time retaining the dignity and status of his own post. Like Prime Minister Asquith, Daniels recognized a young politician's brilliance and enterprise; and as Asquith might smile indulgently at Churchill's caprices and excesses, Daniels gave his colt his head, accepting that he might come a cropper but would have the resilience to survive.

In his determination to bring greater efficiency to the Navy, and above all to stamp out extravagances and suspected corruption, Daniels traveled widely and was away from Washington for long periods, leaving Roosevelt in command. Within a few weeks of his appointment, Daniels announced his departure to Roosevelt: "My dear Mr. Roosevelt, I am enclosing a schedule of my southern trip. . . ."

President Wilson was less aware of the extent to which Roosevelt was broadening the base of his appointment and also stretching out in most directions from that base. Wilson, like Asquith, was no Navy man and had as little to do with the service as he could. He had every confidence in Daniels and let him get on with his work. When it was necessary for Roosevelt to consult at the White House, he usually saw the President's private secretary, Joseph Tumulty. But the two men did meet quite frequently on specific matters, rather than general policy, and on these occasions Wilson would occasionally drop a pearl or two of fatherly wisdom; for example: "It is only once in a generation that a people can be lifted above material things. That is why conservative government is in the saddle two-thirds of the time."

Roosevelt's White House comings and goings were watched by the press and political commentators with special interest. But wherever he went about his business he attracted interest and controversy. Why was this? Why, people asked at the time and in later years, was this young man in a subordinate office the object of so much more speculation and admiration than his superior? One reason lay in his youth, a mere thirty-one years. Then his name. In a much more class-structured and smaller society than today's, the name Roosevelt, representing one of the oldest and most respected families in the land, counted for as much as being a Marlborough-Churchill in Britain; and to be related to Teddy Roosevelt was as great an advantage as to be the son of Lord Randolph Churchill. Teddy Roosevelt as Assistant Secretary of the Navy had not only planned the capture of Manila Bay from the Spaniards; with the Secretary of the Navy absent from Washington, he had ordered Commodore Dewey's historic attack on the Spanish Fleet, which had concluded with the famous victory at Manila. Four years later Teddy Roosevelt was in the White House. How could the parallel be ignored? How long before Franklin emulated him?

Franklin exploited this association and at the time of his appointment laughingly told reporters, "There's a Roosevelt on the job today.... You remember what happened the last time a Roosevelt occupied a similar position."

Again like Churchill, Roosevelt's youth and his name did not count completely in his favor. Some senior naval officers almost twice his age looked askance at "this bright, brash youth." Teddy Roosevelt had his detractors and some of this ill will brushed on to his cousin. But overall the balance greatly favored Franklin Roosevelt.

The Navy was the only department with only one assistant secretary, and a further advantage accrued to Roosevelt's benefit for this reason: When "Uncle Ted" became President he wished to maintain control of the department, just as Churchill appointed a nonentity to the Admiralty when he became Prime Minister in 1940. Roosevelt therefore appointed third-rate men to the post, and men who would do his bidding. After Teddy Roosevelt, President Taft by contrast appointed a strong man as Secretary, but he was away from Washington for much of the time, thus paradoxically raising the status and power of the Assistant Secretary.

But immeasurably the most powerful reason why Franklin Roosevelt attracted so much attention, and mostly approving attention, as Assistant Secretary of the Navy was the style in which he filled the office and performed its functions, and the good looks and fine physique with which he was blessed. It was as difficult to ignore the man as it was impossible for Roosevelt to play any part other than that of the zealous, curious, enthusiastic, ambitious, cheerful young politician hell-bent on success and promotion— with just the right touch of flash on the way. As he wrote to a friend a few days after his appointment, "I now find my vocation combined with my avocation."

A certain amount of ceremonial was built into the job. An American man-of-war gave the Assistant Secretary a seventeen-gun salute, four more than a rear admiral received, and a guard of honor greeted him on the quarterdeck. Roosevelt reveled in all this, and added his own touches. Only the President and Secretary of the Navy enjoyed the privilege of flying their own flags at sea; Roosevelt corrected what he regarded as this anomaly and designed—and flew—one for himself.

He threw all his weight and influence behind the Navy pressure and propaganda group emulating Germany's and Britain's, the Navy League of the United States, and made his first important and widely reported speech to this body. A few months later, he initiated the Roosevelt Cup for the ship's crew with the best swimming record. Swiftly, by these methods, he was building up his name and national recognition.

In his early days Roosevelt, like Churchill, embarked upon a series of inspections of navy yards. Each arrival was marked by fanfares and contingents of marines or sailors lined up for his inspection, his own speech before his departure calculated to resassure the local people of the great future for their Navy and their yard. It was all good political as well as good naval stuff.

At the Panama Pacific Exposition at San Francisco two years after his appointment, Roosevelt toured the stands with the chairman of the government commission wearing top hats and tailcoats, making widely reported speeches. At Roosevelt's side as his aide he had Lieutenant Husband E. Kimmel, who, twenty-six years later, was to play the lead role in the United States Navy's greatest tragedy.

A relatively minor tragedy off Pearl Harbor revealed Roosevelt's rapidly deployed opportunism. The submarine *F-4* was lost with all hands. After publicly expressing his regret, he boarded a submarine at Los Angeles in heavy weather and requested the commander to order it to dive to show that the submarine was really a safe vessel. Then he left for San Diego in a destroyer that "was seen to bury itself time and again in the raging seas."

Two occasions have been recorded when Roosevelt asked to take the helm on board fast new destroyers under tricky navigational circumstances. The commander of one, Lieutenant William F. Halsey, agreed, and was much impressed by Roosevelt's skill and dexterity. The commander of the other destroyer, Lieutenant Harold R. Stark, demurred—"contrary to naval regulations." Both these officers also figured prominently in epochal events when Roosevelt was President and the Navy was fighting for its life.

Roosevelt wanted to be seen as a real sailor's sailor, and the role came to him naturally. He was always ready to don oilskins and embark on the smallest boat in the heaviest sea—as at Boston once in a submarine chaser while promoting the cause of the Naval Reserve, one of his most important contributions to the peacetime Navy, which proved invaluable in war.

Franklin Roosevelt availed himself of his private yacht privileges as frequently as did Churchill with the *Enchantress*, and these cruises were as widely reported. The *Dolphin* was an elegant 1,485-ton armed yacht that Roosevelt increasingly used as his own, cruising up the Hudson to Hyde Park, perhaps with his family on board. Daniels used the *Dolphin* only rarely and strictly on official duties, disapproving of "pleasure trips." From time to time he had to deny Roosevelt the yacht. "It is unnecessary for me to tell you that I would love to do what you wished but I fear that it would not be the part of wisdom to do it," he once responded to a request for domestic use of the *Dolphin*. And on another occasion admonished Roosevelt, "Don't you think it would be a mistake at this time to send the *Dolphin* into Maine upon anything except an official trip?" Roosevelt, who took a most relaxed view of stretching privileges, did not press his claim but continued to sail frequently in the yacht.

In October 1913 a squadron of battleships, off to show the American flag in the Mediterranean and dressed overall and with bands playing, steamed past the *Dolphin*. "The big gray fellows were magnificent as they went past," Roosevelt wrote to his wife, ". . . and I only wish a hundred thousand people could have seen them." This is what the Assistant Secretary most enjoyed, and everyone in turn enjoyed his pleasure. "In sending you as representatives of the United States Navy of today," he said in his farewell speech, "we hope to show to the Old World that the achievements and traditions of the past are being sustained and carried to a still more splendid future. Good luck and God speed!"

"Hot air, by the book," commented one newspaper. But the *New York Herald*'s proud claim that it was "one of the finest naval spectacles since the steaming of the fleet on its world cruise" more accurately mirrored public opinion.

Target practice, evolutions, and maneuvers—at any of these naval occasions there was a good chance that the *Dolphin* would be present, sometimes with Eleanor and the family on board, too. Daniels rarely went to sea, or cast his eyes upon a man-of-war. He had none of Roosevelt's flamboyancy, and his whole approach to the task of running the department was utterly different from Roosevelt's. Daniels held to the belief that "every corporation with a capitalization of more than $100,000 was inherently evil" and that "the Navy was packed at the top with dead wood, and with politics all the way through, and the steel, coal and other big industries were accustomed to dealing with it on their own terms." His first priority was to eradicate corruption and collusion in the supply, construction, and running of the U.S Navy. He would have acted in just the same way if he had been Postmaster General, a post he was nearly given by Wilson. He was after economy, honesty, and efficiency. As a pacifist at heart he certainly was not looking for a bigger navy, and only with reluctance accepted the need for any armed forces. Daniels questioned the cost of bandsmen's instruments while Roosevelt enjoyed their music. Roosevelt felt a deep romantic love for gold braid and respect for flag officers; and, as he was a big-navy man who loved going to sea and knew how to handle a destroyer, the admirals loved him in return.

Roosevelt was as zealous in tackling monopolies, collusion, and inefficiency as Daniels. Their vigor was equal and they worked together very well in the common cause. When, say, they formed a united front against the big steel corporations if they tendered identical prices for the supply of armor plate for a battleship, Daniels determined to force down the price, acting the role of the white knight of efficiency fighting the monster monopoly in the cause of decency; Roosevelt was equally determined, so that the nation could have a bigger navy for the same price. He took a pragmatic view of companies like Bethlehem Steel and Westinghouse, and at the end of any battle was respected for it without further acrimony. Roosevelt was liked and admired by the Navy League, too; Daniels refused to have anything to do with this pressure group headed by the nickel millionaire Colonel Thompson.

As a big-navy man, Roosevelt was swimming with the tide. At the time of his appointment there was growing anxiety about Japan, which had learned big-ship building from the British, who had earlier supplied most of the battleships that defeated the Russians in 1905. In 1913 Japan had five battleships and battle cruisers building in her own new yards and one in Britain, and did not refrain from complaining stridently when the California Legislature passed an act that prohibited Japanese nationals from owning land in the state. The clever, bellicose U.S. Navy aide for operations, Rear Admiral Bradley A. Fiske, warned of a Japanese attack on the Hawaiian Islands and the Philippines (twenty-eight years before Pearl Harbor). According to Daniels, Fiske actually wanted war with Japan; and while Roosevelt wished for nothing of the kind, he counseled readiness and saw the incident as further justification for building a bigger fleet. A lot of people in Washington—and outside—agreed.

Nor was there much cause for complacency to the east, in Europe. The United States had no fear of the British Navy, which had for so long been as sure a shield for America as for Britain. But with the ever accelerating British naval race with Germany, which now possessed the second-largest battle fleet in the world, there was the risk, often expressed by the British themselves, that Germany would catch up and surpass the Royal Navy in size, or so cripple the British battle fleet in war that German expansionism and imperialism could pose a threat to the United States, especially in alliance with a powerful, aggressive Japan.

More ships called for more men, and to attract them Roosevelt led the way for lower-deck reforms and improvements in pay as Churchill was doing in Britain. A new battleship needed more than a thousand crewmen as well as shore-based personnel, even the lowliest trades calling for at least a year's training while no officer could take up his duties in under three years. As the creation of a naval war staff was Churchill's single most important achievement at this time, then Roosevelt's was surely the creation of a naval reserve. It was not his work alone any more than the staff was Churchill's brainchild. And Roosevelt, unlike Wilson and Fisher, who had so strongly opposed Churchill, had Daniels on his side. But Daniels favored a modest-sized reserve, while Roosevelt characteristically advocated and succeeded in getting a substantial number of reservists, who must be offered "greater facilities to make it more attractive to the average private citizen . . . to spend a certain length of time away from his play hours, and do some pretty stiff work."

The application of relentless pressure for a bigger navy and the creation of a naval reserve were two of the tangible successes of Roosevelt during these years. There is again a close parallel with Churchill in less conspicuous aspects of preparing the Navy for war. By his youthful and infectious enthusiasm and evident love for the Navy, in contrast with Daniels and earlier assistant secretaries, his keenness for fighting efficiency and encouragement of the best men in the service, and the everyday evidence that he was a dashing and stylish leader, did as much for the United States Navy in the four years leading to war as Churchill achieved in the near three years before the Royal Navy went to war.

Roosevelt and Churchill also suffered from a common fault. Besides being big-navy men they were battleship men, who advocated ever greater numbers of battleships and battle cruisers at the cost of other requirements of a modern fleet. Since the lightning construction of the *Dreadnought* herself in 1905–06 the judgment of navalists worldwide had been distorted, nowhere as seriously as in the United States and Britain. To build battleships was tangible and statistical: It was reassuring for Americans to hear that the nation had fourteen dreadnought battleships built or building at the end of 1914; and it comforted the British public, so fearful of being overtaken by the Germans, that the Royal Navy would shortly enjoy the power of forty-one battleships and battle cruisers. It was good news politically, too; but unsound when considered in the context of a well-balanced navy.

Blinded by dreadnought-mania, the British Navy found itself dangerously lacking in fully prepared and defended bases when war came. The money had been spent on building battleships. There were no votes or kudos in building bases and it was easy, but foolish and irresponsible, to forget about them.

American dreadnought-mania resulted in a different imbalance. Here battleships were built at the cost of supporting ships. In 1914 the ratio of battleships to modern cruisers and destroyers was 14 : 12 : 49. In the German Kriegsmarine it was 23 : 41 : 164. The lack of auxiliary ships was even more serious. The Japanese crisis of 1913 showed up the inadequacies of the U.S. fleet to contain, let alone defeat, the Japanese at sea. There was an appalling shortage of crews to man the inadequate number of ships; and according to a report to the Navy Department from the senior paymaster, only 25 percent of the required number of colliers could be made available, and that number could be made up only by requisitioning every vessel belonging to the merchant marine.

Roosevelt went some way toward solving the personnel problem with his reserves. Thanks to the British Navy and the restraint of the Japanese, the materially imbalanced U.S. fleet was not put to the test for another quarter century, by which time a new imbalance had manifested itself and the dreadnought was no longer the final arbiter at sea anyway.

THREE

"A Foreboding of Disaster"

I t was not generally known until some time later how fully mo-bilized and ready for war the Royal Navy was in July and Au-gust 1914. For this state of affairs, Churchill was given full credit, mainly because he claimed it so convincingly. The truth is not as simple as history has made it out to be.

Churchill learned early in his political career the importance of establishing and preserving a written record of events that showed him in the most favorable light. With his admirals, who were less concerned with the advantages of credit, and with pos-terity, Churchill acquired the practice of committing to paper an idea put up to him in these terms: "As you know, since I discussed with you the matter of . . ." and then requesting a memorandum on the subject.

Prince Louis as First Sea Lord rumbled these tricks early in his relationship with his First Lord, shrugged his shoulders, and mut-tered to his wife something derogatory about "these politicians." In June 1913 Prince Louis received one of these "As you know . . ." notes from Churchill. This one continued, ". . . this has been in my mind for some long time. I should hope next year to obtain a mobilisation of the whole of the Royal Fleet Re-serve. . . ."

In reality the question of a trial mobilization of the huge Reserve Fleet had been discussed many times between Prince Louis and Jellicoe, and other members of the board. The prince had been pressing for it for ten years. A full-scale test was obviously desirable and necessary to ensure that the complicated arrangements for moving twenty thousand reservists from their homes to their ports and ships worked smoothly.

> In the autumn of 1913 [wrote Churchill in his memoirs], when I was revolving the next year's Admiralty policy in the light of the coming Estimates, I had sent the following minute to the First Sea Lord:
>
> October 22, 1913.
>
> First Sea Lord
> Second Sea Lord
> Secretary
>
> We have now had manoeuvres in the North Sea on the largest scale for two years running, and we have obtained a great deal of valuable data which requires to be studied. It does not therefore seem necessary to supplement the ordinary tactical exercises of the year 1914–15 by Grand Manoeuvres. A saving of nearly £200,000 could apparently be effected in coal and oil consumption, and a certain measure of relief would be accorded to the Estimates in an exceptionally heavy year.
>
> In these circumstances I am drawn to the conclusion that . . . it would be better to substitute instead a mobilization of the Third Fleet [reserves]. . . .

In one written minute Churchill acquired for the record the credit for conceiving this Reserve Fleet mobilization (already agreed to four months earlier), justifying the cancellation of the maneuvers by the fact that data from earlier maneuvers had not yet been studied, and confirming for all to see his desire for economies in the running of the Navy at a time when this was coming up again for minute and hostile scrutiny.

"Prince Louis agreed," Churchill added starkly in his memoirs.

Churchill announced this mobilization in Parliament on

"A FOREBODING OF DISASTER"

March 18, 1914. The timing could hardly have been more fortuitous.

For the family summer holidays Churchill had rented, as he had done before, Pear Tree Cottage at Overstrand near Cromer on the bracing east coast. His brother Jack's wife rented nearby Beehive Cottage. The four children, Clementine's Diana and Randolph and their cousins Johnny and Peregrine, would paddle and play in the sand. It was a memorably hot summer. With the international scene so ominous Churchill did not expect to be able to spend long with his family, but he determined to slip down for one weekend, especially as his wife was expecting another child and was not feeling well.

"Europe is trembling on the verge of a general war," Churchill wrote to Clementine. During a Cabinet meeting on July 24, 1914, a note had been delivered containing the terms of an ultimatum from Austria to Serbia. On this Friday afternoon, Churchill then proceeded to the Admiralty. The First Fleet was at Portland. The Second Fleet was also at Portland after completing exercises and would shortly discharge the members of the reservist crews. The Third Fleet ships manned almost entirely by reservists were heading for their home ports with orders to pay off on Monday.

That night Churchill dined with Cassel and his German industrialist friend Albert Ballin at Brook House, Cassel's stone-and-marble mausoleumlike mansion in Park Lane. Ballin was in a somber mood. During dinner he recounted a prediction of the onetime German Chancellor in 1897. "I remember old Bismarck telling me the year before he died that one day the great European War would come out of some damned foolish thing in the Balkans."

On the following morning, Saturday, July 25, Churchill returned to the Admiralty and spoke to Prince Louis who was to hold the fort over the weekend. Churchill assured his First Sea Lord that he would make special arrangements with the post office switchboard in Cromer to have the telephone manned day and night while he was away so that he could be kept *au courant* with developments, and would telephone himself every few hours. Prince Louis did not approve of the First Lord's absenting himself at this critical time, and later told his younger son, the future Lord Mountbatten, "Ministers with their week-end holidays are incorrigible."

Churchill took the 1 P.M. train to join his family at Overstrand. That evening he telephoned the Admiralty. Prince Louis's news was slightly reassuring. Among the numerous dispatches that had arrived at the Admiralty was a note from the Foreign Office to the effect that Serbia, bowing its head in supplication, had accepted the terms of the Austrian note. Churchill went to bed that night feeling that "things might blow over."

Sunday was a perfect summer day, clear and sparkling. In the morning Churchill took the children down The Land, the two-hundred-yard-long lane leading to the cliff top; and thence down the zigzag path to the beach. "We dammed the little rivulets which trickled down to the sea as the tide went out," he wrote later of this day. He called up Prince Louis again at midday. The Austrians appeared dissatisfied with Serbia's response and remained threatening. At dinner on Friday night Ballin had said, "If Russia marches against Austria," as a result of an Austrian attack on Serbia, "we [Germany] must march; and if we march France must march, and what would England do?" Churchill had told the German magnate that it would be a mistake for Germany to presume that Britain would necessarily do nothing.

The burning question for the Navy was whether or not to halt the dispersal of the reservists. Churchill would not commit himself on his decision, only emphasizing to his First Sea Lord the serious political implications if their demobilization was halted. The telephone line was poor and Prince Louis had difficulty in catching all that Churchill said, but there was no doubt that the decision must be his. Churchill also added that he would cut short his weekend and return late that night. But by then, Prince Louis knew, and Churchill knew, that it would be too late to halt the return home of the twenty thousand reservist sailors, many of whom would be off at once on their own summer holidays and be scattered all over the country.

Prince Louis always believed afterwards that he had been left to carry the can in order that Churchill could not be held responsible and that it would therefore be a service rather than a political decision. "The wrong decision now could seriously damage and even destroy the career of the man who made it," as Prince Louis's biographer has written.

Over the next few hours the news suggested a worsening situation. At 6 P.M., the hour when Austria's ultimatum was due to expire, Prince Louis decided on his own initiative to "stand the Fleet fast," and in his own hand wrote out the orders. Later, Churchill gave him full credit—"his loyal hand had sent the first order which began our vast naval mobilization"—and was relieved to hear late that night on visiting the Foreign Office that the announcement of this grave step "might have the effect of sobering the Central Powers and steadying Europe."

As the situation worsened still further, all precautions and contingent arrangements worked out by the new Naval War Staff were put in hand. Coastal guns were manned day and night, bridges guarded, naval bases and barracks closed to all but authorized personnel, magazines and other vital stores protected. After Monday's Cabinet meeting, Churchill drew up "a very secret warning" to all commanders in chief.

In consultation with the Chief of Naval Staff, Admiral Doveton Sturdee, and Prince Louis, at 10 A.M. on Tuesday, July 28, the decision was made to dispatch the First Fleet to its war stations. This fleet, soon to be renamed the Grand Fleet, was the Navy's first line and comprised the battle squadrons and supporting cruisers and destroyers of the latest and most powerful ships. It was to leave Portland, and during the hours of darkness and with all lights extinguished, the battleships and battle cruisers, eighteen miles long in all, would steam fast through the Strait of Dover and head north for Scapa Flow, Cromarty, and Rosyth in Scotland, where all ships would refuel and be put on a war basis.

By the morning of July 31 they were ready for action, and eager for it, too. Morale was good, self-confidence as high as it had been in Nelson's day. The stroke fell four days later. At 11 P.M. on August 4, Churchill flashed the signal, "Commence hostilities against Germany." The civil head of the Royal Navy in peacetime was now responsible to Parliament and the nation for the efficient maintenance and running of the Royal Navy in time of war.

The duties of a first lord were almost as undefined as the British constitution. "Accepted practice" was an expression much used and much abused by Churchill. He had never once transgressed the law, let alone the constitution, in his eleven hundred days in office. But he had departed from the practices of his predecessors in almost every department. His early excesses, which had caused such outrage, had been somewhat mitigated. There was less friction with his admirals in 1914 than in 1912 but that was largely because these admirals had come to terms with his style and behavior and complained less because they were on the whole a stoic body of men and could see that nothing was to be gained by getting upset. Moreover, his most stubborn opponents had by now been overthrown. Relative calm reigned. As the German naval attaché wrote home in one of his last dispatches, "On the whole the Navy is satisfied with Mr Churchill. . . ."

There was no hint, in Churchill's style of leadership as First Lord in peacetime, to lead Prince Louis and the Naval Staff to believe that he would be less exacting and less commanding in time of war. But the keenness with which he followed every move, the depth of detail into which he at once plunged, and the authoritarian and completely dominating manner in which he took over control of the main thrust of events, came as a great shock to that professional body of men within the Admiralty who had trained for years in their roles. Like some maritime Marlborough, Churchill *was* the Admiralty, *was* the Navy—supremo, admiralissimo, dictator.

Churchill, in conducting the naval war, listened to Sturdee, listened to Prince Louis, sought answers to his questions, delegated relatively minor matters—there were, after all, only eighteen working hours in the day. But there was never any shadow of doubt about the position of the hub of this giant steel wheel. It was not in the office of the Chief of Naval Staff, nor that of the First Sea Lord. It was midway between the Admiralty war room with its charts of the world's oceans upon its walls, and Churchill's private office overlooking the Horse Guards Parade. Because Churchill reigned supreme, increasingly when absent he left a vacuum, a sense of impotency almost, initiative shriveled among those whose real business it was to supervise the conduct of the war at sea. Because he *was* the dynamo, when it was switched off the lights went out.

The public, who had expected an immediate and glorious victory in the North Sea, were disappointed. The Germans remained in harbor in home waters. It was in distant seas, where they had a scattering of ships, some of them powerful, that the first naval events occurred, and they were disappointing to the British. In the Mediterranean, the modern German battle cruiser *Goeben,* supported by a light cruiser, escaped from a more powerful British force and was welcomed with open arms by the sympathetic, but still neutral, Turkish people. Unfortunately, Churchill had just ordered the seizure in British shipyards of two dreadnoughts being completed (and paid for) for the Turkish Navy.

On the same day that Churchill learned of the safe arrival of the German ships in Turkish waters, Prime Minister Asquith noted, "We had a Cabinet this morning as usual. The only interesting thing is the arrival of the *Goeben* in the Dardanelles & her sale to Turkey! The Turks are very angry—not unnaturally—at Winston's seizure. . . . As we shall insist that the *Goeben* shall be manned by a Turkish instead of a German crew, it doesn't much matter: as the Turkish soldiers cannot navigate her—except on to the rocks or mines. . . ."

Thus, with stratospheric arrogance and complacency, Asquith disposed of *that* incident in the war that was seven days old. David Lloyd George, Asquith's Chancellor of the Exchequer, thought quite otherwise. He was convinced later that Churchill had forced Turkey into the war in 1914, and told him so, to his outrage.

There were several setbacks for the Navy during the month of August besides the failure to intercept the *Goeben,* including the loss in a minefield (after sinking the German minelayer) of the light cruiser *Amphion.* From now on, almost until the war's first Christmas, the Admiralty had almost nothing but bad news to report, and Churchill became more and more depressed. On October 24, Captain Herbert Richmond, the assistant director of operations, who had Churchill to dinner that evening, noted that he was "oppressed with the impossibility of *doing* anything. . . . I have not seen him so despondent before." Far from fighting a fleet action with the Germans, Jellicoe had been obliged to retreat from his insecure base at Scapa Flow for fear of submarine attack. Even on the west coast of Scotland it seemed that the fleet was not safe from the much feared underwater weapons. The new superdreadnought *Audacious* was sunk by a mine off Lough Swilly in Ireland three days after Churchill dined with Richmond. So finely balanced numerically were the two battle fleets now that if the German Navy had sought a major action at this time it could very well have inflicted a decisive defeat—and that would have meant the end of the war.

On September 22, 1914, soon after dawn three old Bacchante-class cruisers, the *Aboukir, Hogue,* and *Cressy,* manned in all by over twenty-two hundred men, were steaming in a straight line on patrol, unescorted (the weather had been too bad for destroyer escort) at ten knots. A single, small, obsolescent German U-boat stalked them and put a torpedo into the *Aboukir,* which sank in twenty minutes. The other two big ships came alongside her to lower rescue boats and were in turn themselves sunk. Twelve hundred officers and men perished, and being reservists were mostly married men with families, an infinitely worse loss than the worthless ships, which should never have been there.

Churchill in his account of the catastrophe made much of a minute he had written four days earlier—"the *Bacchantes* ought not to continue on this beat"—and recounted the chapter of accidents that had led to action being taken too late. He failed to mention that Commodore Roger Keyes had warned of the risks being taken on this patrol in a letter he had written on August 21. "For Heaven's sake," he pleaded, "take those 'Baccchantes' away! . . . the Germans must know they are about, and if they send out a suitable force, God help them!" It is unlikely that Churchill, with his eye on everything, failed to see this or have his attention drawn to it, especially as it came from a real fire-eating commander.

Up at Scapa Flow during those anxious autumn weeks of 1914, fears grew of U-boats entering the anchorage and causing mayhem. Jellicoe was becoming jittery and there were early signs that his health was being affected by the weight of his responsibilities. As he wrote to a friend, "I am laid up for a bit. It is of course due to the worry of trying to get things done which ought to be done without my having to step in. . . ."

It was the lack of a secure anchorage for his great fleet that was his first concern. "I *long* for a submarine defense at Scapa; it would give such a feeling of confidence," he wrote to Churchill a week after the loss of the three cruisers. "I can't sleep half so well inside as when outside, mainly because I feel we are risking such a mass of valuable ships where, if a submarine did get in, she practically has the British Dreadnought Fleet at her mercy. . . ."

Churchill had already attracted strong professional and public criticism for what came to be known as his Antwerp escapade. From the earliest days of the war the Navy had to concern itself with the German advance through Belgium. Not only were the Channel ports at stake, but if they fell the supply lines to the British Army fighting in France would be cut. The Naval Air Division was soon operating from French soil near Dunkirk, and by the middle of September a large quantity of guns and ammunition had been supplied to the Belgian defenders and the Royal Marines brigade of three thousand men dispatched as support.

The most important Belgian port was the fortified city of Antwerp, which was still holding out, the King and the government in residence, at the end of September. Once Antwerp had fallen, the way was open for the Germans to advance upon Dunkirk, Calais, and Boulogne. With the fall of Brussels, the Germans turned their attention on Antwerp, bombarding the forts with howitzers. The Belgians' morale slumped; by October 2 it was clear that they would not hold out for long without help and the Belgian government announced that it would evacuate the next day. Churchill was informed of the depth of the crisis and was recalled from a visit to the naval aerodrome at Dunkirk. Encouraged by Kitchener, Churchill decided to go to the rescue of the Belgians personally, to put spine into the Antwerp defenders, reinforce and reorganize the city's defenses, and prevail upon the King and his government not to quit.

Churchill left London in his personal train at 3 A.M. on October 3, promising a report as soon as possible. The spirit of Marlborough was already flowing through his veins. He observed with an expert eye German howitzers demolishing the powerful Belgian forts. The principles of land warfare were something that he had fully comprehended and fully mastered many years ago, and the prospect of saving a great city and changing the course of the war filled him with anticipatory excitement. "I cannot but think that he will stiffen them up to the sticking point," Asquith commented. And he was right. The Belgian government agreed not to evacuate if the British agreed to give strong support. Churchill called for the naval brigades from their base in England and toured the city's defenses in a Rolls-Royce with a rifleman in the front seat.

The rifleman, many years later, recalled this picture of Churchill the soldier far from the First Lord of the Admiralty's office: "He put forward his ideas forcefully, waving his stick and thumping the ground with it. After obviously pungent remarks, he would walk away a few steps and stare towards the enemy's direction. On other occasions he would stride away without another word, get into the car and wait impatiently to go off to the next area."

With the scent of battle in his nostrils—he was under fire more than once—Churchill decided that he would like to stay and see it through "provided that I am given necessary military rank and authority, and full powers of a commander of a detached force in the field." He wished to resign from the Cabinet, and his post as First Lord, and become a soldier again. "I feel it my duty to offer my services, because I am sure this arrangement will afford the best prospects of victorious result. . . ." He even proposed a successor at the Admiralty.

Asquith read out this startling document to the Cabinet, members of which were anxiously inquiring about the likely date of his return as he was too often given to these dashes across the Channel, which were not welcomed by the government or the Admiralty. Asquith later reported the Cabinet reaction. "I regret to say that it was received with a Homeric laugh. W. is an ex-Lieutenant of Hussars, and would if his proposal had been accepted, have been in command of 2 distinguished Major Generals, not to mention Brigadiers, Colonels &c. . . ." In fact, Asquith had already telegraphed his refusal to Churchill's proposal.

By October 8, Churchill knew that it was all over. "Poor Winston is very depressed," Asquith wrote to his confidante, Venetia Stanley, "as he feels that his mission has been in vain."

Arthur Gwynne, editor of the *Morning Post* and a violent Churchill-hater, published these patronizing injunctions: "What we desire chiefly to enforce upon Mr Churchill is that this severe lesson ought to teach him that he is not, as a matter of fact, a Napoleon; but a Minister of the Crown with no time either to organise or to lead armies in the field." Being photographed under fire (as indeed he was), the *Morning Post* charged, "is an entirely unnecessary addition to the risks and horrors of war."

Sir John French did not agree. Churchill enjoyed a great fellow feeling with the Commander in Chief of the British forces in France. Churchill had frequently visited him at his headquarters to discuss the problems and progress of the war on land as well as on sea. "You did splendid work at Antwerp," French wrote to Churchill when he was at his lowest. "When are you coming to me again? For God's sake don't pay attention to what those rotten papers say."

Churchill could not entirely avoid doing so, but felt able to reply, "I clear my heart of all hostile reflections and sterile controversies. It is vain to look backwards."

But the Navy's fortunes did not prosper. The German armed merchantman *Kaiser Wilhelm der Grosse* (her name alone a provocation) was responsible for a number of losses in the Atlantic before being tracked down and destroyed by a British cruiser. The German cruiser *Karlsruhe* in the Caribbean and off Pernambuco in Brazil evaded a powerful force sent in search of her and notched up a steady toll of victims, seventeen in all, by November 1.

The career of the *Emden* in Indian and Southeast Asian waters became something of a *cause célèbre,* and for a while she paralyzed trade over a wide area. She, too, was still untraced, still continuing her depredations, at the beginning of November, her captain assuming even in British eyes something of the guise of a heroic privateer of old.

The most serious commerce-raiding problem, however, was in the vast reaches of the Pacific, where it could truly be said for a time that Britannia no longer ruled the waves. Besides the *Goeben* and *Breslau* in the Mediterranean, the German Navy had had on station at the outset of the war a powerful squadron in China, consisting of armored and light cruisers under the command of a skillful and determined officer, Vice Admiral Count Maximilian van Spee.

After detaching the *Emden* from his squadron, Spee disappeared from sight, posing a threat to all Australasian shipping, and later, as he took his force from west to east, to the equally important Pacific South American trade routes. A veritable armada of searching men-of-war—French, Australian, New Zealand, and

Japanese as well as British—spread out to locate the German force, listening all the while for the faintest message on the wireless telephone.

The force most likely to intercept Spee was a squadron of mainly elderly cruisers under the command of a gallant but unwell and sketchily organized officer called Christopher Cradock. Admiral Cradock finally caught up with the overwhelmingly superior German squadron off the Chilean coast on November 1, 1914. His flagship and his second armored cruiser were instantly sunk with no survivors.

With unforgivable self-righteousness, Churchill declared later, "I cannot accept for the Admiralty any share in the responsibility" for this tragedy. Moreover, he presented to Asquith and the Cabinet a wholly distorted account of the events, and the exchanges of signals, leading up to the Battle of Coronel. Cradock, Churchill told his fellow ministers, was at fault in disobeying "his instructions, which were express to the effect that he must concentrate his whole squadron. . . ."

But the truth was that, however ill judged was the action of the courageous British admiral, he had been confused by contrary orders stemming from Churchill personally and the Admiralty's craven, inexperienced, and not very brainy Naval War Staff.

Prince Louis of Battenberg, a German by birth, escaped all blame for the disaster in the Pacific because three days before Coronel he had resigned his office as First Sea Lord, his own battle finally lost after weeks of bloodless struggle. Before the war Lloyd George had warned that the public would not stand for a German-born admiral being professional head of the Navy in war. Asquith, too, thought that there might be trouble but that if everything went well Prince Louis might expunge the "crime" of being a blood relation of the German hierarchy—after all, the Kaiser was King George's cousin. But that was not to be.

Of Churchill at this time, Asquith wrote to Venetia Stanley on October 28, "Poor boy, he has just been pouring out his woes." The sinking of the *Audacious* was a great worry, but "Winston's real trouble however is about Prince Louis & the succession to his post. He *must* go, & Winston has had a most delicate & painful interview with him—the more so as his nephew Prince Maurice was killed in action yesterday."

So the deed was done, and Prince Louis was told to go, and at the outset of a war for which he had spent his life in preparation.

And whom was Churchill to choose to replace his First Sea Lord, now that the pressure had, by Prince Louis's involuntary sacrifice, been lifted from his own shoulders? A friend had written to Churchill a few days earlier, "The nation thoroughly believes in you. I should like to see Fisher and Wilson brought in." Their advent, he claimed, "would make the country feel that our old spirit of the Navy was alive and come back."

The more Churchill thought about Fisher as his partner, the more he liked the idea. Conflicts they had had, but these had been inevitable in the turbulent times in which the Navy had lived recently, and they had always come out beaming at one another in the end, to settle down to another ferociously long talk, sparks flying, beating the best out of each other. Fisher the stimulant was what Churchill was in need of in these pallid days of worry and inaction.

"Lord Fisher used to come occasionally to the Admiralty, and I watched him narrowly to judge his physical strength and mental alertness," Churchill wrote later. "There seemed no doubt about either . . . he left me with the impression of a terrific engine of mental and physical power burning and throbbing in that ancient frame."

Churchill sounded him out forthwith and found, unsurprisingly, "that he was fiercely eager to lay his grasp on power, and was strongly inspired with the sense of a message to deliver and a mission to perform. . . . I was well aware that there would be strong, natural and legitimate opposition in many quarters to Fisher's appointment, but having formed my own conviction I was determined not to remain at the Admiralty unless I could do justice to it. So in the end, for good or for ill, I had my way."

Churchill and Fisher had a mutual compulsion for one another, drawn to some shared drug that raised them to a new high of hyperstimulation. Contentment lay in rapid debate, sparks flying, which was a wonder to others present, who were themselves stunned into silence. When these two wanted one another, nothing was allowed to stand in their way—not even the words of caution to her husband uttered by sensible Clementine. As for Fisher, the lust for renewed power, like one of his battle cruisers under forced draft, swept him ever more swiftly back to the Admiralty, listening to no one. The newspaper proprietor Lord Northcliffe wrote to the journalist Hugh Massingham, "I expended one hundred and twenty minutes of as much energy as I possess in giving him [Fisher] my views of Churchill's character— its many good qualitites, its many bad—gained in a great many years of acquaintance with Churchill. I might have been talking to a stone. . . .

The King argued that the service did not trust Fisher, he would open up old wounds, and so on. George V was joined by other doubters. Besides those who had never been in the fish pond, several admirals, including a future first sea lord, Rosslyn Wemyss, experienced forebodings for the future. "They will be as thick as thieves at first until they differ on some subject," wrote this percipient and highly experienced sailor, "probably as to who is to be No. 1, when they will begin to intrigue against one another."

But the newspapers, with few exceptions, were delighted at the news, as were the public at large. Churchill was right. The Admiralty's reputation was redeemed overnight, and with it his own reputation even before anything had been accomplished.

The wheels of vengeance for Coronel were thrust into motion within just one hour of the news being confirmed that Cradock and his two cruisers had gone down off the Chilean coast. Fisher was in his element, in command again at this hour of need for his beloved Navy and his country. At the Admiralty it was at once evident that, for the first time since October 1911, professional control was no longer exclusively in the hands of the First Lord. Fisher changed all that overnight. There was no branch of the elaborate and powerful Admiralty machinery with which he was not familiar. He knew all those in command, their strengths and weaknesses, and could identify without a glance his enemies and friends.

After clearing out all weak elements, Fisher got down to the business of running the war at sea with Churchill. At this stage it was Fisher who made most of the operational decisions, the new Chief of Staff, Henry Oliver, being no more than a rubber stamp. The new dispositions were entirely Fisher's and characteristically positive they were, too. He proposed to send to the South Atlantic without delay two battle cruisers, each capable of outgunning and outpacing Spee's entire squadron. They did so, in short order, and on December 8, 1914, a British squadron caught and sank all but one of Spee's five cruisers off the Falkland Islands—the fifth was caught later. The Navy and the Admiralty were reinstated in the hearts of the people. "A brilliant feat of arms," "Coronel avenged," and simply "A Great Naval Victory" were the expressions used by the press. Letters from his friends and contemporaries in the service, from politicians, from the general public poured into the Admiralty for Fisher. But the message he treasured most was from Churchill:

December 10

This was your show and your luck. . . . Your *flair* was quite true. Let us have some more victories together, and confound all our foes abroad—and (don't forget) at home.

Churchill had not been so politically secure since the outbreak of the war, the partnership with Fisher had never been so close, and they were soon to share in another victory at sea, this time in home waters.

Two days after the British defeat at Coronel, German cruisers had struck again, this time in the North Sea. On November 3, four battle cruisers under the command of Admiral Franz von Hipper had crossed the North Sea to cover a mining operation and bombarded Yarmouth on the east coast of England. Only a few shells were fired, damage was negligible, and no one was hurt. But the implications were serious. For the public, it was a rude slap in the face.

Fisher at once matched his preparations for a counterattack here with those he was taking against Spee on the other side of the world. By happy chance a set of German cipher and signal books had come into the hands of the British recently through the good offices of the Russian Admiralty. (They had been found on the corpse of a German sailor: Churchill referrred to them as "these sea-stained priceless documents.") With the guidance of these codes and the extremely sophisticated listening-in and direction-finding devices installed along the English coast, the Admiralty could by this time not only locate and listen in to German men-of-war and to German shore transmitters, but through its hush-hush "Room 40" learned in advance of certain German operations.

Thus, on the evening of December 14, Fisher was informed that Hipper's battle cruisers were about to embark on an operation against the English coast again. There was plenty of time to prepare a trap. All the auguries were favorable. A crack battle squadron of dreadnoughts and battle cruisers were poised to destroy the German force as it advanced across the North Sea. The Germans fell into the British trap and lost a powerful battle-cruiser-cum-armored-cruiser, the *Blücher*.

The action was hailed as a great British victory and photographs of the sinking *Blücher* on her side were relished by millions. Referring to Hipper (who had earned the sobriquet Baby-Killer) one newspaper noted with satisfaction, "It will be some time before they go baby-killing again." And *The Times* rejoiced "to announce that the German battle-cruiser squadron was caught by the Royal Navy in the North Sea yesterday while steaming at full speed towards the east coast of England on another of its murderous raids. The powerful cruiser *Blücher* was sunk, and two other German battle-cruisers were seriously damaged. Such is the crushing reply of British sailors to the raiders who bombarded undefended towns and slaughter helpless women and children."

For Churchill the Battle of the Dogger Bank was another much needed gift. How fortunes had swung in the Admiralty's favor since he had recalled Fisher! But never for one moment did he relate Fisher's return to the relative noninterference in operational matters Churchill was now permitted as a result of Fisher's firm control and total authority over the day-to-day running of the Royal Navy and all matters of communication between the Admiralty and commanders at sea. Churchill, while following events in the Dogger Bank with intense keenness, limited himself to informing the King about what was happening rather than shooting off loosely worded instructions like those sent to Admiral Cradock.

The Dogger Bank battle marked the completion of a brief but critically important phase in Churchill's relations with the Royal Navy. Since Fisher's return he had handed over numerous controls of the great and complex Admiralty to Fisher, who was handling this ship with all the old brilliancy and fervor he had demonstrated when, as a younger man, he had run the Navy virtually unaided from 1904 until 1910.

But it would be quite wrong to deduce from this that Churchill had in any way reduced his own steam pressure. His mind did not rest during any waking moment in the long day and half the night when he worked, and he was soon back to his old tricks, trying to run everything. The range of his thinking was infinitely wider than Fisher's, embracing, as it did, not just the needs and activities of sea power but the entire broad spectrum of the war and how and where it must be won.

Back in 1911 Churchill had prepared a long memorandum for a meeting of the Committee of Imperial Defence, "to instil into this important body an alertness such as he felt himself." It assumed an alliance among France, Russia, and Britain and a joint attack on this alliance by the Central Powers, Germany and Austria. On the Western Front, Churchill predicted, a massive German advance would break through the line of the Meuse on the twentieth day, after which the French armies would fall back on Paris. But, claimed Churchill the military prophet, the rate of the advance would be slowed by the Germans' losses, by the need to guard their extended lines of communication and supply, by the vast diversion (half a million men) required for the investment of Paris, by the growing pressure from the east as the vast Russian armies gained momentum, and by the arrival of the British Army. By the fortieth day Germany would be at full strain and the "opportunities for the decisive trial of strength may occur."

Three years later, as the German armies poured through Belgium, Churchill circulated copies of this document to the Cabinet, not as a boast of his prophetic powers but to put some steel into their spines. As Balfour wrote at the time, "It is a triumph of prophecy!" This prediction did not, however, reach beyond the fortieth day. It did not predict the land war's lapse into stalemate, ineffective and bloody attrition in the tortuous maze of trenches and barbed wire, blasted dwellings and forests. But even before the fortieth day had come and the German Army had ground to a halt, Churchill was seeking an alternative to an impasse in the west.

THE GREATEST CRUSADE

Churchill's strategic eye was attracted to the east. Here Russia was the partner in the alliance whose armies and geographic advantage of vast spaces could exhaust the enemy. Influenced historically by Napoleon's exhaustion and final retreat, Churchill saw on the Russian front the means for the eventual crushing of Germany and Austria—if contact could be made and lines of communication and supply set up.

For almost as long as Churchill had known him, Fisher had preached the "Baltic Project" as the masterstroke, the decisive campaign, to win a war against Germany. In common with received opinion in the Navy, Fisher disapproved of sending the small, professional British Army on the outbreak of war to France, where it must soon be surrounded and destroyed. He wanted it reserved for amphibious warfare. "Fisher's view was that a country like Britain with a relatively large and highly trained Navy, but only a small professional Army, could use that Army to the best effect by throwing it, at a critical moment, on the flank or in the rear of the main body of the enemy."

The Baltic Project provided this opportunity. The British Fleet would force its way into the Baltic and, with an armada of hundreds of shallow-draft landing vessels, put a Russian army ashore on Pomerania. Churchill was much taken with this concept, had digested it over the years, and when war came, even before the stalemate in the west, began to make projections. He first sounded out the Russians on a joint amphibious attack on August 19, 1914, in a memorandum addressed to Grand Duke Nicholas, the C in C of the Russian Army.

Any kind of offensive action in the Baltic, was the burden of this message, must depend on either defeating the German High Seas Fleet in battle or effectively blocking the Kiel Canal. Presupposing success, "it is important that plans should be prepared *now* to make the best use of our getting command of the Baltic," Churchill wrote, wishing "the Russian General Staff to tell us what military use they would think it worth while to make of that command."

Fisher, not yet back in the First Sea Lord's office, inquired anxiously from Churchill about his own favorite Baltic Project. Churchill confirmed enthusiastically that it was by no means dead. "But you must close up this side first," he wrote to Fisher.

"A FOREBODING OF DISASTER"

"You must take an island and block them in. . . . The Baltic is the only theatre in which naval action can appreciably shorten the war."

These schemes came to nothing, frustrated by lack of enthusiasm or downright disapproval from inside the Admiralty, and the looming of new priorities. But the fundamental need to establish links with Russia and to support her in her isolation remained steady in Churchill's mind.

With the British declaration of war on Turkey on November 5, 1914, attention turned sharply to the ever troubled, mutually antagonistic states of southeast Europe and Asia Minor. Serbia looked set for being crushed by the Central Powers; no one trusted Bulgaria, least of all her neighbor Greece, who was in turn at daggers drawn with the Turkish Empire. Turkey also threatened Egypt and the Suez Canal and the Russian frontier in Armenia. Italy continued to sit on the fence, ever alert to the tides of military failure and success. German influence and military infiltration in Turkey was by now total.

The key to the Russian Caucasus and the crushing of Turkey lay in the Gallipoli Peninsula and the Dardanelles, that surrealist example of geographic extension that just splits Asia from Europe and forms the narrow, hazardous sea link between southern Russia and the rest of the world. Since mankind had become mobile and bent on conquest, this fast-flowing (four-knot) natural canal had figured in eastern Mediterranean military considerations, from Xerxes in 480 B.C. and Alexander the Great in 334 B.C. to a meeting of the British Committee of Imperial Defence in 1906, when Turkey and Britain came close to war.

The seizure of the Gallipoli Peninsula and the passage through the Dardanelles of the British Fleet would be sufficient to force the Sultan to his knees—or so were the findings of a report by this committee at the time. But how this was to be accomplished was not explained. The recent British record in this part of the world was not encouraging. In 1807 a British fleet had got through the Sea of Marmara, but took a savage drubbing returning down the Dardanelles. When, during the Armenian massacres eighty-eight years later, a repeat of this operation was considered, this time with powerful ironclads, the commander on the spot advised against it. Suicide, he said.

THE GREATEST CRUSADE

Once again in November 1914, with Britain in desperate need of an alternative to the Western Front, where the small British Army—the "old Contemptibles"—was being savaged, the Dardanelles came up on the agenda. Churchill, strongly supported by Fisher, presented the idea of a joint military-naval attack on the Gallipoli Peninsula, which initially would allay the worst fear in this theater now that Turkey was an enemy—a Turkish attack on Egypt.

The tall, grave, revered figure of Field Marshal Kitchener at once took the center of the stage as Churchill, the leading actor, completed his opening lines in the Dardanelles drama now unfolding. Kitchener at once made it abundantly clear that no troops would be available for such an operation. And that was that.

Churchill and Kitchener had enjoyed the barest minimum of social or professional contact since the Boer War. When Kitchener was C in C Indian Army in 1905 and wished to extend the power of the military administration against the viceroy, Lord Curzon, Churchill expressed himself opposed to acquiescing "in the handing over of the Indian Empire to an ambitious and indocile soldier." He wrote to his mother, "Of course I am all for Curzon as against Kitchener, and for Constitutional Authority against military power. I cannot believe a Liberal Government will allow the Commander-in-Chief in India to engross himself in so much power."

In 1912 the two men met in Malta when Kitchener was agent general in Egypt, and reached a formal agreement over naval strength and dispositions in the Mediterranean. When Kitchener became Secretary of State for War in 1914, the two men came into close contact again for the first time in a dozen years. The gulf between their processes of thought and standards of conduct was as wide as it had been in Egypt and South Africa. For Kitchener, Churchill, the clever, cocky braggart on the make, three-quarters scribbler for the gutter press, one-quarter bogus soldier, had grown into a self-seeking, untrustworthy politician; and to Kitchener politicians, like journalists, were a breed that he both despised and utterly failed to understand.

Churchill took a more relaxed and pragmatic view of the most famous soldier of his day. He did not see Kitchener as an alien species. He disliked him as much as ever, but feelings of antipathy were of no consequence when it came to working in harness with him. Kitchener was head of the Army; Churchill was head of the Navy. A sudden dreadful danger had struck Britain and the empire and they were fighting for their lives against a gross tyranny.

Kitchener's staff and paperwork were appalling and rapidly became notorious in the War Office, where he became known as "Kitchener of Chaos" rather than "Kitchener of Khartoum." But Churchill was at first as impressed as he expected he would be at Kitchener's apparently firm and decisive leadership, and they worked together satisfactorily over arrangements for the transportation of the Army to France. It was Kitchener who encouraged Churchill to rush to Antwerp during those desperate days before the city's investment and was undisguisedly admiring of the manner in which he rallied the Belgians and organized the Royal Marines and scratch naval divisions. When Asquith read out to the Cabinet Churchill's offer to give up the Admiralty and remain to continue the fight, Kitchener did not, like the others, laugh the idea to scorn; he said he would make Churchill a lieutenant general on the spot.

To Churchill's amazement Kitchener's enthusiasm and admiration for him in these early days appeared to know no bounds. "My dear Churchill . . . Please do not address me as Lord as I am only yours Kitchener." When Churchill approached Kitchener about finding some war work for his cousin the duke of Marlborough and Kitchener responded, Churchill wrote to him: "I am touched by the promptness with wh you have looked after Marlborough. It is a gt pleasure to work with you, & the two Departments pull well together. . . ."

Within a very short time, a matter of about four weeks, cracks began to show in Kitchener's relations with Sir John French. Kitchener felt obliged to make a visit to his C in C in France. It was not a success. Churchill, as an old friend of French, tried to mediate by letter. French replied about Kitchener's behavior in the same terms as Churchill's admirals might have complained of his relentless interference with them: "I do beg of you, my dear Friend, to add one more to all the many & great kindnesses you have done me & *stop this interference* with the field operations. Kitchener *knows nothing* about European warfare. . . ."

THE GREATEST CRUSADE

When matters went from bad to worse, Kitchener asked Churchill to act as liaison between himself and his commander. Bedeviled by a thousand problems in his own department, Churchill agreed and made his first visit in this capacity on September 15. His visits to General French became more frequent and were soon being made on his own account. To his detractors, this activity was seen as "Winston playing soldiers again." Kitchener took a more serious view. From being a mediator, was Churchill not now becoming a collaborator with his difficult field commander? Churchill's wife, ear to the ground as always and a shrewd observer and judge, counseled caution before he embarked on his fourth visit to French's H.Q. "Of course I know you will consult K," she wrote. "Otherwise the journey will savour of a week-end escapade & not of a mission. You would be surprised & incensed if K slipped off to visit Jellicoe on his own. I wish my darling that you didn't crave to go. . . ."

Churchill took his wife's advice, asked for and received Kitchener's assent. "How right you were about telling K," he wrote to Clementine humbly.

But no amount of advice, no words of warning, seemed able to curb Churchill's involvement in every theater of war, by land, sea, and air, and this inevitably led to the first serious clash with Kitchener. On December 17, Churchill proposed to cross the Channel yet again to "see the working out of the plan." The temptation to become involved on the spot was irresistible. But he took the precaution this time of informing Asquith first. Asquith replied that "I do not think that you ought to go again to French without first consulting Kitchener & finding that he approves."

So Churchill did as he was told: Have you any objection to my staying with French as he wd like . . . ?" Instead of answering direct, Kitchener went to see Asquith at 10 Downing Street to present his objections and persuade him to prohibit Churchill from staying with French again.

> My dear Winston,
>
> There can, of course be no objection to your going to Dunkirk to look into naval matters, but after talking with Kitchener, who came to see me this morning, I am clearly of opinion that you should not go to French's headquarters or attempt to see French.

"A FOREBODING OF DISASTER"

These meetings have in K's opinion already produced profound friction between French & himself. . . .

Yrs always
HHA

"Profound friction" indeed! Who had begged Churchill to act as a peacemaker? That same afternoon (December 18) Churchill stormed out of the Admiralty and made his way to Downing Street. He was furious at Kitchener's back door methods of bypassing himself and going to the top without a word directly.

After Churchill left, the Prime Minister wrote to Venetia (sometimes he wrote three times a day), "He has just been to see me, very sore & angry with K, upon whom he poured a kettle-full of opprobrious epithets. Of course he acquiesced in the decision. . . ."

As the Prime Minister's daughter had already observed of Kitchener and Churchill at Malta during their meeting in 1912, "Their relationship has always been a prickly one." From this time, the prickliness had hardened into a hostility between the two men that was as total and relentless as the war itself, camouflaged as it might be to the outside world, and even to members of the Cabinet, by the courtesies of correct public behavior. Private communication was something different.

"The question I asked was one wh you cd easily have answered yourself," Churchill snapped in a letter he wrote the same day. ". . . It was not necessary to trouble the Prime Minister; and some of the statements you appear to have made to him are not well founded, & shd certainly in the first instance have been made to me."

Asquith directly, and Venetia Stanley indirectly but promptly, were at once wide-eyed amused witnesses, and conciliators in this fracas between the two war leaders at this critical hour.

Kitchener replied with an even heavier shell:

My dear Churchill,

I cannot of course object to your going over to discuss naval co-operations with Sir J. French; but at the same time I think I ought to tell you frankly that your private arrangements with French as regards land forces is rendering my position and responsibility as S of S impossible. I consider that if my relations with French are strained it will do away with any advantage there may be in my holding my present position and I foresee that if the present system continues it must result in creating grave difficulties between French & myself. I do not interfere with Jellicoe nor do I have a personal correspondence with him.

He concluded with the extraordinary suggestion that Churchill should take over the War Office and let Fisher become First Lord—"then all would work smoothly I hope." Although this was not sent, Kitchener was not going to deprive himself of the satisfaction of telling Churchill that he had written it and been persuaded by Asquith not to send it, with all the implied dark hints about its contents.

Back came Churchill on this hectic day (December 19) of hurled Whitehall insults with messengers running hither and thither. Claiming reasonably that he had on every possible occasion and by every possible means promoted confidence and goodwill between Kitchener and French, Churchill said bluntly that "there was no need to make charges or statements of the character to wh I have referred. They are vy unfair to a colleague," he concluded, "who has worked with you with the utmost loyalty."

To clear the air, and calm down "my stormy petrels," as Asquith described Churchill and Kitchener, he decided to bring Sir John French over secretly from France for conversations. These covered a whole range of subjects, but during them French let drop that, much as he admired and felt affection for Churchill, he did find his judgment "highly erratic." But then he also told Churchill later that "Kitchener *ought* to be shot!"

Acrimony, then, was rife, optimism a rare commodity, disenchantment widespread early in 1915. The small British Army in France—what was left of it—was exhausted and in the judgment of its commander incapable of offensive action. Casualties during the first months of the war had been far beyond anyone's reckoning. At sea Jellicoe complained of inadequate strength, inadequate bases, the deadly and continuous threat of the mine and the U-boat; he also complained about his health, pyorrhea and piles in particular.

"A FOREBODING OF DISASTER"

The German armies beat their way farther into Russia and the Turks opened an offensive in the Causasus. It was this attack and the *cri de coeur* from the Russian C in C, that forced the Cabinet and the War Council to take some sort of positive action and at last break the frustrating and gloomy impasse that had gripped the nation's war-making powers for so long.

The Russians' appeal for action to relieve the pressure being applied to them was received on January 2. The response was immediate. The Foreign Office dispatched a telegram promising some sort of action against Turkey. Gallipoli and the Dardanelles became the military planners' first target. And again Fisher, by a long way the oldest member of the War Council, was first off. He drew up, within twenty-four hours, a new strategic plan, written characteristically with many capital letters, underlinings, and exclamation marks. "I CONSIDER THE ATTACK ON TURKEY HOLDS THE FIELD!—but ONLY if it's IMMEDIATE! However, it won't be! . . . We shall decide on a futile bombardment of the Dardanelles which wears out the irreplaceable guns of the 'Indefatigable' which probably will require replacement. . . . And so the war goes on! You want ONE man!"

Not a very helpful beginning. Then, more positively, it went on to recommend the formation of an expeditionary force of seasoned troops from France (replacing them with Territorials from Britain), a Greek attack on Gallipoli, and a Bulgarian attack on Constantinople. There were two main snags to this plan: Bulgaria and Greece, archenemies anyway, were both neutral; and neither Kitchener nor the French command would countenance for one minute the withdrawal of seasoned troops from France.

There was, however, a last paragraph that caught Churchill's eye: Force the Dardanelles with old battleships. "But as the Great Napoleon said 'Celerity'!" Fisher concluded, "—without it— 'FAILURE'!"

Ignoring the complementary proposals for combined attacks by land, Churchill seized the last item in Fisher's proposal in isolation, regarding it as an inspired idea that, if successful, could reverse the damage done by the escape of the *Goeben* and the seizure of the Turkish battleships back in August, and force Turkey to surrender. Suddenly he saw British battleships, white ensigns flying, cleared for action, and flinging shells at the Turkish batteries, steaming up The Narrows to the Sea of Marmara, and

thence to the Bosporus and the Muslim seat of power itself—
Constantinople.

Acting on Fisher's plea for speed, Churchill dispatched a telegram that afternoon to the C in C Allied Forces Eastern Mediterranean.

3 January 1915   Admiralty
1.28 p.m.
Secret

Do you consider the forcing of the Dardanelles by ships alone
a practicable operation.
It is assumed older Battleships fitted with mine-bumpers
would be used preceded by Colliers or other merchant craft
as bumpers and sweepers.
Importance of results would justify severe loss.
Let me know your views.

W.S.C.

The C in C was Admiral Sir Sackville Hamilton Carden, a
fifty-six-year-old Irishman who had earlier been placed in command of Malta dockyard in order to serve out his time in relative
obscurity. No one seemed able to explain how or why he had been
given this later appointment. Fisher had no time for him: Churchill was "not aware of anything that he has done which is in any
way remarkable." In the light of his future responsibilities, the
only remarkable thing was that Churchill was prepared to retain
the unenterprising and negligible Carden at this critical juncture.

Carden replied to Churchill's inquiry on January 5. He did
not think it possible to "rush" the Dardanelles, "but they might
be forced by extended operations with a large number of ships."
Churchill came back the next day asking the admiral to "forward
detailed particulars" and assuring Carden that "high authorities
here concur in your opinion."

It is difficult to identify these "high authorities." The original
plan expressly called for attacks by land, on three fronts, *in conjunction with* a purely naval attempt to force the Dandanelles. Certainly Fisher was not among them.

Lloyd George once wrote that when Churchill had "a scheme
agitating his powerful mind . . . he is indefatigable in pressing it
upon the acceptance of everyone who matters in the decision." If

Churchill could sway the War Council with the blast of his argument, what sort of chance had admirals who neither had his brains nor "had the training" in persuasion?

In these early days of January 1915, then, Fisher was negatively acquiescent to the Navy-only plan and preparations, and to his later regret even made one positive contribution. The *Queen Elizabeth,* the first of the mighty 15-inch-gunned, fast, oil-burning superdreadnoughts of the 1912 program, had now been completed and was due to carry out her all-important gunnery trials off Gibraltar. Rather than firing off her 15-inch shells into the sea, why not lay her guns on the Turkish forts? Churchill responded enthusiastically to Fisher's proposal. Surely even the most strongly defended fort could not stand up to salvos of these almost one-ton projectiles.

But on January 21, Fisher wrote uncompromisingly to Admiral Jellicoe, "I just abominate the Dardanelles operation unless a great change is made and it is settled to be made a military operation, with 200,000 men in conjunction with the Fleet."

In making much of Jellicoe's inadequate strength and emphasizing the need to concentrate the Navy in "the decisive theatre at home," Fisher had a second reason that he never raised in his arguments at this time, knowing that it would carry less weight because, in the eyes of many of his enemies, it was his hobbyhorse. This was the Baltic Project, so recently supported by Churchill and now lost in the cordite smoke of the Dardanelles battleships. In every shipyard in the land, vessels big and small, all of shallow draft, were being hastened to completion. And Fisher knew deep in his heart that all were likely to be swallowed up in the Eastern Mediterranean instead of the Baltic.

This was the reason why his opposition to the Dardanelles project, at least in War Council meetings, was mainly silent; this silence alas, being taken by many as, if not assent, at least muted agreement.

In spite of Kitchener's implacable opposition to the loss of any troops from Britain or France for Churchill's Dardanelles expedition, Fisher still prayed that it was not too late to make him change his mind. He wrote despairingly to Churchill, "I hope you are successful with Kitchener in getting a Division sent . . . *tomorrow!*"

Then, as if by magic, a bright shaft of light appeared, bringing into view an entirely new aspect of the operation. In spite of Kitchener's total intractability up to now, while approving of the Navy-only plan in principle, the field marshal suddenly let it be known to the War Council that a regular professional division, the 29th, based at home but intended eventually for France, could be diverted to the Mediterranean and the Dardanelles to support the two battalions of Royal Marines already assigned to that theater, and any troops that could be spared from Egypt.

So it was no longer to be Navy-only but a combined operation as it should have been all along. In a few words, delivered with stately deliberation, Kitchener had transformed the operation. Asquith was greatly relieved; Churchill was delighted and his soldier's mind was already full of plans of how best to utilize this sudden access of strength. He ordered transports for their passage and arrangements of all kinds.

As if Churchill's difficulties with Fisher were not enough, there then took place the most acrimonious exchange yet with Kitchener. The subject in dispute was the naval division in France. The timing could not have been worse. Churchill had offered to French over Kitchener's head a brigade of the naval division and two squadrons of his armored cars—"those famous Armoured Cars which are being hawked about from pillar to post," as Asquith referred to them. "My conversation with French was of course quite unofficial," Churchill wrote later in mitigation. But knowing as he must have known by now on past experience, it was an ill-considered step. He may not have realized how arrogant and overbearing this kind of behavior seemed to others. But he certainly knew how ultrasensitive the equally arrogant, not to say megalomaniacal, Kitchener was about interference in his department.

It was an afternoon of high hopes and expectations at the Cabinet on February 19, 1915. The decision to send out the 29th Division urgently was to be confirmed. Details and dates were to be discussed. Kitchener spoke first, and his words broke over the assembled members like the first salvos of the Dardanelles bombardment, which had opened that morning at 8 A.M. "In view of the recent Russian setback in East Prussia," ran the minutes, "he was averse to sending away the 29th Division at present." For the time being any troops required to follow up the naval bombard-

ment must come from the corps of New Zealanders and Australians—the "Anzacs"—encamped in Egypt, fresh, enthusiastic,
but only half trained.

As Churchill's biographer has written, "Churchill was totally
unprepared for such a volte-face. It was ony three days since
Kitchener had agreed to release the 29th Division without detri-
ment to the European situation." What had brought about this
reversal of decision? Could it be coincidence that in those three
days the situation had changed so dramatically for the worse on
the Eastern Front? Or was the real reason the sudden plummeting
to new depths of relations between Kitchener and Churchill during those three days?

The minutes do not record Churchill's fury, only: "MR CHUR-
CHILL said it would be a great disappointment to the Admiralty if
the 29th Division was not sent out. The attack on the Dardanelles
was a very heavy naval undertaking. It was difficult to over-rate
the military advantages which success would bring. . . . We
should never forgive ourselves if this promising operation failed
owing to insufficient military support at the critical moment," he
ended ominously.

Asquith appealed to Kitchener to change his mind, emphasizing the dangers of weakening the force by depriving it "of the one
Regular Division so necessary to its effective composition." Churchill was not quite right in claiming that "the whole Council,
with the exception of Lord Kitchener, were of one mind. I urged
the Prime Minister to make his authority effective," Churchill
later wrote, "and to insist upon the despatch of the 29th Division. . . . I felt at that moment in an intense way a foreboding of
disaster. I knew it was a turning-point in the struggle as surely as I
know now that the consequences are graven upon the monuments
of history." But Asquith wrote in his diary that night, "Kitchener,
I think on the whole quite rightly, insisted on keeping his 29th
Division at home." So what *did* Asquith think? It really does seem
as if he did not know what to make of the whole business and was
stunned into silent acquiescence (not for the first time) by the
omniscience of the stern field marshal. Thor had spoken, and that
was that.

Kitchener did not rule out the prospect that the division
might be allowed to leave at some time in the future. On the day

after the meeting as a further slap in Churchill's face he canceled, without authority and without informing Churchill, all the arrangements for the dispatch of the troops, and the numerous transports were dispersed.

In renewed fury Churchill wrote to him: "The War Council on the 18th instructed me to prepare transport inter alia for the 29th Division, and I gave directions accordingly. I now learn that on the 20th you sent . . . a message that the 29th Division was not to go, and acting on this the transports were countermanded without my being informed. . . . I have now renewed the order for the preparation of the transports; but I apprehend that they cannot be ready for a fortnight. . . ."

On the same day Churchill took the precaution of circulating a note recording his opinion that the alternative military force to the 29th Division "is not large enough for the work it may have to do; and that the absence of any British regular troops will, if fighting occurs, expose the naval battalions and the Australians to undue risk . . . the weakness of the military force may compel us to forego a large part of the advantages which would otherwise follow."

At length, Kitchener changed his mind again and released the 29th Division on March 10. Due in part to the cancellation of the transports, the last of the vessels carrying these professional regulars did not get away until March 23, three weeks later than it would have done if Kitchener had not canceled the order. Characteristically understating the consequences, Asquith wrote in his diary, "There is no doubt that this delay . . . gave the Turks time to improve their defences."

It was not possible then, and remains impossible today, to discern and analyze all the motives for this grave and infinitely damaging decision to cancel the departure of this division. But a strong if not a dominant influence was the abiding hatred and jealousy Kitchener felt for Churchill; young, aristocratic, happily married to a beautiful woman and with three children, journalist and successful political careerist, and in every aspect of his being and character the diametric opposite to Kitchener. Fifteen years after their African confrontations—fifteen years when Kitchener saw himself as loyally carrying out his imperial duties in India and Egypt and Churchill was ruthlessly hewing out political advancement—fate had brought them together again. But now the onetime insubordinate lieutenant was head of the Navy, and as powerful as Kitchener was.

But even as Kitchener made the decision to support Churchill's Navy-only plan, he was assailed by doubts. As A.J.P. Taylor has written, "Again there was no rational calculation, no cool determination. . . ." *If* the Navy pulled it off on its own it would enjoy enormous popular acclaim and prestige. So would Churchill. If it failed, the danger to Egypt would greatly increase and would demand further troop reinforcements from Britain anyway. Kitchener's excuse for holding back the 29th Division because German successes on the Eastern Front might lead to greater pressure can be quickly discounted. Churchill wrote that Kitchener "gave as his reason the dangerous weakness of Russia and his fear lest large masses of German troops should be brought back from the Russian Front to attack our troops in France. I cannot believe that his argument had really weighed with him. He must have known that, apart from all other improbabilities, it was physically impossible for the Germans to transport great armies from Russia to the French front under two or three months at the very least, and that the 29th Division—one single division —could not affect the issue appreciably if they did so." Churchill concluded significantly, "He used the argument to fortify a decision which he had arrived at after a most painful heart-searching on other and general grounds."

The conclusion of the Dardanelles Commission, a body set up to investigate the cause of the failure of the expedition, was uncompromising: "We think that Mr Churchill was quite justified in attaching the utmost importance to the delays which occurred in despatching the 29th Division . . . from this country."

Had Asquith had the courage and strength of will to overrule the Secretary of State for War, as was his perfect right; had Balfour, Churchill's successor at the Admiralty, or McKenna his predecessor, been First Lord in these critical weeks of 1915, there can be no doubt that the 29th Division would have sailed in the transports Churchill had made ready on February 22. Personal prejudice played its disagreeable part in what Arthur Marder has called "the three weeks of shilly-shallying." Perhaps after two of those weeks had passed Kitchener's doubts began to disperse, like the transports for his troops' rapid embarkation. Perhaps he began to recognize a different balance of accruing kudos from a successful joint attack. Be that as it may, when he announced to a greatly relieved War Council that the eighteen thousand professionals of the 29th Division could go with his blessings after all, and when he appointed his old crony from the days of the Boer War, General Sir Ian Hamilton, as commander of all land forces for the Gallipoli campaign, his orders were to capture Constantinople. "If you do," Kitchener told him, "you will have won not only a campaign, but the war." And the contribution of the Navy and of Churchill personally would be seen as very small beer by contrast with his own and the Army's.

Two feuds broke the Dardanelles Expedition, and Churchill himself: Churchill's naval feud with Fisher, and his Army and personal feud with Kitchener. A number of men who knew Fisher and Churchill had predicted the clash of wills, which was an overture to catastrophe. Only one man, and he was not the supine, complacent Asquith, anticipated the even more dangerous jealousies, competition, and resentment, with their roots deep in earlier wars, that would develop between Churchill and Kitchener. And that man was Kitchener himself, who had first begged Churchill to go to Antwerp and then done his utmost, when the opportunity so fortuitously occurred, to recruit him as a subordinate lieutenant general in the Army rather than continue to suffer him as an equal in the Cabinet.

"A ship can no more stand up against a fort costing the same money," wrote the American naval historian Alfred Thayer Mahan in 1911, "than the fort could run a race with a ship." Horatio Nelson, one of Mahan's heroes, learned the same lesson, as did so many more naval commanders, including the commander of the Dardanelles naval force, Admiral Sir John de Robeck, who had now replaced the inadequate Carden. In addition, the naval mine, which had already proved itself in the Russo-Japanese War, had been developed into a lethal weapon that, more than the Turkish guns, spelled doom to Churchill's Navy-only attack. By the time a substantial landing force had arrived, the Turks had prepared, under German guidance, an almost impregnable defense of the peninsula. The catastrophe of the Dardanelles, which resulted in the deaths of so many Australians, New Zealanders, and British troops and the eventual withdrawal of the expedition, was ascribed, in the public mind and many professional minds, too, to Churchill.

But Churchill's downfall occurred long before the evacuation. Cordiality and cooperation between Churchill and Fisher had virtually ceased by the end of March 1915. And Kitchener, now that he had belatedly and reluctantly spared the 29th Division, which could have caused the defeat of the Turkish defenders, viewed the whole operation in Army terms and declined all offers of naval cooperation.

There were numerous reasons for the self-destruction of Fisher and resulting destruction of Churchill's political career in the crisis of mid-May 1915: Fisher's age and increasing hysteria; Kitchener's mad obduracy and hatred of Churchill, which distorted all judgment; the vacillations of the weak, indolent Asquith (who almost went mad himself over the loss, to one of his ministers, of Venetia Stanley in the middle of it all); the inadequate and muddled command on the spot; and the inexperience of the sublimely brave Australians and New Zealanders.

Churchill clung on to the bitter end, reaching out for support even to the Conservatives. But the Conservative party wanted none of him, except his blood; and the public saw the resignation of the admired, professional old Admiral Fisher as the work of the devil Churchill. Asquith's government fell, and with it Churchill.

On May 21, 1915, just one week after the advent of the crisis, Churchill was finally out of office. He said he would be prepared to take any post, however lowly, but only the chancellorship of the Duchy of Lancaster came his way, a sinecure for "distinguished politicians who had reached the first stages of unmistakable decrepitude," as Lloyd George venomously put it.

There was worse to come. Almost all the newspapers expressed relief and there was scarcely a good word about his record, let alone appreciation for what he had done in three and a half years as First Lord. Almost alone, J. L. Garvin, the editor of *The Observer*, offered a morsel of cheer. "His is young. He has lion-hearted courage. No number of enemies can fight down his ability and force. His hour of triumph will come."

The Navy, too, expressed its heartfelt relief from almost every quarter and every rank. Beatty, whose cause and career had been so strongly supported by Churchill, wrote that "the Navy breathes freer now it is rid of the succubus Winston." Vice Admiral Sir Stanley Colville, a past naval aide-de-camp to the King's father, wrote to George V, "He was, we all consider, a danger to the Empire." Jellicoe wrote that he had for long "thoroughly distrusted Mr Churchill because he consistently arrogated to himself technical knowledge which, with all his brilliant qualities, I knew he did not possess." Writing in general terms of the Navy's reaction to Churchill's resignation, the *Times* naval correspondent believed that "the news that Mr Churchill is leaving the Admiralty has been received with a feeling of relief in the Service, both afloat and ashore."

Lord Kitchener, exuding dignity and consciousness of the forgiving spirit he was demonstrating, called at the Admiralty to deliver the last rites. "I had the honour of receiving a visit of ceremony from Lord Kitchener," wrote Churchill with a touch of irony. ". . . He asked what I was going to do. I said I had no idea; nothing was settled. He spoke very kindly of our work together. . . . As he got up to go he turned and said, in the impressive and almost majestic manner which was natural to him, 'Well, there is one thing they cannot take from you. The Fleet was ready.' After that he was gone."

After the last rites were over, Churchill's old friend Wilfrid Blunt found him "deeply embittered" and considered that if it had not been for Clementine's support "he might have gone mad." Churchill was distracting his mind with painting a portrait when Blunt arrived, and broke off to speak to him. Blunt recalled his saying, " 'There is more blood than paint on these hands', showing his paint-smeared fingers with a queer little tragic gesture. 'All those thousands of men killed. We thought it would be a little job, and so it might have been if it had been begun in the right way. . . .' "

For Clementine the pain was instant and quite unendurable. Cynthia Asquith, the Prime Minister's daughter, lunching at the Admiralty before the Churchills moved out, found Clementine alone for a moment. "She looks very sad, poor thing." Edwin Montagu reported to his fiancée—Asquith's recently lost confidante—that he found her "so miserable and crying all the time." Later, he wrote to Clementine:

"A FOREBODING OF DISASTER"

My dear Mrs Winston,

    My heart bled to see you so unhappy and I came back from your house to write a line in the hope of atoning for my lack of capacity to express myself verbally.

    It is a hard time and it is true that Winston has suffered a blow to prestige, reputation and happiness which counts above all. . . .

    But it is also indisputably true that Winston is far too great to be more than pulled up for a period. His courage is enormous, his genius understood even by his enemies and I am as confident that he will rise again as I am that the sun will rise tomorrow. . . .

    Be as miserable as you must about the present; have no misgivings as to the future. . . .

                   Yrs ever to command
                   Edwin S. Montagu

    Many years later Clementine told Churchill's biographer, "The Dardanelles haunted him for the rest of his life. He always believed in it. When he left the Admiralty he thought he was finished. . . . I thought he would never get over the Dardanelles; I thought he would die of grief." Churchill's private secretary Eddie Marsh said that the blow to Churchill was "a horrible wound and mutilation . . . it's like Beethoven deaf."

    Churchill's quiet dignity and the brave face he presented to the outside world gained him great credit, even among his enemies. However unjustly he felt he had been treated, however deep his regret that if he had remained he could have done great things to help bring the war to a conclusion, and however bitterly he felt he had been let down by his friends and treacherously dealt with by his enemies and supposed friends like Asquith and Lloyd George, he made no public word of complaint.

    Churchill was proud of his youthfulness. But in the final judgment, his youth combined with his zeal and intolerance and impatience, his consuming self-admiration for his instinct for war, his unusual blend of romanticism and ruthlessness, told against him fatally. At forty years of age he had not yet tamed his dictatorial manner of commanding a department—it had been worse still at the Home Office but there, there was not, by an infinite margin, so much at stake. Whatever he did for the Royal Navy in those months of peace when he worked so hard and against such odds to prepare the Royal Navy for war, the overall results of his performance in time of war were more baleful than beneficial.

Certainly the ineptitude of the Naval War Staff was a contribution on a massive scale to the failures and disasters at sea, and the performance of a number of admirals at sea left a great deal to be desired, too. But while Churchill justly took the credit for creating a staff against the sternest opposition, it was he, more than any of his less power-assuming predecessors, who must be charged with selecting or retaining these men.

It was not only for political reasons that Churchill was the object of so much criticism in 1915, some of it of an extreme nature. He was notorious for his arrogance and offhand manner, his intolerance of people with views different from his own and the way he rode roughshod over them, his relentless need to interfere in everything concerned with the conduct of the war even when his experience and knowledge were sketchy. "Undisciplined in mind, Churchill was not a success," wrote Richmond, the only really intelligent officer on the Naval War Staff. "He had studied war, but not sea war." But in what Churchill himself liked to call "the great sweep of history," his mistakes and failures at the Admiralty were as nothing. The great mass of the British public, while not expressing themselves in such terms, made what appeared to be a bad investment in Winston Churchill, the young politician and war leader. But the trials Churchill underwent and the lessons he learned in those tumultuous ten months of war in 1914–15 were to pay incalculable dividends in the fifty-seven months of war from 1939 to 1945, and lead to the renown that made him by a wide margin, the greatest Briton of the century.

The shrewd, perceptive wife of the Prime Minister confided to her diary a sparkling thumbnail sketch of Churchill in this brief wartime period when he was head of the Admiralty:

> What is it that gives Winston his preeminence? [asked Margot Asquith.] It certainly is not his mind. I said long ago and with truth Winston has a noisy mind.
> Certainly not his judgement—he is constantly very wrong indeed (he was strikingly wrong when he opposed McKenna's naval programme in 1909 and roughly speaking

he is always wrong in his judgement about people). It is of course his courage and colour—his amazing mixture of industry and enterprise. He can and does always—all ways put himself in the pool. He never shirks, hedges, or protects himself—though he thinks of himself perpetually. He takes huge risks. He is at his very best just now; when others are shrivelled with grief—apprehensive, silent, irascible and self-conscious morally; Winston is intrepid, valourous, passionately keen and sympathetic, longing to be in the trenches—dreaming of war, big, buoyant, happy, even. It is very extraordinary, he is a born soldier.

Churchill resigned his sinecure appointment in November 1915. "My regiment is awaiting me," he had said; and so it was. After training with the Grenadier Guards, the "born soldier," took over command of the 6th Battalion, Royal Scots Fusiliers. Kitchener, the great survivor, retained the public's but not the government's esteem to his end and created Britain's first great Continental Army of recent times. He was never a friend of the Navy, and ironically, met his end on board H.M.S. *Hampshire* when it was sunk en route to Russia on June 5, 1916.

There is little that makes attractive reading following Churchill's departure from the Admiralty. The shell scandal, which jointly with Fisher's resignation brought down Asquith's government, continued for many weeks and led to many more thousands of unnecessary deaths. It was eventually resolved under the control of Lloyd George as Minister of Munitions.

Futile and extravagant trench warfare continued into infinity, or so it seemed to the participants on both sides of the barbed wire. U-boat warfare was intensified until the German dream of starving Britain into submission came near to fulfillment. Nothing much changed until the Americans came into the war two years later, and then only slowly. The war ceased with the moral and military disintegration of Germany, brought about by the drain of manpower and lack of food. If any one branch of arms was responsible for destroying the Teutonic imperial dreams of the Kaiser and his Prussian military, it was the Royal Navy, which with its unbreakable blockade in the end squeezed the life and spirit out of the Central Powers. No major battle was sought by the High Seas Fleet, and when by chance it met the Grand Fleet head-on at the Battle of Jutland a year after Churchill left the Admiralty, it was concerned only with escape, as at the Falklands, at the Dogger Bank, and in the Mediterranean. The fact that it sank some British ships before disappearing into the mist and dusk was of no strategic consequence whatever. The fifty-one-month-long Great War was the greatest victory in the Royal Navy's history.

FOUR
Dinner at
Gray's Inn

While Churchill, admired distantly by Roosevelt, fought pugnaciously and publicly for the Royal Navy against the "Little Navalists" and scarcely less publicly against inadequate and unsubservient admirals, then bloodied himself against Kitchener, the Germans, and the Turks, that other "naval person" continued his own fight for a stronger and more efficient United States Navy. In relative terms it was a less violent business than Churchill's struggles; Roosevelt's chief obstacle was his own boss and for this reason devious tactics were demanded.

During the years 1913–17 Roosevelt's chief allies were, first, the worsening situation in Europe leading to the outbreak of war, and the ever growing threat from across the Pacific where a bellicose Japan was causing increasing anxiety.

When the news was flashed that Germany was at war with Britain, Roosevelt was away from Washington, on a trip as Assistant Secretary of the American Navy. He at once returned to his office, only to find that the news had made little or no impact on the Navy Department, or any other department for that matter. Daniels, he discovered, was "feeling chiefly very sad that his faith in human nature and civilization and similar idealistic nonsense was receiving such a rude shock. So I started in alone to get things ready and prepare plans for what *ought* to be done by the Navy end of things," Roosevelt later wrote. As his biographer has written, "Roosevelt regarded Daniels's idealistic devotion to peace as being dangerously anachronistic in a warring world."

The one step Daniels was prepared to take was purely humanitarian—to dispatch the fleet to Europe to bring back American citizens. Roosevelt was horrified. "Aside from the fact that tourists (female etc.) couldn't sleep in hammocks and that battleships haven't got passenger accommodations, he totally fails to grasp the fact that this war between the other powers is going inevitably to give rise to a hundred different complications in which we shall have a direct interest." Three days later, buoyant and excited about all the activity, he told Eleanor, "Alive and very well and keen about everything. I am *running* the real work, although Josephus is here! He is bewildered by it all, very sweet but very sad!"

For the next thirty-two months, between August 1914 and April 1917, Roosevelt played the part of the impatient reformer and prophet, convinced that the European war would draw the nation into the fighting and determined to do what he could to prepare for that day. Against him he had indifference, isolationism, political caution, and a chief who combined these characteristics with Methodist pacifism. Supporting his cause directly were the more aggressive and realistic big-navy congressmen and admirals; of priceless indirect assistance were British naval setbacks like the German bombardment of east coast English towns (what was to stop a bombardment of New York?), and U-boat outrages like the sinking of the *Lusitania* (May 7, 1915) and *Sussex* (March 24, 1916) with American passengers on board.

Within two months of the outbreak of war in Europe, Roosevelt was taking the risky course of advocating giant naval rearmament, far beyond what Wilson, let alone Daniels, thought necessary. While most Americans believed that the war would be a short one, and bankers believed that both sides would run out of cash in six months at most, Roosevelt predicted a long war. Pressing for the immediate recruitment of eighteen thousand more enlisted men to keep 13 second-line battleships in commission, he knew the risk he was taking. He also believed that "the country needs the truth about the Army and Navy instead of a lot of the soft mush about everlasting peace which so many statesmen are handing out to a gullible public," as he wrote at the time. He was also quite prepared to go behind Daniels's back to his strongest political opponent, the Republican congressman Augustus P. Gardner, to relate to this big-navy advocate facts about specific weaknesses of the Navy, such as the poor reliability of submarines, to feed in turn to the press and help the rearmament campaign. "I just *know* I shall do some awful unneutral thing before I get through!" he once wrote in mock anguish.

When the Mexican troubles* were at their height, Wilson ordered the fleet to concentrate in the south. The fleet was still there eighteen months later and after war had broken out in Europe. Roosevelt was as alarmed at this state of affairs as Admiral Fiske. Training was being seriously interfered with. The battleships, Fiske complained to Daniels, were simply "doing gunboat duty. . . . In the matter of general fleet training for war in strategy and tactics the year and a half that has just elapsed has been almost a total loss." Roosevelt supported this complaint until at last something was done.

Even in politics fortune sometimes rewards the honest and brave, and Daniels's tolerance was never stretched quite to breaking point. And the American public warmed to Roosevelt's youthful sincerity and earnestness. "If you cut off the United States from all trade and intercourse with the rest of the world you would have economic death in this country before long," he told one audience in December 1915. And, pressing for higher appropriations for the services, he upbraided another audience, "Why, we spend more money per year for chewing gum . . . than we do to keep our Army, and more money is being spent for automobile tires than it costs to run the Navy." He reminded his listeners that while Americans would balk at paying more than 2 percent tax, the English income tax was from 10 to 30 percent.

A sharper and more urgent note is evident in communications between Roosevelt and his superior, whose stately, cautious response towards reforms and expansion were exasperating Roosevelt. *"The actual present danger of this situation should be explained to the Secretary and he must understand that immediate*

---

* Internal disorder and resistance to American intervention.

legislation is necessary," we read in one memorandum; and this brief, exasperated note has also survived:

WASHINGTON, April 1917

Dear Mr. Daniels:
Do please get through two vital things *today:*
1. Get that Interior Building or give it to War Dept. & let us take latter's space here.
2. Authorize calling out Naval Militia or Reserve—It is essential to get them if we are to go ahead.

F.D.R.

Roosevelt had drawn up plans for a large naval training cruise in the summer, a cruise that would be paid for at cost by participants but would offer them experience and, it was hoped, would encourage new recruits to the reserve. Daniels did not much care for the idea, seeing it as an east coast upper-class outing for the rich. Roosevelt tried to reassure him. "I fear you have some kind of an idea that the cruise will be taken advantage of only by college boys, rich young men, well-to-do yachtsmen, etc. I want to remind you of the fact that I have twice been elected to office in a fairly large and cosmopolitan kind of district and that I can rightly claim to be in touch with every element in the community. You may, therefore, I think, with perfect propriety accept my word for it that the proposed naval training cruise would be carried out on absolutely democratic lines."

Towards the end of 1915 it was evident that the navalists' cause was beginning to prevail. The war in Europe had lasted not weeks but fourteen months with no end in sight and the strength of the German Fleet was growing, especially in U-boats. The expected twentieth-century Battle of Trafalgar had not taken place. Wilson was at last pressed into calling for a building plan that would give the country a navy "second to none." It would cost five hundred million dollars and include sixteen battleships and battle cruisers and sixty-seven submarines. By the end of August 1916 the Naval Act was passed, with only one amendment: The plan should be completed in three and not five years.

With the failure of the British Grand Fleet to destroy the German Fleet at Jutland and the approval by representatives of the

American people of this giant program three months later, we can see the first hint of the historic handing over of naval supremacy to the United States.

It is indeed a strange paradox—and surely unique—that the head of a navy should deplore a vast increase in its size. As America was pushed further towards war in early 1917 with the renewal of unrestricted U-boat warfare from February 1, Daniels even opposed the defensive arming of American ships entering the danger zone, fearing for those who would man the guns. But he had to give way on this, too, and a diary entry for March 13, 1917, when he signed instructions to naval officers commanding armed guards on merchant ships, reflected his concern: "It was a rather solemn time, for I felt I might be signing what would prove the death warrant of young Americans, and the arming of ships may bring us into war."

To authorize the arming of merchantmen destined for Europe was one step in the right direction, in Roosevelt's judgment, but where were the guns to be found? The Navy was allowed to sell only unserviceable "ordnance material," and Roosevelt balked at the subterfuge of condemning serviceable guns and selling them to shipowners as unserviceable. But he had an idea, which he put to Daniels: "Under the law, however, guns may be *loaned*. . . . Frankly I believe that an intolerable situation is beginning to arise. . . . It is clear that American ships cannot get guns suitable for arming themselves except from the government, and they cannot square it with their conscience to let their passenger ships leave New York without some protection, either convoyed or armed. . . . I would suggest that we can properly loan these guns with their mounts and ammunition. . . . If we refuse to let this source become available to private companies we close absolutely the only door open to them. . . ."

In the event of war—which, Roosevelt believed, could not be long delayed—there was a very real risk of U-boat attacks on American shipping in the Caribbean. The Germans were already building large ocean-cruiser U-boats, such as Fisher had for so long advocated for the Royal Navy, capable of crossing the Atlantic. For Roosevelt this reinforced the policy pressed upon the department by Admiral Fiske to secure American bases in the Caribbean. In 1916 Roosevelt had warned the House Naval Affairs Committee that an enemy was certain to strike in this area of many islands, most of them under weak and corrupt rule, and stressed that it was America's duty to protect these islands for themselves and for the security of the United States.

Roosevelt, therefore, warmly approved of the American occupation of Haiti in 1915 and the purchase from Denmark of the Danish West Indies. He even made plans personally to raise the American flag for the first time at St. Thomas on the renamed Virgin Islands. "We have simply got to control those [Caribbean] islands as a whole—the sooner the better—The next step is to purchase the Dutch interests!" he pronounced in his best Teddy Roosevelt manner.

Appropriately, Roosevelt was a dinner guest of the marine commandant and his wife in the old palace in Santiago, Santo Domingo, on February 3, 1917, when a message arrived from Washington asking him to return immediately. The "political conditions" to which the message referred were the German announcement of the renewal of unrestricted U-boat warfare. This was in defiance of the pledge given to America after the loss of American lives in the sinking of the steamer *Sussex* incident, and the German ambassador in Washington was now given his passport.

Roosevelt was in a state of high excitement. Surely, he believed, this marked the end of procrastination, when even Daniels must recognize that war was inevitable and the navy must be put on full alert. "As we headed north through Caicos Island passage on our way to Hampton Roads no lights were showing, the guns were manned and there was complete air [radio] silence," wrote Roosevelt.

On his arrival in Washington, the anticlimax seemed like a rerun of August 1914—"no diplomatic relations with Germany broken off, no excitement, no preparations, no orders to the Fleet at Guantanamo [Cuba] to return to their home yards . . ."

Like "Uncle Ted" in 1898, Roosevelt was acting as Secretary of the Navy at this time of crisis, because of the absence of Daniels. Shortly after Roosevelt's return he went to the White House and asked the President, "May I request your permission to bring the Fleet back from Guantanamo, to send it to the Navy Yards and have it cleaned and fitted out for war and be ready to take part in the war if we get in?"

Wilson replied, "I am very sorry, Mr. Roosevelt, I cannot allow it."

Roosevelt pleaded in vain, and was given no reason for the negative reply—only "No, I do not wish it brought north."

Like a good Navy man, Roosevelt said, "Ay, ay, sir." But on his way from the room the President called him back and said, "I am going to tell you something that I cannot tell to the public. I want history to show not only that we have tried every diplomatic means to keep out of the war; to show that war has been forced upon us deliberately by Germany; but also that we have come into the court of history with clean hands."

This was the conversation Roosevelt recalled many times in later years. Wilson later gave to Daniels a more pragmatic explanation for his decision:

"There are two reasons why I am determined to keep out if possible.

"The first is that I cannot bring myself to send into the terrible struggle the sons of anxious mothers, many of whom would never return home.

"The second is that if we enter this war, the great interests which control steel, oil, shipping, munition factories, mines, will of necessity become dominant factors, and when the war is over our government will be in their hands. We have been trying, and succeeding to a large extent, to unhorse government by privilege. If we go into this great war all we have gained will be lost and neither you nor I will live long enough to see our country wrested from the control of monopoly."

But events and public opinion were racing ahead of the "peace party" and even the President. Every outrage at sea committed by the Germans nudged the nation closer to outright war. The mood and will of the people could no longer be denied. On March 18, 1917, three American ships were torpedoed. Many more would certainly be lost unless steps were taken to protect American trade. Congress was summoned for April 2, and on that evening Roosevelt took his wife to the Capitol to hear the President deliver an important message.

For Franklin Roosevelt it was "Now's the day, and now's the hour/See the front of battle lour." One of his biographers has written, "Here at last was the excitement, derring-do, and grand-scale conflict for which he had longed. Momentous decisions faced the Navy, and he eagerly helped solve them." He might equally have been writing of Churchill in August 1914. Even now Daniels was still procrastinating, working on the principle that this was to be a limited war for the United States and that there was no need for haste, which might lead to rash decisions.

On the day Wilson declared war Roosevelt was asked by a newspaperman if the fleet had been mobilized. In contrast with Churchill in the same situation, Roosevelt had to plead that he did not know. He took the reporter directly into Daniels's office and told his superior that the press wished to hear. Daniels replied calmly, "Tell the young man that an announcement will be made in due course."

Outside, Roosevelt turned to the reporter. "You see it was the best I could do," he said.

Whatever defense may be made of Daniels's policy of caution before the United States entered the war, none is possible after the declaration when his delaying tactics led directly to the loss of thousands of lives at sea. U-boat warfare, which had brought America into the war, remained the first and gravest threat and Roosevelt gave by far the greatest part of his time and energy to "the submarine menace" during the 17 months before the Armistice. In February he had convened a conference of naval experts to draw up plans to fight the U-boats, which that month sank no fewer than 86 British ships, rising to 103 in March and 155 in April, when total Allied and neutral losses reached the catastrophic figure of 869,000 tons. The decision was made at this conference to concentrate naval construction on destroyers and light craft, which were to be used to hunt down U-boats and protect convoys from them.

The destroyer program demonstrated for the first time to the world the unprecedented strength and flexibility of American industrial power. Some 280 were laid down and, although many were not completed until after the end of the war, great numbers of them put to sea and joined the older destroyers that took up Atlantic convoy and U-boat patrol duties. Their specifications varied only in detail, the average displacement being around 1,300 tons, the armament, of 4-inch and 3-inch guns and 12 torpedo tubes, heavier than that of contemporary German and British destroyers, and the speed very commendable at 35 knots maximum. They were flush-decked for speed of construction and economy, somewhat basic in their finish, and were not very good sea boats. But they performed their function and did a significant part in turning the tide of the first Battle of the Atlantic. They remained a tribute to Roosevelt's zeal and powers of organization until long after their notable reincarnation a quarter century later.

Roosevelt was particularly enthusiastic in his promotion of mass-built wooden U-boat hunters. He later declared that these 110-foot wooden boats with 3 gasoline engines were "extraordinarily successful boats; i.e. large enough to be sea-keeping and to cross the ocean under their own power, and to stay out for long periods." Some 330 of them were built, mainly in small yards from Jacksonville, Florida, to Milwaukee Wisconsin. They displaced 85 tons full load and were armed with a 3-inch gun and depth charges. They did indeed prove to be highly useful, but not in the American coastal waters for which Roosevelt had initially intended them, for the U-boat never became a serious threat along the American coastline.

Daniels did not share Roosevelt's faith in these small craft. "Roosevelt ordered more motor boats to be used for patrol," he wrote in his diary. "Will order many, but are they valuable? How much of that sort of junk shall we buy?"

Daniels also discouraged the construction of smaller patrol boats and in this case he was correct, which was galling for Roosevelt. Frank Feidel has commented on Roosevelt's relations with Daniels at this time, "His skirmishes with his chief repeatedly illustrated a major strength and weakness stemming from the same characteristics: his rather uncritical willingness to listen to almost any novel ideas, his strong support of the proponents of these whether they were worthy or not, and his optimistic confidence that through slashing red tape he could achieve the impossible and in record time." Here once again we see the essence of the qualities and weaknesses of Winston Churchill in his dealings with the Royal Navy in his early days.

Quite as formidable and spectacular an achievement as the building of these vast anti-U-boat flotillas was the construction of a mine barrage across the North Sea, for which Roosevelt can claim equal credit. He wrote after the war: "The first week we were in the war I had been studying a map of European waters, had measured the distances across the English Channel, across the North Sea from Scotland to Norway. . . . I had examined the depths of the waters in those places, and had come to the conclusion that some kind of barrier, if it could be worked out on the technical side, offered the proper strategical solution of keeping German submarines out of the Atlantic and out of the Mediterranean."

The proposal that developed from these thoughts and calculations predictably met resistance on both sides of the Atlantic, although the British admiral Reginald Bacon had proposed a similar scheme in 1916. The Admiralty in London pooh-poohed the idea: The Royal Navy had had difficulty in manufacturing enough mines to close the twenty-three-mile-wide Channel; Roosevelt was talking about a thousand miles of nets and a half-million mines at a cost of anything up to five hundred million dollars. The British Foreign Office feared the diplomatic effects of mining Norway's territorial waters; the C in C of the Grant Fleet, now Admiral Beatty, feared for the loss of free movement of his ships.

Roosevelt persisted with his plan, and on June 4, 1917, made his proposal to President Wilson. The President asked for a report; he got it the next day. Roosevelt proposed that the board should make a speedy full report on the subject. Extensive experiments were not necessary, Roosevelt claimed. "There is enough data in regard to mines, buoys, currents, etc. to enable [members] to report on the advisability of making the attempt on a large scale, and I cannot help feeling," ran the report, "that time is of the essence of the plan, especially because during the next three or four months the weather conditions will be good for carrying out the preliminary work."

Under the pressure of despair at U-boat sinkings and American naval opinion, the Planning Section of the British Naval Staff also made a study and announced that the barrage was technically feasible. Jellicoe, who was now First Sea Lord, was not convinced. But then he had not been convinced by the arguments (strongly supported by America) in favor of convoy, which at length defeated the U-boat. Where would the mines come from? The Americans guaranteed the supply. But it was not until November 2, 1917, when millions more tons of shipping and thousands more lives had been lost, that an agreement was reached between the two governments. The mine to be employed was of the new "antenna" type, which could be laid at any depth, a thin copper cable projected to within a few feet of the surface, supported by a small buoy. Contact with this antenna activated the mine.

Back in America, where Roosevelt had been observing wearily the too-familiar delaying tactics by many of the parties involved, he prepared what he called "a very stinging memorandum" for Daniels, in which he expressed forcibly his hope that "his" barrage would be completed "with a different spirit from any of the operations up to now. It will require prompt decision all along the line." Prompt decision making was not among Daniels's strongest attributes.

The Americans did work valiantly on this mammoth barrage, in conjunction with their allies, and by the end of the war seventy thousand mines had been laid at a cost of eighty million dollars. It was by no means complete, but Roosevelt's claim that even in its incomplete state it destroyed some U-boats and was feared by U-boat commanders was justified. The grinding down of the German war spirit and the cutting off of supplies by the four-year-long British naval blockade was the first cause of Germany's defeat. But the U.S. Navy's contribution in providing hundreds of small men-of-war for the Battle of the Atlantic, and these many thousands of mines for the greatest barrage ever conceived, was of fundamental importance. Roosevelt may not have turned the tide in the war at sea in 1917–18, but history will honor him as the most effective and farsighted American concerned with naval affairs in the First World War. And that is enough.

A summary of Roosevelt by a perceptive newspaperman reveals in a few words much of the man at this time:

> He is young but not too young; has a natural manner, but a keen interest, and is well poised. He works in one of the thousand square, high-ceilinged rooms in the State, War and Navy building, with maps of Europe and ocean routes around him, a bronze bust of John Paul Jones on the inevitable mantelpiece and his commission from President Wilson framed on the wall. . . .
>
> His face is long, firmly shaped and set with marks of con-

fidence. There are faint wrinkles on a high straight forehead. Intensely blue eyes rest in light shadow. A firm thin mouth breaks quickly into a laugh, openly and freely.... He is a young man, a young man with energy and definite ideas, as well as a definite objective, who can be generous and fair, but firm in his own cause. He recalls Conrad's description of the young Malay "war comrade" in *Lord Jim,* "unobscured vision, tenacity of purpose" ...

By the summer of 1918 there was a very substantial American naval presence in Europe, with five battleships serving with the Grand Fleet and three more in Irish waters. "The relations of both myself and our forces over here with the British service and Admiralty are excellent, and all that could be desired," wrote Admiral William S. Sims, commander of American naval forces in European waters, to Roosevelt.

The British admiral Sir Lewis Bayly, who commanded the Western Approaches force fighting the most dangerous U-boat attacks, integrated into his command with complete success large numbers of American destroyers and patrol craft. The American rear admiral Albert Gleaves, responsible for ferrying some two million American soldiers across the Atlantic, commanded forty-five large transports and twenty-four cruisers to escort them. He accomplished this task through waters threatened by U-boats without the loss of a single life.

By July 1918 it had become clear that someone senior in U.S. Navy administration should visit Europe, meet the officers on the spot, inspect depots and bases, and report on everything from civilian contracts to the state of morale up at Scapa Flow, where Admiral Hugh Rodman commanded the American battleships. Roosevelt decided to go himself, and in characteristic style arranged to cross the Atlantic in a small destroyer bound for the war zone, flying his own flag and wearing a uniform of his own design—"khaki riding trousers, golf stockings, flannel shirt & leather coat—very comfy and warm, does not soil or catch in things," as he told his wife. For the length of the voyage he occupied the stateroom of the captain, who had to make do with the chart room.

The destroyer, the U.S.S. *Dyer,* formed part of the escort for a troop convoy of five transports, and Roosevelt reveled in every stage of the passage, from New York to the Azores, where he was to inspect the American naval base. He enjoyed himself whether it was "warm, bright, sunny, smooth, really smooth" or conditions forced "one to hang on all the time." He particularly relished the element of danger and the feeling of participating in the real war—"a lovely night for submarines"; "the alert whistle had blown and everybody was dashing to gun stations"; "we headed [for the U-boat periscope] at full speed about a mile away and fired three shots."

The alarms were false ones, the convoy was never seriously threatened, and the only serious incidents were engine breakdowns and a near miss by one of the *Dyer*'s gunners. "It seems that one of the 4" deck house guns was trained fore and aft and that one of the gunner's mates was working on it," Roosevelt's naval aide in the Second World War recalls being told. "The ship was in the war zone and the gun was loaded. Roosevelt was on the wing of the bridge, on the port side in the vicinity of the compass repeater. He left this position, moved inboard directly behind the helmsman. Just as he cleared the wing of the bridge, the gun was accidentally discharged, the shell taking off through the area just vacated by Roosevelt."

Roosevelt's appetite for excitement and danger was partly satisfied by the time the destroyer tied up alongside at Portsmouth on July 21, 1918, to be met by admirals and officials of both nations. "I wish I could travel all the way in my destroyer costume," Roosevelt lamented. But protocol deemed otherwise. Roosevelt traveled far and wide that summer, from London to Ireland, to France and Italy.

The extremely able Sir Eric Geddes was now First Lord of the Admiralty, and he agreed to accompany Roosevelt on a visit to Bayly's command at Queenstown, crossing the Irish Sea in an American destroyer. "As you know, British officers are not much in the habit of running around on vessels flying a foreign flag," Roosevelt crowed in a letter to Daniels. On the way they talked about the integration of building plans for naval vessels "in order that between us we may not build too many of one type of vessel"—a degree of close cooperation that was not matched until the Second World War.

"Things at Queenstown are running well in every particular,"

Roosevelt reported. "Sir Lewis Bayly is at first a diffident sort of man to deal with, but everybody has come to swear by him on closer acquaintance. He and his niece have been very kind to all our officers. . . . The American and British forces are run absolutely separately and yet in complete harmony, that is to say, although the British have a Navy Yard there, we make all our own reports."

Traveling close to the front line in France, Roosevelt witnessed the cataclysmic consequences of modern war, and of the fearful paralysis of trench warfare, which was to have as great an effect on his war thinking in the future as Churchill's months in the trenches were to have upon his strategic policy in the Second World War.

From the remains of the citadel at Verdun where so many Frenchmen had died, he looked down over the town, and later wrote in his diary:

> Great gaps showed where buildings had once stood. Detached and jagged walls were everywhere, and of the houses still standing not one roof remained intact. It was a scene of colossal destruction. . . . We returned to lunch in the tiny underground dining room of the Commandant and his staff. The first thing that met our eyes on one of the walls was the memorable original signboard which was posted near the entrance of the citadel during the siege, and on which the thousands of troops going forward to hold the line read the words which, for the French people, willl sum up for all time their great watchword of four years—"ils ne passeront pas."

While taking a photograph of a destroyed village, he was hustled away by a French colonel who had noticed two German observer balloons to the north, the inevitable overture to shelling. A few minutes later, from a position of greater safety: "Sure enough the long whining whistle of a shell was followed by the dull boom and puff of smoke. . . ."

But this was not simply a sight-seeing trip. Roosevelt also kept his eyes wide open for urgent needs and shortcomings. "Not a single American navy airplane in France can operate offensively," Roosevelt cabled Daniels. Motors and spare parts were both short. "Drastic action on part of all bureaus necessary as present conditions are scandalous."

DINNER AT GRAY'S INN

In London, Roosevelt met the Prime Minister, the First Lord of the Admiralty, and the First Sea Lord. All doors, and all confidences, were open to him; he learned of H.M.S. *Furious* "being fitted as an airplane ship, with a clear deck aft upon which airplanes could take off and land"; of aircraft production at the remarkable figure of 550 a week and destroyer production of 8 a month.

It was an exciting time to be in London. After four years, British commitment to the war remained total in spite of the cataclysmic casualties. A great German spring offensive had been beaten off, albeit with terrible loss of life. And now the Germans were engaged in a retreat that seemed likely to conclude with final defeat.

"A very interesting day yesterday," wrote Roosevelt of July 29, 1918. It was indeed a day of memorable and historic meetings for the future President. First, at 10 A.M. he went to Buckingham Palace for an audience with King George V. They got on famously, the "Sailor King" loved hearing of Roosevelt's transatlantic passage in a destroyer, and they both lamented that fate had prohibited their taking part actively in the war. "Uncle Ted" had written the King "a nice letter." The stories of German atrocities and wanton destruction, the King assured the Assistant Secretary, were perfectly true—"I can tell you frankly," this grandson of a Saxe-Coburg declared, "that in all my life I have never seen a German gentleman."

On a lighter note, the King told him of a visit to a hospital in Scotland where sailors wounded in the Battle of Jutland were recovering. One of them had a large portrait of the King tattooed on his chest. When the King congratulated him on his patriotism, the sailor pointed to a portrait of the Queen between his shoulder blades, the Prince of Wales on one arm, his sister Princess Mary on the other arm.

"That ain't the 'arf of it, Your Majesty," declared the sailor. "You should see me behind. I 'ave two other portraits—I'm a-sittin' on the Kaiser and Von Hindenburg."

"The King was a delightfully easy person to talk to," noted Roosevelt in his diary, "and we got going so well that part of the time we were both talking at the same time."

Roosevelt next attended a luncheon at the Savoy Hotel given by the American Luncheon Club in London in honor of Sir Eric Geddes and himself, at which Roosevelt gave a short speech. "It has taken me just four years to get to this country," he began amidst laughter; and claimed, "Our naval plans have struck their stride, and there are now over 250 American naval ships on this side." Everyone loved it.

In the afternoon Roosevelt mixed with American and Canadian soldiers and sailors at the Y.M.C.A., and in the evening attended a formal and impressive dinner at Gray's Inn. Here General Jan Smuts spoke for South Africa, Sir Robert Borden for Canada, and the Italian ambassador for his country. Without warning, Roosevelt was invited to make a speech on behalf of the Allies. Its spontaneity, charm, and good sense were given a fine accolade.

Roosevelt met many other notable people on that summer evening when the world war was straining through its dying weeks, Germany was close to defeat, starvation, and revolution, and large areas of France and Belgium had been blasted into a wilderness. Among them was the controversial statesman Winston Churchill, now Minister of Munitions. Roosevelt had admired Churchill from across the Atlantic for many years for his "imaginative and vigorous method of coping with war and naval problems." This was in fact their first meeting, the editor of Roosevelt's letters confusing Churchill with the novelist of the same name in reference to a lunch in Washington in July 1917. They were not to see another again until the conference in Placentia Bay twenty-three years later.

Like many fellow Americans returning home in 1918, Roosevelt was taken ashore on a stretcher. But for the Assistant Secretary, it was only a case of pneumonia. When he had recovered sufficiently, he tried to resign his appointment in order to put on a uniform and join the fighting in Europe. President Wilson firmly refused his request. By contrast with Churchill's experience three years earlier, there was little fighting left, and the President told Roosevelt that he had received the first overtures for an armistice with Germany. Roosevelt was deeply disappointed. He relished the prospect of becoming a fighting soldier. Churchill had demonstrated at Omdurman and in South Africa the political value of heroism. And Roosevelt's years with the U.S. Navy had confirmed him, finally and irrevocably, in his ambition to give up his life to politics.

DINNER AT GRAY'S INN

As Churchill regretted the failure to be awarded any gallantry decoration, so Roosevelt believed that his name should appear on the school tablet of honor among other Grotonians who had faced action. "Though I did not wear a uniform," he wrote, "I believe that my name should go in the first division of those who were 'in the service,' especially as I saw service on the other side [of the Atlantic], was missed by torpedoes and shells . . ."

In the early weeks of 1919, while Churchill as Secretary of State for War was tackling the administrative problems of running down an immense military war machine and "bringing the boys back home," Roosevelt sailed for Europe again to conduct a similar operation on behalf of the U.S. Navy. Admiral Sims had expressed his confidence that he could tackle the complex task of winding down the naval presence in European waters, and on land. Roosevelt, wishing to do the job himself, had told Daniels, "I am absolutely certain that a civilian is needed in charge of this demobilization." But Daniels had at first insisted that Roosevelt was needed in Washington. In any case, he wrote (December 7, 1918), "Our experience has been that our men in the service handle these matters better than civilians called from private life." Roosevelt argued that service experience did not equip an officer to deal with the tough bargaining and financial skill required; and Daniels at length (December 24) yielded. "You will proceed to New York," he ordered his Assistant Secretary, "and take passage on the *Leviathan* to Brest. . . ."

In the event, Roosevelt sailed, in the greatest luxury and with Eleanor, on board the liner *George Washington.* En route they learned of the sudden death of Teddy Roosevelt. "We were shocked by the news of Uncle Ted's death," Eleanor wrote home to her mother-in-law. And later she wrote, "I knew what his loss would mean to his close family, but I think I realized even more keenly that a great personality had gone."

Roosevelt's task in Europe in 1919 was the biggest he had ever undertaken entirely on his own. He was in supreme command of some 350 ships, 54 shore bases, 25 port offices. All these ships had to be sent home, all the installations dismantled or sold off, batteries of heavy guns, radio stations, and a hundred small cogs that had operated the naval machine in European waters over almost two years disposed of on the best economic terms. Roosevelt accomplished his task with the same smooth efficiency as Churchill was exercising for the British Army.

But he received the minimum cooperation from Admiral Sims, who was much put out by being usurped by Roosevelt and received him on arrival coldly and even discourteously. Roosevelt had to admonish him. It was one of the few occasions when he fell out with one of his admirals. Later Sims became ensnared in domestic politics; his attack on the Wilson administration's conduct of the naval war was repudiated by an official committee's inquiries, leading to the ruin of the admiral's career.

This exercise in running down a vast organization also represented the rundown of Roosevelt's period of naval administration, during which he had gained immense experience and a high reputation, not least because he had succeeded in surviving through peace and war a successful partnership with Josephus Daniels. On the return voyage, his task completed, Roosevelt enjoyed the company of Woodrow Wilson. The President was returning from the meeting that had drawn up the Covenant of the League of Nations. Wilson told Roosevelt of his deep wish for the United States to be included in the covenant, and Roosevelt became a total convert to the cause of internationalism through the league. Like all the European war leaders, Wilson was determined that the popular subtitle for the Great War, "the war to end war," must be ensured by a community of nations dedicated to peace and cooperation.

No one embraced the cause of the League of Nations more ardently than the Assistant Secretary of the Navy during his last months in office. Roosevelt and Eleanor shared in the tumultuous welcome accorded to the President on their return, and over the following months Roosevelt made numerous speeches up and down the land in support of the United States' ratifying the covenant. "I have faith that the League of Nations will go through in the end with the support of the great majority of our nation to the unutterable delight of millions of downtrodden in Europe. . . .

"Among all the peoples of the Allies," Roosevelt declared, "and I believe Germany, too, there is a demand that out of this war we shall get more than a mere treaty of peace—something nobler and higher. . . ."

But, alas, the people of the United States were not yet ready for conversion to the faith of internationalism as expressed a generation later through the United Nations, which Roosevelt, more than any single individual, did so much to bring about. In 1920 the seed lay in cold soil, unready for germination. With James M. Cox as presidential nominee for the Democratic party at the 1920 Democratic Convention, Roosevelt was nominated for the vice-presidency at the age of thirty-eight, two years older than Churchill when he had been appointed First Lord, but four years younger than Teddy Roosevelt when he had been nominated as Vice-President. "If he did not actually create a record in the number of speeches he made and the amount of ground he covered," it has been written of Franklin Roosevelt, "he came near to it; and everywhere he left the impression of being a man of boundless strength and enthusiasm." But the Democratic party was doomed from the start and no amount of campaigning could turn the tide.

The 1920 presidential campaign was Roosevelt's Dardanelles. Warren Harding was the new President, Calvin Coolidge Vice-President. Roosevelt retired from the political scene, resumed his law practice, and was appointed vice-president of an insurance company instead of the nation. He had little time to brood over political defeat or enjoy the pleasures of a fuller family life.

On August 6, 1920, Roosevelt wrote a farewell letter to Daniels, marking the end of one of the most interesting, most productive, and in many ways most touching relationships in the history of naval administration. It is a letter that marks out some of the qualities of both men.

> Mr. dear Chief:
>
> This is not goodbye—that will always be impossible after these years of the closest association—and no words I write will make you know better than you know how much our association has meant. All my life I shall look back . . . on the wonderful way in which you and I have gone through these nearly 8 years *together.* You have taught me so wisely and kept my feet on the ground when I was about to skyrocket—and in it all there has never been a real dispute or antagonism or distrust.
>
> Hence, in part, at least, I will share in the reward for which you *will* get the true credit in history. I am very *happy* to have been able to help.

THE GREATEST CRUSADE

We will I know keep up this association in years to come—and please let me keep on coming to you to get your fine inspiration of real idealism and right living and good Americanism.

So *au revoir* for a little while. You have always the

Affectionate regards of
(signed) Franklin Delano Roosevelt

The friendship did indeed live on, and when he became President, Roosevelt appointed his old friend ambassador to Mexico. Daniels outlived his onetime Assistant Secretary by three years, dying in 1948.

In August 1921 Roosevelt was struck down by infantile paralysis, which he had feared for his children and against which he had taken every means to protect them. He lost total use of both his legs and faced the prospect of being a cripple for life, becoming an invalid at Hyde Park with winters in Florida. For three years the progress of his recovery was negligible. Then in October 1924, in the same month when Churchill recovered the lost reins of his own political career, Roosevelt heard of the curative qualities of some springs in Georgia. The waters were to not only bring about a partial cure of his terrible paralysis, but refresh the spring from which eventually flowed the spirit of determination to return to the politics that were the mainstream of his life.

FIVE
"Disentangled from the Ruins"

For a man who was a soldier to his fingertips, as distant from fear as were the Western Front trenches from Whitehall, it is no surprise that Churchill acquitted himself with élan and success as a battalion commander when he left politics in December 1915. His example and dedication, his intelligence and courage, were admired by officers and men, and his superiors. He shared all their dangers, was several times close to death, supported the wounded, wrote letters of sympathy to the next of kin of those who died. "He would often go into no-man's-land," one of his lieutenants recalled. "It was a nerve-racking experience to go with him. . . . He never fell when a shell went off; he never ducked when a bullet went past with its loud crack."

If Churchill had stuck to soldiering after Omdurman he would by 1916 have been promoted to a very high command with strong influence on the way the war should be fought. As it was, this period in France and Belgium served only to underline in his mind the futility and waste of trench warfare and led him to regret ever more bitterly the unreliability of Kitchener and the uneven support the Asquith government had given to the Dardanelles Expedition.

In all Churchill's early life no event more clearly reveals the dichotomy of his mind that his decision to return to politics in May 1916. And it was a typically quixotic turn of fate that within a few days, the Royal Navy's greatest battle of the war took place off the coast of Jutland, and within a few days more his arch-enemy, Herbert Kitchener, had drowned in an armored cruiser off Scapa Flow while on his way to Russia.

Already by March 1916 the acrimonious murmurs of White-hall were sounding louder in Churchill's ears than the artillery barrages of Ploegsteert in Belgium. He returned on leave for the naval estimates debate, savagely attacked the Admiralty for its supine passivity, and—to the astonishment of every listener—de-manded the recall of Fisher, the man who had helped Kitchener to seal Churchill's fate. Balfour replied with a very much more ef-fective and balanced counterattack. It was a bad new start in poli-tics for Churchill, and when two months later he resigned from the Army he was able to recognize perhaps for the first time how few were his friends and numerous his enemies. Throughout the country he was deeply distrusted, and even if Asquith had wished to do so he could not have offered him even a junior post in 1916. The Dardanelles fiasco hung over his political career like a dark shadow. "Whenever I open my mouth in Parliament," he com-plained to his old friend and confederate Lord Hankey on June 5 (a few hours before Kitchener drowned), "someone shouts out that I am the man who let us in for the Dardanelles mistake, and the papers are perpetually repeating it. My usefulness in Parlia-ment is entirely ruined until my responsibility is cleared."

It was the lowest period in Churchill's political life so far. "I remain inactive & useless on the edge of the whirlpool," he wrote miserably to Archibald Sinclair, his old friend and second-in-command of the battalion. He knew that he could never be rein-stated in political esteem until his public reputation had been cleared. A great part of his time and talents was therefore now devoted to the unedifying but necessary task of gathering evi-dence to justify his actions while at the Admiralty. This was eventually accomplished, but with only partial success, by press-ing the Asquith government, itself in a state of terminal sickness, to set up a commission of inquiry into the Dardanelles campaign. This prolonged and exhaustive investigation led finally to the Dardanelles Report, which was debated in the House of Commons on March 20, 1917. In his own speech Churchill was critical of many points but did concede that it was "an instalment of fair play." With Lloyd George now Prime Minister, Churchill was back in office, as Minister of Munitions, four months later.

The Dardanelles Commission's final report was not published until November 1919, twelve months after the war ended. Churchill was not singled out for blame but it was also not the total vindication he sought and that he believed he needed to ensure his political future. He therefore decided to write his own account of his years at the Admiralty in peace and war, at first confined to two volumes but subsequently enlarged to become a history of the entire First World War. He wanted to use the title *The Great Amphibian;* his American publishers, Scribner's, wisely insisted upon *The World Crisis.*

Churchill went about the task as if it were a military operation, gathering a team of subordinates about him with their special tasks, while he orchestrated the whole work, eventually into seven volumes. Reading *The World Crisis* today, self-justification, even special pleading, intrudes too evidently and accuracy is too suspect in the chapters covering the sea war up to May 1915. A more subtle hand could have made out a stronger case more convincingly and less intrusively. As to the rest of the narrative, it takes the reader through the war years at a fine pace, with much rolling of drums and fluttering of banners. It may not be standard history but it is a good, rich read.

Just how damaging the Dardanelles failure had proved to be for Churchill became evident again when his first peacetime appointment was announced in January 1919. Loyd George had reformed the coalition government that had at last brought victory and peace in the previous November. The Conservatives were still unforgiving of Churchill and the most outspoken of the Conservative newspapers, the *Morning Post,* commented, "We have watched his brilliant and erratic course in the confident expectation that sooner or later he would make a mess of anything he undertook. Character is destiny; there is some tragic flaw in Mr Churchill which determines him on every occasion in the wrong course. . . . It is an appointment which makes us tremble for the future."

THE GREATEST CRUSADE

The appointment was to have been to the Admiralty again, which Churchill had indicated to Lloyd George would be his choice, and would offer him the best opportunity for reinstating his reputation with the Navy. Instead the onetime lieutenant of the North-West Frontier and Omdurman and brigadier and battalion commander in the Royal Scots Fusiliers took Kitchener's old office as head of the Army—Secretary of State for War, which also involved responsibility for the R.A.F. as Secretary of State for Air. In this second role Churchill ensured that this force, which was not yet a year old, remained independent of the other two services. But even at the War Office, where he took in hand the enormous problem of demobilizing a restless and even mutinous army in the shortest possible time, and became disastrously involved in counterrevolutionary activities in Russia, he also made his influence felt at the Admiralty.

Churchill's strengthening of the independence of the R.A.F. also led to the unsatisfactory dual control by the R.A.F. and the Navy of the Navy's aviation. The Royal Naval Air Service, which had come into being during Churchill's period at the Admiralty before the war, had become the largest and most advanced in the world. As Japan had earlier come to Britain for guidance on building her Navy, so the now powerful Imperial Japanese Navy created its own air arm in the mould of the R.N.A.S., importing British naval aircraft and using British aircraft-carrier experience. Now with R.A.F. control of aircraft flying with the navy over the sea from shore bases, and from carriers, the Royal Navy's air arm operated more as a poor cousin of the R.A.F. than as the flying branch of the Senior Service. Only the enthusiasm and dedication of a small body of aircrew sustained morale through the difficult years until 1937. Then, too late for another world war, Churchill changed his mind, and the paper he prepared on the future of the Naval Air Service advocated the return of total control to the Navy. In terms of the effect on the Navy of Churchill's brief tenure of the War Office, 1919–21, his critics' fears were realized. Admiral of the Fleet Earl Beatty, the First Sea Lord (as Sir David Beatty he had commanded the battle cruisers and the Grand Fleet during the war after serving as Churchill's secretary), at first supported the Smuts Plan, which effectively destroyed the R.N.A.S., and was blamed by the Navy for doing so. He, too, changed his mind too late.

"DISENTANGLED FROM THE RUINS"

At the same time as the Navy's air arm was being weakened by this dual control, faith in the battleship's future was being confirmed; and in the long-drawn-out battleship-versus-bomber debate Churchill believed there was "an overwhelming case for the capital ship." "He wanted to initiate building programmes of four [battleships] a year for four or five years," Stephen Roskill has written, "just as he had done with Germany in view as the probable enemy in 1912. This was surely a case where his previous experience and his sense of history misled him badly, since in 1920 the circumstances were quite different. No possible enemy except the U.S.A. was in view, and all Ministers and service chiefs regarded war with that country as 'unthinkable'."

All this nonsense of international battleship competition, mainly among Japan, the United States, and Great Britain, was ended at the Washington Conference of 1921–22. But Churchill's faith in the battleship as the ultimate weapon of sea power remained until, and after, he came back to the Admiralty in 1939.

But whatever the eventual outcome of the battleship-versus-bomber contest, Churchill in 1924 found himself involved in one of the political somersaults that had punctuated his political life for twenty years. After losing office, and his seat in Parliament, in 1922, he was reelected on October 30, 1924, as a pro-Conservative, crossing the floor of the House for the second time. This one was a double somersault, for to his delighted surprise, the new Prime Minister, Stanley Baldwin, offered him the Treasury.

As Chancellor of the Exchequer, Churchill saw it as his business to turn round on the Royal Navy, and clip not just its wings but its men-of-war, too. It was a replay of 1908–9 with the important difference that he was now not merely a supporter of the Treasury's economy moves against the Navy, but was the Chancellor himself.

In studying possible economies, the first task of any Chancellor, Churchill at once stated that more money might have to be found for the R.A.F., that the Army's expenditure was already lean enough, but that the Admiralty was behaving extravagantly, as it had in 1908 but with the difference that there was no possible enemy on the horizon let alone within range. Beatty wanted more ships, wanted to make Hong Kong into a submarine base and Singapore into a full-scale base for a Far Eastern fleet in the event of war against Japan. In Churchill's judgment this was all rubbish. Overlooking his recent advocacy of four battleships a year (only two in all were laid down and completed between the wars), he prepared a long document in the form of a letter to the Prime Minister on the folly of increasing naval expenditure. How would a stronger navy be financed? It was impossible to borrow the money; there would be nothing for the taxpayer, nothing for social reform. And who was this enemy Britain was rearming against? Germany was bankrupt and impotent, Russia bankrupt, impotent, and in political turmoil. The Americans were Britons' cousins; and Japan? "A war with Japan!" Churchill exclaimed. "But why should there be a war with Japan? I do not believe there is the slightest chance of it in our lifetime."

Churchill also introduced the "Ten-Year Rule," which operated on the comforting assumption that there would be no major war for ten years. This was not altogether unreasonable in 1924; but then the Treasury made it into a "rolling" ten-year assumption, every new year marking the start of a fresh decade of peace.

Throughout this struggle Churchill remained puzzled, and sometimes outraged, by the Admiralty's constant harping on the danger from Japan. Even his long familiarity with the Admiralty had not taught him that a navy has to have a theoretical foe. "The Navy always needed an 'enemy,' " Peter Kemp has written. "At the turn of the last century it was Russia, then until 1904 it was France, and after 1904 Germany. Pretty well the whole Navy accepted Germany as the 'enemy' mainly because there was no one else (one or two admirals put forward the U.S.A. as a possible threat but no one took them seriously)."

When the announcement had been made of Churchill's appointment to the Treasury, Beatty had written a letter of congratulation, to which he had replied gracefully—"I am one of your greatest admirers." Beatty was, according to Churchill "an inheritor of the grand tradition of Nelson." If only, claimed Churchill, "I could have guided events a little better and a little longer, Jutland would have had a different ring if the plans already formed in my mind after the Dogger Bank for securing you the chief command had grown to their natural fruition." So it appeared that but for the Dardanelles fiasco and Churchill's resignation, Jellicoe would have lost his command, probably less than a year after he had been pushed into it.

"DISENTANGLED FROM THE RUINS"

Clementine Churchill, who was always inclined to take a more jaundiced view of her husband's admirals, certainly did not revere the onetime heroic battle-cruiser commander. By March 1925, with the first contest with Beatty over the estimates warming up, she wrote to her husband urging him to "stand up to the Admiralty. Don't be fascinated or flattered or cajoled by Beatty. I assure you the Country doesn't care two pins abut him. This may be very unfair to our only War Hero, but it's a fact. . . . Beatty is a tight little screw & he will bargain with you & cheat you as tho' he were selling you a dud horse which is I fear what the Navy is."

For once Churchill did not require advice from his wife. He knew very well how to stand up to Beatty. And as a mature politician he knew, like any legal advocate, the importance of holding a fight to a professional level and avoiding personalities. Churchill's admiration and affection for Beatty never wavered, even at the height of the struggle over the naval estimates in 1925 and 1926. As for Beatty, he told his wife, "I have had some bitter struggles in the past, but never so bitter as this—although there is no bad feeling about it. Winston and I are very good friends."

Because the Washington treaty had ruled out the construction of battleships and battle cruisers, in the "naval race" of the 1920s and early 1930s cruisers were the contestants, and the size and numbers of these the main bone of contention between the Treasury represented by Churchill and the admirals represented by Beatty, with Bridgeman as a latter-day McKenna behind him. In the final count the compromise solution left the Royal Navy with an insufficiency of all classes of warships but numbers a great deal higher than if Beatty had not struggled so hard and for so long.

David Beatty was succeeded as First Sea Lord by Admiral Sir Charles Madden, a less belligerent and implacable leader, in 1927. By now the fire had gone out of the battle, and only glowing embers remained when Churchill left office two years later with the fall of the Baldwin government. Ten more years were to pass—"the wilderness years"—before he again became an active figure in the affairs of the Royal Navy. But he never lost faith in himself during the 1930s nor entirely his belief that when a renewal of war with Germany occurred, his services would be called upon. Meanwhile, as a back-bench M.P. supported by a small group of loyal disciples who shared his fear that war would indeed be renewed, he fought publicly and privately, and intrigued, for rearmament—for an increase in the size of the Navy, and especially of the R.A.F. in the face of the ever growing German Air Force.

All that he had feared came to pass, and reluctantly the appeasers were forced to recognize the true face of Adolf Hitler's Nazism. Finally, at nine o'clock on the morning of Sunday, September 3, 1939, the British government under the leadership of Neville Chamberlain dispatched an ultimatum to Hitler's government. It demanded that German troops that had invaded Poland must halt or Britain would declare war. Hitler was given three hours to comply. He did not trouble to reply. Germany had embarked upon almost six years of conquest, pillage, corruption, tyranny, mass murder, and destruction—and final retreat—in a war that was to become many times more destructive than Germany's earlier attempt to conquer and impose her will upon Europe.

No one had done more than Churchill to warn the timorous and supine British governments of Stanley Baldwin and Neville Chamberlain of the dangerous and evil intentions of Nazi Germany. No one had appealed more strongly for measures to defend Britain and the British Empire from this second threat within a quarter of a century from German paranoia, greed, and militarism. An increasing number of people had listened to Churchill's warnings, but less than a year earlier the nation had been united in joy and relief when Chamberlain returned from the last of several critical meetings with Hitler and informed the world that it was to be "peace in our time."

During those intervening months when the last British illusions dissolved in the heat of German threats and the last voices calling for further appeasement were drowned by the tread of German jackboots, Churchill was increasingly recognized as the one man to lead the nation if war came again. He had never experienced such popularity since his return from South Africa almost forty years earlier. But the hatred and suspicion within the established hierarchy of the Conservative party were as ferocious as in 1915, and Neville Chamberlain withheld office from Churchill until he was forced to do so under the threat of a back-bench revolt with the support of millions outside Parliament.

It was not until after the ultimatum to Germany had expired that the Prime Minister asked Churchill to call on him. The country was already at war, the sirens—falsely as it happened—warning of the first air raid had already sounded out over London, when Churchill was offered a seat in the War Cabinet and the office of First Lord of the Admiralty again. Now, at the age of sixty-four and almost a quarter century since he had been forced out of office, Churchill was confident that there would be no repeating of history, except that the Germans would again be defeated. He also believed, as did the ever watchful, ever percipient Roosevelt, that he would before long displace as Prime Minister the nationally discredited, weak figure of Chamberlain, And then he would recover not only his own reputation after past defeats and years in the wilderness, but that of his father, too. Robert Boothby, one of Churchill's most powerful supporters, believed that it was within Churchill's power "to go to the House of Commons tomorrow and break him [Chamberlain] and take his place." And Leopold Amery wrote in his diary, "I think I see Winston emerging as PM out of it all by the end of the year."

Instead, early that evening Churchill arrived at the Admiralty to take over from Lord Stanhope, as weak and ineffective a first lord as McKenna had been. Nothing could have done the Navy more good, nothing could have raised higher its spirit, than Churchill's return to power at the Admiralty, all his past "misdeeds" forgotten, now the hero of rearmament and the warning voice of what had indeed come to pass. Guy Grantham, at the time a captain and naval assistant to the First Sea Lord, got early wind of the news. "I managed to get the buzz into the Admiralty, which led to the signal 'Winston is back!' " he recalls. "It made our day, a great relief to everyone. The news shot round the fleet, everyone was cock-a-hoop." "There was immense relief when Churchill became First Lord," an officer in the Intelligence Centre recalls. "A doer was going to take over. I think the top brass knew Churchill was going to get them hard at it, and they said, 'Well, never mind—it's a good thing.' "

As a traditionalist, with a touch of the superstitious in his makeup, Churchill wanted everything to be as it had been left in 1915. "It was very inconvenient," recalls Sir Clifford Jarrett, private secretary to the First Lord for most of the war. "He wanted all his old furniture back and his notorious lampshade. This was an enormous affair of green silk with butter muslin to diffuse the light, and a long fringe of beads, the whole thing faded and filthy. Eric Seal [Churchill's principal private secretary] had to find and dig out all these objects. After much difficulty, by some miracle he found the lampshade in the vaults of the India Office."

Churchill felt more comfortable and at home when everything was just as it had been, the old octagonal table placed immediately under the lampshade. Even some of the faces about him were the same as in 1915, notably and most important of them the First Sea Lord, Admiral Sir Dudley Pound, who had once been on Fisher's staff.

More ominously, a great many of the ships were familiar, too. All but three of the fifteen operational capital ships had been under construction or completed in Churchill's earlier period as First Lord. Some of the cruisers and many of the destroyers dated back to the First World War. Only the aircraft carriers provided an entirely new configuration.

To counter the threat from the air, all men-of-war were now equipped with many more anti-aircraft guns than in 1915, and the 4.5-inch high-angle gun had been widely introduced. The 8-barrel 2-pounder pom-pom, the "Chicago piano," was a much vaunted weapon against aerial attack, and multibarrel machine guns and, more recently, the Oerlikon 20-millimeter cannon gave great comfort to those facing air attack. More than that, they induced a sense of false security, much as the quick-firers of the late nineteenth century had been regarded as the battleship's complete answer to the torpedo boat. "An air attack upon British warships, armed and protected as they now are," Churchill had written earlier that year, "will not prevent full exercise of their superior sea power."

The truth was that the Royal Navy might have only a modest-sized battle fleet compared with 1914, but it was still battleship-minded. The battleship was still regarded as the final arbiter of sea power, and five new battleships were under construction to meet the new German construction of battleships, just as if history had stood still in 1914 and the torpedo-carrying plane and the heavy bomber and dive bomber had never been invented. Churchill did not question these dated beliefs; he shared them, and wrote of a proposed new battleship as being "absolutely proof against air attack."

"DISENTANGLED FROM THE RUINS"

Neither did Churchill conflict with received "battleship" opinion in the Navy that the answer to the U-boat had been found in asdic, an echo-sounding device that could locate submarines when submerged. Some peacetime exercises seemed to confirm its reliability and accuracy, just as anti-aircraft fire against slow, steadily moving targets at a moderate height appeared to confirm that the bomber was not the menace the "fanatics" claimed it was. It made the admirals happy.

Jellicoe would have understood, and no doubt admired, the rewritten *Fighting Instructions* prepared for the fleet in 1938. This document "was written on the basis that the naval war would be little different from 1914–18," the Staff Officer Plans remembers. "The war at sea would be fought with battleships in line of battle," Admiral Pound, one of the authors, insisted, envisaging war with Japan. In action there would be A, B, C, or D formation with a line of scouting cruisers ahead and a single signaling cruiser between them and the battle fleet. Pound's fellow author, Admiral Charles Forbes, reluctantly agreed. The only feature of these instructions that would have puzzled Jellicoe was that they were triple-paged. "Because the authors were at loggerheads and could agree about nothing else," Admiral Grantham continues today, "every time a passage was drafted by one the other would turn it down, and if one approved the other automatically disapproved. In the end the only way to cope was to print the instructions three pages to a page, the third page being the compromise conclusions in red ink of Terence Back and myself."

But on the whole the admirals, who had mostly been lieutenants or lieutenant commanders in the previous war, were of a higher quality than the previous generation, the "pleasant, bluff old sea dogs with no scientific training; endowed with a certain amount of common sense but with no conception of the practice or theory of strategy and tactics, who had spent their lives floating round the world showing the flag, and leaving behind them a most admirable impression of the nature of the British gentleman," as Stephen King-Hall has described them. The younger officers were drawn from a broader—but still not broad enough—spectrum of the nation's classes. There was still too much class distinction, arrogance, and philistinism. A clever brain was more respected than in 1912, but not much more.

The gunnery officer still ruled and other weaponry was regarded as of secondary importance. There was no fault to be found in the spirit of the Senior Service, however, and the failure to destroy the German High Seas Fleet in 1914–18 in no measure clouded the Navy's confidence that it would always beat the Germans in a straight fight—or with odds against, for that matter.

One department in which the Navy was very advanced, though no more so than the Germans, was in radar, unknown in the American and Japanese navies at this time; but radar was regarded as so secret, and also with so much suspicion, that its existence, with all its novel and fundamental implications, was not recognized in the *Fighting Instructions.*

The first task of the Navy was to escort the new British Expeditionary Force to France, where it would take up its position in the French defensive line, just as in 1914. A blockade of Germany had to be reinstated, and German commerce raiders loose on the oceans had to be rounded up. Perhaps, then, Churchill had been right to surround himself with the same objects and equipment, for the tasks ahead were almost identical. "A few feet behind me, as I sat in my old chair," he wrote, "was the wooden map-case I had had fixed in 1911, and inside it still remained the chart of the North Sea on which each day, in order to focus attention on the supreme objective, I had made the Naval Intelligence Branch record the movements and dispositions of the German High Seas Fleet."

Confirmation of the new spirit that was to run through Admiralty affairs was evident on that first evening, and the first evening of the war, when Churchill convened a meeting of the board and senior Admiralty officials at 12:30 A.M. The board room rapidly filled, and Churchill took his old seat at the head of the long table. He was clearly deeply moved by the occasion, and by the words of welcome uttered by Dudley Pound. Like the host toasting his guests at dinner, he cast his eyes from officer to officer in turn, studying each face critically. Then he told them what a pleasure and honor it was to be there. "There will be many difficulties ahead but together we shall overcome them." Then he adjourned the meeting—"Gentlemen, to your tasks and duties."

There was a strong element of déjà vu in the opening situation and the opening moves of the Second World War. Scapa Flow, as was soon to be tragically proved, was still insecure against U-boat attack. The German Navy showed as few qualms as before in attacking merchantmen without warning, and within a few hours of Churchill's appointment, the liner *Athenia* was sunk with the loss of 112 lives, including 28 Americans. The German mine proved markedly superior to the British mine, and, being activated by a magnetic mechanism, proved for a while to be highly lethal and difficult to contend with. As a parallel to an air raid on Cuxhaven in Germany during 1914, twenty-nine aircraft of Bomber Command attacked German men-of-war with equally unsatisfactory results.

Churchill wasted no more time than in 1914–15 in starting his "search for the offensive." No one believed more strongly than he did that when not attacking the enemy you are offering him victories by stealth. A revived Baltic Project was the first major naval offensive operation Churchill proposed, just as if the ghost of Fisher could not be laid. He even proposed bombardment monitors of shallow draft for the operation, combined with attacks on the Kiel Canal. It was the control of the Baltic Sea upon which Churchill had his eyes, and thus the cutting off of the important Swedish iron ore traffic with Germany, rather than the landing of troops on the Pomeranian coast. But if all naval operations in the Baltic, other than by submarines, qualified for the realm of fantasy in 1914–15, their fatal nature in 1939–40 was multiplied many times over.

"I cd never be responsible for a naval strategy wh excluded the offensive principle," Churchill wrote in a memorandum to Pound, "and relegated us to keeping open lines of communication and maintaining the blockade." "The entry of the Baltic," he wrote a few days later, "for instance would soon bring the [German warship] raiders home and give us measureless relief."

A great deal of Admiralty time was employed on proving the impracticability of Churchill's wilder schemes. The suspicion and natural distaste he felt for anything that could be described as negative was as strong as ever and the Admiralty staff, many of whom were equally imbued with the offensive spirit, found it depressing to have to spend so much time finding reasons for not supporting certain positive Churchillian offensive operations.

Dudley Pound himself was the first target for "Winston's ideas," or "Winston's notions" as they were also called. "His ideas poured out in a torrent, almost all impractical," says Sir Clifford Jarrett. "The Naval Staff and the technical departments became practiced in seeing that the impractical schemes were abandoned. That there were great contests over these 'notions' is not true; if the other services were also concerned they nearly always supported the Admiralty's objections." Admiral Grantham also observed with fascination these countermeasures. "Churchill would blow into Dudley Pound's room exclaiming, 'I've got an idea. Now . . .'. If Pound did not agree he always said, 'I've noted that and will look into it right away.' Then when he had got onto paper all the evidence he needed he would show it to Churchill." That was usually the end of that.

The institution of convoys at the height of the U-boat war in 1917, two years after Churchill had left the Admiralty, had undoubtedly saved the Allied cause. But Churchill, like Jellicoe though for different reasons, did not care for the principle of convoy, which he regarded, quite wrongly, as a defensive practice. Contingency planning long before the war had decreed the immediate introduction of convoys in time of war, however, and Churchill did not attempt to interfere with this lifesaving operation. What he did attempt to bring about, however, was what he called a "loosening up" of the convoy system with a higher degree of risk by employing smaller convoys in order to segregate the faster from the slower ships. He was much concerned at the slowing up of trade that the convoy system caused.

He also wanted to employ in the Western Approaches small groups of anti-U-boat vessels in sweeps over likely areas, rather than concentrating them all on patrol escort work. It was the old story of his military imagination visualizing groups of fast men-of-war seeking out the enemy—on the offensive, not defensive. But logic and experience showed that there was not one chance in a thousand of finding U-boats in this haphazard way. In the real world of U-boat war you protected your convoys and waited for the wasps to come to the honey and then swatted them, preferably before they had dipped in their mouths, or failing that after they had given proof of their presence. In mixing his terminology when advocating these groups—"independent flotillas working like a cavalry division"—he revealed the confusion in his mind between military and naval practice that he had not been able to throw off after all these years.

"DISENTANGLED FROM THE RUINS"

The folly of offensive sweeps was demonstrated in the first month of the war when two precious aircraft carriers with destroyers were detached from the Home Fleet for anti-U-boat operations in the Atlantic. The new carrier *Ark Royal* was narrowly missed, the older *Courageous* sunk. Then, up at Scapa Flow, another U-boat succeeded in penetrating the defenses and sinking the battleship *Royal Oak* with the loss of a further 833 lives.

The toll of U-boat sinkings of merchantmen rose, too, although it was not until 1941–42 that they became serious, just as the buildup of losses in 1914–15 had been relatively slow. The depredations of German surface raiders again caused much anxiety, and it did seem for a time as if the pattern of ill luck was again dogging Churchill as First Lord.

The most threatening and elusive of these raiders was the *Graf Spee,* appropriately named after the German admiral who had been hunted all over the Pacific in 1914. This vessel was one of Germany's "pocket battleships" built under the restriction of a 10,000-ton maximum imposed by the Versailles Treaty, although this figure was secretly increased to about 11,700 tons. These were cleverly designed compromise men-of-war, tough, fast (26 knots), carrying 11-inch guns and fuel to give a range of more than 10,000 miles. They were equipped with radar, which came as a nasty shock to the Admiralty, and two spotting seaplanes, which greatly extended the range of vision. By contrast with 1914, the Royal Navy had only three old battle cruisers with the speed and gunfire to ensure the destruction of one of these pocket battleships.

The *Graf Spee* began her operations in the Southern Hemisphere towards the end of September 1939 and sank merchantmen in the Indian Ocean and South Atlantic. Now, however, almost all merchantmen were equipped with radio, and her movements could be followed by the signals sent out by her victims before they were silenced.

By clever calculation and anticipation, a force of three cruisers under the command of Commodore Henry Harwood intercepted the *Graf Spee* in the South Atlantic off the river Plate. The *Graf Spee*'s shooting was exemplary, quite as good as the *Gneisenau* and *Scharnhorst*'s in 1914, and early and destructive hits on the biggest British cruiser, the *Exeter,* gave warning of another possible Coronel disaster. But Harwood maneuvered his three smaller

131

ships cleverly and scored so many hits on the *Graf Spee* that she took refuge in neutral Uruguayan waters at Montevideo.

Before and during this action Churchill remained in a frustrated fever of inaction in the war room, some of the time in his flowing dressing gown emblazoned with dragons, longing to dispatch a series of signals to direct the battle. "Why isn't he sending any signals?" he kept demanding of Pound. In fact, Harwood's signals had to be sent in cipher to the Falkland Islands, relayed to Gibraltar, then again to Cleethorpes wireless station in England, and finally to the Admiralty. The news was coming in faster from N.B.C. in America, which infuriated Churchill.

Harwood was in tactical command from the start, and demonstrated brilliantly how the Royal Navy could have run the *Goeben* to destruction in 1914. It was Falklands luck again for the First Lord. The German captain having been deceived into believing that an overwhelming British force was assembling to greet him if he left neutral waters, the *Graf Spee* was scuttled and the captain shot himself. The nation rejoiced, and the cry "Good old Winnie!" sounded throughout the land.

(A photograph of the *Graf Spee* before she was sunk published in *Life* magazine was the first intimation to the British that Germany had shipborne radar, too. Churchill tried unsuccessfully to buy the wreck from the Uruguayan authorities in order to learn about this radar and recover the ship's code machine.)

In spite of his numerous and time-consuming "notions," Churchill attracted little of the obloquy he had suffered from within the Navy in the First World War. He was, by contrast, far more mellow, far less abusive and overbearing; not less tolerant of inefficiency but more susceptible to reason. There was none of the harsh setting of junior against senior, and he was altogether more human to work with. Small differences from that earlier period mattered out of all proportion. For instance, there was no conflict of working hours with Pound as there had been with Fisher: Pound worked almost twenty-four hours a day anyway, or so it seemed to those who worked under him, and, besides, Pound was sane and selfless. The regime in the Admiralty could not by any means be called mellow, but it could be called less abrasive. And it was certainly as vibrant as ever.

One has only to read his memoranda, or his "prayers" (as they were called because demands so often began, "Pray, let me have without delay . . .") of 1939–40 to observe the reflected change from the forty-year-old First Lord. Churchill early made clear, for example, that he now wanted his ideas (*he* never called them notions) to form the basis for a discussion and not be regarded as the final word. For instance: "The First Lord submits these notes to his naval colleagues for consideration, *for criticism and correction,* and hopes to receive proposals for action in the sense desired." He would not have written in those terms in 1912.

In his brief period in office, Churchill succeeded in instituting a number of reforms. The most important with the greatest long-term effect were in welfare matters and in fighting the still significant elements of class distinction that impaired efficiency. He proposed an improvement in the roster of destroyer crews, who endured the toughest conditions at sea, in order to give them more rest. He instituted better leisure facilities at the bleak anchorage of Scapa Flow, where he installed a theater and cinema ship. He ferreted out inequalities in the methods of appointing cadets, learning, for example, that three young bright men had been rejected because they came from a humble background, one with, horror of horrors, "a slight cockney accent"! "But the whole intention of competitive examination is to open the career to ability, irrespective of class or fortune." All three made useful officers.

The war for the Royal Navy from September until the onslaught of April–May 1940 was by no means a "phony war." The Navy was the only service that saw continuous activity, and arduous activity in the submarine and destroyer branches. This greatly strengthened Churchill's power and influence in the War Cabinet, which he exploited to the utmost, and which later led to his additional appointment as chairman of the War Cabinet's Military Coordination Committee. He was certain that Germany, having settled the fate of Poland and divided up that unfortunate state with the equally rapacious Russians, would swing round and attempt to devour France, the Low Countries, and Britain itself. He fretted for offensive action and at the same time recognized that none would come from France, which he believed to be corrupt, politically unstable, and militarily weak and incapable. It was not only the unprecedented cold of the European winter of 1939–40 that had the French shivering; it was fear of provoking the Germans into taking action against them. For the same reason the French war government opposed any signs of positivism in her ally. When Churchill proposed floating mines down the river Rhine in retaliation for German indiscriminate magnetic mining in British waters, the French opposed the plan for fear of reprisals, and continued to do so until April 1940, which Churchill rightly found contemptible.

Another mining offensive proposed by Churchill was to be in Norwegian territorial waters. Besides being across the Baltic, the German war machine drew considerable supplies of Swedish iron ore through the Norwegian port of Narvik, deep inside the Arctic Circle, and thence by freighter hugging the serrated Norwegian coast. By forcing this traffic outside the "Inner Leads" within the chain of islands, Churchill planned to capture the ships and close that route completely. The War Cabinet did not share Churchill's sense of urgency on this matter and the project hung fire while varying degrees of nervousness were reflected in War Cabinet opinion, from fear of offending neutrals to fear of countermeasures by Norway. "Oh, surely it's not as important as all that!" was the received opinion in the Cabinet.

But Churchill insisted that with the cutting off of all German iron ore supplies from Sweden through 1940 Germany would suffer a blow "at her war-making capacity equal to a first-class victory in the field or from the air, and without any serious sacrifice of life."

Minor victories scored with the British people a success rating out of all proportion through that long, cold, drear, anticlimactic winter; a German plane shot down, a reconnaissance by a party of a dozen or so troops towards the German Siegfried Line on the Western Front, made headline news. The *Graf Spee* victory had caused great joy and satisfaction. Now, in the third week of February 1940, Churchill provided another display of good old-fashioned cheeky gallantry so beloved of the British people.

The German naval tanker *Altmark*, which had worked in company with the *Graf Spee* and had taken on board captured British seamen, succeeded in reaching Norwegian waters en route to Germany. But she was spotted by British aircraft, and when anchored was approached by the British destroyer *Cossack*, under Captain Philip Vian, who had been informed of her suspected cargo. The

Lieutenant
Winston Spencer
Churchill, Fourth
Hussars, 1895

Churchill as First
Lord of the
Admiralty

Churchill with the First Sea Lord, Admiral Prince Louis of Battenberg, father of Lord Mountbatten and soon to be cast into the wilderness because of his German connections

(Left to right) William Jennings Bryan, Josephus Daniels *(partially hidden)*, President Woodrow Wilson, and *(far right)* F.D.R., in front of the State, War, Navy Building, June 14, 1914

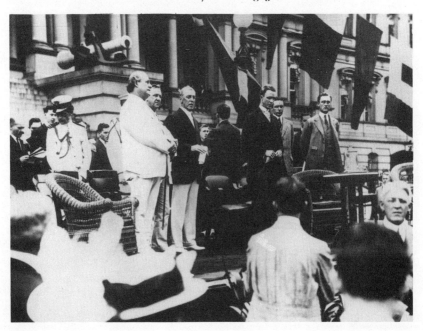

F.D.R. with Rear Admiral Charles J. Badger, Commander of the U.S. Atlantic Fleet, Josephus Daniels, an unidentified man and Rear Admiral Archibald A. Scales aboard the U.S.S. *Dolphin*, October 25, 1913

The top brass at the Army-Navy football game of November 29, 1919. Group includes *(left to right)* General Payton March, Chief of Staff of the U.S. Army; Newton D. Baker, Secretary of War; General John J. Pershing; Josephus Daniels; F.D.R.; and Rear Admiral Archibald A. Scales, superintendent of the Naval Academy

Admiral of the Fleet Lord Fisher *(above left)* and Field Marshal Earl Kitchener *(above)*, who were responsible for Churchill's downfall in May 1915. Churchill never lost his love and admiration for "Jacky" Fisher and never ceased to despise Kitchener. Under the influence of Fisher, Churchill at first admired Admiral Sir John Jellicoe *(below left)* and ensured that he was appointed Commander in Chief of the Grand Fleet at the outbreak of war in 1914. Later, his confidence waned.

Admiral of the Fleet Alfred von Tirpitz *(above)* and Kaiser Wilhelm II *(above right)*, who together led the massive buildup and modernization of the German Navy and the creation of the High Seas Fleet of 1914. Herbert Asquith *(below right)*, the Prime Minister who was forced to replace Churchill as First Lord of the Admiralty during the shell scandal and Dardanelles crisis of May 1915.

F.D.R. and Josephus Daniels in top hats at a Washington, D.C., review
for the Prince of Wales, November 1919

F.D.R. and Josephus Daniels with the U.S. Navy aviators who planned
the first transatlantic flight, April 1919

Dear Franklin — Do you remember
the miles of red tape you cut
to make the first Transatlantic
flight successful! A quarter of a century
ago! Dick Byrd

A solemn and moving moment at Sunday service on board the *Prince of Wales* at the first Atlantic meeting, August 1941

(Below left) Admiral Sir Dudley Pound, First Sea Lord during the difficult and dangerous first years of the war. Churchill learned to love and respect him; *(below right)* Admiral Sir Andrew Cunningham, "valiant in action and in facing adversity . . . staunchly loyal to his superiors and generous to his equals"—the Nelson of World War II, but later less happy in the Admiralty.

(Above left) Fleet Admiral Chester W. Nimitz, Commander in Chief Pacific Fleet, who had just been decorated with the Order of the Bath, Knight Grand Cross, by Admiral Bruce Fraser *(above right: left to right)* Admiral Nimitz; Admiral Ernest J. King, who was Commander in Chief United States Fleet and was suspected, in Washington, of hating everyone and everything, especially the British; and Admiral William "Bull" Halsey, who commanded in the South Pacific

(Left to right) Churchill, F.D.R., and Stalin at Yalta, where the shape and power structure of the postwar world was arranged to the benefit of Soviet Russia thanks to the ailing Roosevelt

"DISENTANGLED FROM THE RUINS"

Norwegians proved intractable and refused permission for a British search of the ship, claiming falsely that they had already done so and there were no British on board. When Vian pressed the point, he was threatened with destruction by the two Norwegian gunboats present. Vian signaled for instructions. Churchill took the matter into his own hands, and without reference to the War Cabinet drafted a signal in his best uncompromising 1914 style— "You should board *Altmark,* liberate the prisoners and take possession of the ship. . . . If Norwegian torpedo-boat interferes you should warn her to stand off. If she fires upon you, you should not reply unless attack is serious, in which case you should defend yourself. . . ."

When negotiations with the Norwegians broke down, and the officer in command refused to accompany Vian on board the *Altmark* to confirm what Vian now knew to be the truth, Vian took his ship alongside the *Altmark* and boarded her in true Nelsonian style, killing four Germans who resisted while the rest surrendered or fled ashore. Below the hatches were 299 Britons facing what they had regarded as certain confinement for the rest of the war.

The *Altmark* affair raised mountainous excitement. King George VI, who like his grandfather, but not his father, greatly admired Churchill, sent him a personal letter of congratulation. Churchill replied, "It is a vy gt encouragement & gratification to me to receive Your Majesty's most gracious & kindly message of approval. . . ."

Churchill was prepared to go much further than this to risk good relations with Norway, and Sweden, too. In early March he returned to the attack over the question of mining Norwegian waters, and, taking a more dramatic step forward, proposed landing a force at Narvik to occupy the port and the Swedish iron ore fields a short distance away across the frontier. Chamberlain opposed the concept. "If we took such action, we should completely alienate the sympathies of Norway and Sweden at the very moment when they are feeling a sense of relief from the danger of being involved in hostilities." The equally craven Lord Halifax, Foreign Secretary, also expressed his shock at such a suggestion. This, Churchill suddenly realized, was worse than the Asquith-Grey lineup of 1915 before the Dardanelles. The proposed action was, pleaded Churchill, "the only hope of securing the iron ore

143

and of thus shortening the length of the war, and perhaps obviating the slaughter . . . on the Western Front." Shades of the Dardanelles indeed!

Worse still, there was even serious talk of a truce with Germany among some political elements, especially in the Foreign Office. Both Halifax and his Undersecretary of State, R. A. Butler, were muttering about the desirability of coming to terms with Germany. The voice of the National Peace Council, articulated through the melifluous voices of theatrical dreamers, like John Gielgud, Sybil Thorndike, and George Bernard Shaw, were heard in the land. And if they later claimed that they could hardly know that the plans for a Nazi spring offensive, including the rape of half of Europe, were already settled, a glance at the German record since 1933 might have suggested that the "peace in our time" of the Prime Minister a year earlier was doomed and that it was "tyranny in our time" unless something was done.

What little that was done, was done, needless to say, by Churchill during the critical month of March 1940 when stronger and stronger rumors filtered out of Europe of German plans to assault the Netherlands and Denmark and Norway. He finally received War Cabinet authority to lay the minefields, with a strong landing force ready to sail if the expedition aroused German countermeasures. The date of the mining was fixed for April 5. And then, like the voice of Kitchener echoing down the years, the word "No!" sounded out—this time, inevitably, from the French War Cabinet, expressing terror of German reaction. Three days passed, days as critical for the Norwegian operation as the days between February 22 and March 10 in 1915 when the 29th Division had been forbidden to sail for the eastern Mediterranean. Then on April 8 the minelaying was carried out, the minelayers, being escorted by destroyers and the battle cruiser *Renown*. The assault troopships were still in harbor when the Germans struck. They were too late, by three days.

Churchill later recounted how, "on the evening of Friday April 5, the German Minister in Oslo invited distinguished guests, including members of the Government, to a filmshow at the Legation." The film, continued Churchill, "depicted the German conquest of Poland, and culminated in a crescendo of horror scenes during the German bombing of Warsaw. The caption read: 'For this they could thank their English and French friends.' "

The party, according to Churchill, "broke up in silence and dismay." And with good reason; for virtually the entire German Navy, accompanying numerous troop transports and supported by a substantial proportion of the German Air Force—the Luftwaffe—had either already left German ports or were making last preparations for the invasion and occupation of Denmark and Norway. On the morning of April 8 the Norwegian government was busy drafting protests to Britain concerning the mining off their coast, which had been announced at 5 A.M. in a broadcast from London. Late on that same day, German warships were seen approaching Oslo. Already reports were arriving of German attacks on other Norwegian ports. The defense of the Norwegian capital rested on a single 1,600-ton minelayer armed with four 4.7-inch guns and a pair of diminutive minesweepers, and some aged shore batteries. The resistance was stout, in the finest tradition of Norse gallantry. The German cruiser *Emden* was disabled, two destroyers held off, and the new powerful German heavy cruiser, *Blücher,* like her namesake in 1915, was sent to the bottom, together with members of the Gestapo and the German staff intended to administer the conquered nation. It was a bad start for the German Navy. Oslo was taken later by German troops landed by air and from shore landings close by.

Elsewhere up the Norwegian coast, German forces landed at and occupied Bergen, Stavanger, Kristiansund, Trondheim, and, evading British naval forces, at Narvik. Churchill remained optimistic in the face of this news, confident in the overwhelming superiority of the Royal Navy and relishing the crippling damage British men-of-war now had it in their power to inflict, the German Fleet being out and scattered far from its bases. "The German forces which had been landed," Churchill noted, "were commitments for them, but potential prizes for us"; and he predicted that "we will liquidate them in a week or two."

The Deputy Chief of Naval Staff, Admiral Sir Tom Phillips, "Winston's blue-eyed boy" as he was called, was equally optimistic. Phillips was a battleship man with a quick mind and good judgment; and Pound, though more cautious and thoughtful about the whole business, also calculated that the Navy stood to gain a series of scattered victories. The C in C Home Fleet, Admiral Sir Charles Forbes, was as vigilant, eager, and self-confident as his subordinates. Nowhere, on land or sea, did there appear to be a revisionist-realist like Herbert Richmond who recognized the deadly danger from shore-based aircraft to a fleet with inadequate air cover and inadequate air power to strike back effectively.

First contacts between the adversaries were, however, ship-to-ship actions that appeared to substantiate British confidence and optimism, and certainly British gallantry. The small destroyer H.M.S. *Glowworm* chanced upon the twelve-thousand-ton modern German heavy cruiser *Hipper* and two enemy destroyers. By brilliant maneuvering, the *Glowworm* attacked the destroyers and, when the *Hipper* appeared, concealed herself behind a smoke screen and then emerged to ram, the only means she had left to damage the massively more powerful vessel. The *Glowworm* tore a forty-foot hole in the armored side of the cruiser, then blew up and sank. The details of this action were not known for five years, until a handful of survivors were released from prison camps. Lieutenant Commander Gerard Roope was awarded the Victoria Cross posthumously.

The next action was almost as one-sided, when the fast, modern battle cruisers *Scharnhorst* and *Gneisenau* were sighted by the old Fisher-inspired and lightly armored British battle cruiser *Renown* in appalling weather off Narvik. In a brisk, brief exchange of fire the *Renown* scored a hit that temporarily put out of action all the *Gneisenau*'s main armament. The two German ships, in marked contrast to their predecessors of the same names with odds on their side, fled to the north, the *Gneisenau* receiving two more hits before disappearing in snow squalls. Admiral Lütjens, it seemed, was no Admiral von Spee.

In Narvik fjord on April 10 the Royal Navy, in spite of being overall far superior in numbers to the German Navy, was again unfortunate in facing severe adverse odds. Captain B.A.W. Warburton-Lee with five destroyers made a surprise raid on the German-held port, sank two more powerful German destroyers, damaged three more, and sank a number of transports. Then he, in turn, overwhelmed by superior numbers, lost his ship and his life in a desperate battle that earned him the Victoria Cross posthumously. Another British destroyer had to be beached and two more were damaged.

In describing this engagement to the House of Commons the next day, Churchill said, "I do not think we ought to have a kind of mealy-mouthed attitude towards these matters. We have embarked on this war and we must take our blows." He also used the occasion, recalling Norway's anti-British behavior over the *Altmark* and the constant traffic in war-sustaining iron ore inside Norwegian waters since the war began, to remind the House that "it is not the slightest use blaming the Allies for not being able to give substantial help and protection to neutral countries if they are held at arm's length . . . until those countries are actually attacked. . . ."

If he had waited a day or two longer, Churchill could have recounted in his marvelously rotund and adjective-rich delivery the annihilation of all eight German Narvik destroyers, together with a U-boat, by a British force. George VI, noting Churchill's increased responsibilities as chairman of the Military Coordination Committee, added: "I would like to congratulate you on the splendid way in which, under your direction, the Navy is countering the German move against Scandinavia."

German naval losses continued over the following days. British submarines found the pocket battleship *Lützow* and put her out of action for many months; another found the cruiser *Karlsrühe* and damaged her so badly that she had to be sunk. But the fact remained that the Germans were there in Norway, strongly established, within a few days of the invasion, with powerful elements of the Luftwaffe that made difficult any blockage of the Norwegian ports. As Churchill admitted to Pound, "We have been completely outwitted." He began his memorandum, "The Germans have succeeded in occupying all the ports on the Norwegian coast, including Narvik, and large-scale operations will be required to turn them out of any of them. . . . It is now necessary to take a new view. . . . We must . . . concentrate on Narvik, for which long and severe fighting will be required. . . ."

The failure of the Navy, with its superiority over the enemy greater than at any time during the First World War, to intercept and destroy the German invaders was raising old doubts about Churchill's ability to lead the Navy effectively. He counter-attacked stoutly but the truth could not be denied. "Everyone must recognise the extraordinary and reckless gambling which has flung the whole German Fleet out upon the savage seas of war," he told the Commons." . . . This very recklessness makes me feel that these costly operations may be only the prelude to far larger events which impend on land. . . ."

For the present at least, the events on land continued to be confined to Norway and their shape began to assume more and more closely that of the Dardanelles. The De Robeck of 1940 was Admiral of the Fleet Lord Cork, who had been brought out of retirement by Churchill at the outset of the war and placed in an office in the Admiralty to work on the proposed Baltic operations, like Admiral Wilson in 1914. Now, at the age of sixty-five, three years older than Admiral Callaghan had been in 1914, he was appointed Flag Officer, Narvik, to command naval forces in the recovery of that vital iron-ore town. The General Hamilton of this latter-day Dardanelles was Major General Pierse Joseph Mackesy, whose main base was Harstad, a short distance from Narvik. He was not the most aggressive of soldiers; moreover his supplies had been wrongly loaded, leaving him short of artillery and ammunition. Although the Germans occupying the town had been badly shaken by the mutilation of their naval forces, Mackesy refused to attack with what he regarded as his inadequate forces.

"The similarity between De Robeck's signals from the Dardanelles and Cork's signals from Norway twenty-six years later is quite remarkable," Martin Gilbert has commented. On April 20, Lord Cork began bombarding the German-held forts with the *Queen Elizabeth*'s sister ship *Warspite*. "Starting harassing fire today," he reported to Churchill. "H.M.S. Warspite much appreciated. Intend her to engage pill-boxes at point-blank range. . . ." Greatly encouraged by this positive attitude, Churchill answered, "It seems to me that you can feel your way and yet strike hard"; and put Cork in overall command.

By this time the War Cabinet, and Churchill, were forced to concede that, in spite of all their supply problems and the elimination of a large part of their fleet, the German control of the air, almost without a break from Oslo to Narvik, was making the liberation of Norway impossible. French and British troops put ashore farther south in the Trondheim area were being constantly harassed by German fighters and bombers, and it was not until

"DISENTANGLED FROM THE RUINS"

R.A.F. fighters could be put ashore near Narvik that an assault on the town could be contemplated, such was the recent rapid buildup by the Luftwaffe. But the "larger events" predicted by Churchill were now about to break. On May 10, 1940, the German blitzkreig burst upon the frontiers of Holland, France, and Belgium, and the last pretense that Hitler was interested in only a "phony war" was shattered in the scream of Stuka dive bombers, the silent descent of paratroops, and the swift advance of panzer divisions.

Narvik was later occupied by Allied troops only in order that installations could be destroyed, and the evacuation of Norway, the first of so many evacuations over the coming months and years, was carried out with the same consummate skill and efficiency that had marked the evacuation of the Dardanelles by the Navy.

Misfortune and good fortune alike accompanied this retreat. The three surviving German heavy men-of-war, the cruiser *Hipper* and the battle cruisers *Scharnhorst* and *Gneisenau,* chanced upon one transport, fortunately empty, and a tanker, which were sunk. Then the battle cruisers, steaming farther north, caught sight of the distant chunky silhouette of the aircraft carrier *Glorious.*

Besides her naval planes, the *Glorious* carried a squadron of R.A.F. Hurricane fighters that had just been obliged to make a deck landing without arrester gear or experience of any kind. The pilots had little time to congratulate themselves. The eleven-inch shells set the carrier ablaze, and she went down shortly after.

The glory of this operation was provided by the officers and crews of the two escorting destroyers, which laid smoke screens and then attacked the massive ships at point-blank range. One torpedo struck the *Scharnhorst* right aft doing damage that put the ship out of action for many weeks. Only a handful of survivors from the *Glorious* were picked up.

The damage to the *Scharnhorst* led the German force to abandon its efforts to intercept any further convoys to the north, and it returned to Trondheim harbor, thus missing the opportunity that otherwise would have been wide open to the battle cruisers to destroy the cruiser *Devonshire,* a mere hundred miles distant, which was carrying the entire Norwegian royal family to Scotland.

The *Gneisenau* was later badly damaged by the submarine *Clyde.* As Churchill has written, "From all this wreckage and confusion there emerged one fact of major importance potentially affecting the future of the war. In their desperate grapple with the British Navy the Germans ruined their own, such as it was, for the impending climax . . . the supreme issue of the invasion of Britain." The Royal Navy had suffered some grievous losses, but at the end of the Norwegian campaign the German Navy had almost ceased to exist. It could call immediately on just one heavy cruiser, two light cruisers, and four destroyers.

By contrast with the First World War, the German Navy had been handled recklessly and had paid a terrible price. Nor had it shown the same skill and courage as the Kriegsmarine of 1914–18, and from the Norwegian campaign was born Hitler's disillusionment with his surface fleet. As for the Royal Navy, it had been forced within a few weeks and at a high cost to face the realities of sea power in the age of the bomber. Ships on both sides had been sunk by dive bombers and high-level bombers, the first to suffer this fate in war. And in spite of the presence of British anti-aircraft cruisers bristling with guns, the Navy had to accept that it could not survive and perform its functions in combined operations without control of the air. Where this was acquired, as briefly at Narvik, the Army could operate successfully. Where it was lacking, the Army was virtually helpless. The threat of invasion of Britain was still some weeks away, but already Churchill could see with prescient eye that the survival of the country must depend primarily on the R.A.F. and only secondarily on the Royal Navy.

Treated as a real-life exercise, the Norwegian campaign was of priceless value. The same mistakes had been made as at the Dardanelles. The Admiralty had many times interfered with operations, with dire results. Looking back, for example, on the Admiralty's cancellation of a potentially successful attack on Bergen, Churchill wrote that "I consider the Admiralty kept too close a control upon the Commander-in-Chief, and after learning his original intention to force the passage into Bergen we should have confined ourselves to sending him information." Once again memories of the Dardanelles, with Churchill, lacking full information, urging a course of action that could prove fatal to those on the spot.

The decisive, underlying fault that led to the disasters and miscalculations of the Norwegian campaign rested in prewar planning by the Naval Staff, which had established to its complete satisfaction that Norway could not be successfully invaded and held by German arms while the British Fleet at Scapa Flow dominated the North Sea. Churchill had had seven months in office in which to question this accepted view. He did not do so and fell comfortably into the illusion that the nature and function of sea power had little changed.

The chief blame, however, lay with the Admiralty, blinkered and still living between the wars as if nothing had been changed by the First World War. The Germans knew better. The German planning staff had had their eye on Norway for years. Vice Admiral W. Wegener had written (in *Die Seestrategie des Weltkrieges*) to advocate an attack on Norway and the establishment of bases along the long saw-toothed coast. "England could then no longer maintain the blockade lines from the Shetlands to Norway but must withdraw approximately to the line of the Shetlands–the Faeroes–Iceland. But this line was a net with very wide meshes. . . . Moreover [it] was hard for England to defend, for in the first place it lay comparatively near to our [new Norwegian] bases and, above all, as the map shows, we should considerably outflank the English strategic position to the north."

This influential and authoritative book was readily available before 1939. No one at the Admiralty appears to have read it.

It remains the greatest blessing and good fortune for Britain—and for the United States and the whole free Western world—that, far from hounding Churchill out of office after his second Dardanelles, the disastrous Norwegian campaign led to his becoming Prime Minister on May 10, 1940.

How could Churchill be "disentangled from the ruins?" a later prime minister, Harold Macmillan, recalled wondering when writing about the parliamentary debate on Norway. But he was. And it was at Neville Chamberlain, not Churchill, that the finger was pointed and "the terrible words" as Churchill called them were uttered: "Depart, I say, and let us have done with you. In the name of God, go!"

SIX

"As Naval People ..."

There was little surprise in the White House when the words "In the name of God, go!" appeared in the American newspapers the following day; and Roosevelt, President now for seven years, had been increasingly confident that Chamberlain's successor would be Winston Churchill—the man he had admired as First Lord of the Admiralty back in 1913 and met so briefly twenty-two years ago when he had been a fit and mobile young politician.

Three years after that dinner at Gray's Inn, the Washington Conference to stem the flow of naval competition—by common consent one of the chief causes of the First World War—had been convened, just as Roosevelt was struck down by polio. It was widely believed in American naval circles that the outcome of this conference was as crippling to the Navy that Roosevelt had done so much to enlarge and strengthen as his disease was to Roosevelt himself. Under the Wilson administration the U.S. Navy had been on the way to becoming the largest and most modern in the world. But under the terms of this treaty over six-hundred thousand tons of capital ships under construction were to be scrapped. "Here was a magnificent potential of sea power," Commodore Dudley W. Knox has written, "upon which we had already spent upwards of 300,000,000 dollars, tossed overboard in a magnanimous gesture for international goodwill and peace, neither of which was subsequently realized."

During the following decade, while Roosevelt fought his disease and courageously reentered the arena of politics, the U.S. Navy—"his" Navy, as he always regarded it—maintained a fine spirit and prepared itself for the imminent naval revolution of the mid-twentieth century. In 1932 it was, like the British Navy, still a battleship navy with tactical concepts based on the line of battle and the big gun. And, because of the Washington treaty, the American battle fleet was an aging instrument of war. All but one of the fifteen battleships had been laid down during or before the First World War. Even the much reduced British battle fleet had nothing as ancient as the twelve-inch-gunned *Arkansas* or the fourteen-inch-gunned *New York* and *Texas*. A modernization plan was under way but no new battleship construction was contemplated. The destroyer flotillas, too, were all obsolescent, being made up largely of the simple and rapidly built "thousand-tonners" and "flush-deckers" of war years.

On the material side, however, the U.S. Navy was, like the Royal Navy, blessed with a skilled and enthusiastic air arm. Back in Roosevelt's time—May 1919—the General Board had made a report "to insure air supremacy." It stated that "to enable the United States Navy to meet on at least equal terms any possible enemy, and to put the United States in its proper place as a naval power, fleet aviation must be developed to the fullest possible extent. Aircraft must become an essential part of the fleet." By 1929 two giant aircraft carriers were operating on fleet exercises along with the much smaller pioneering carrier, the *Langley*.

An indirect benefit of the Washington treaty was the ban on the development by the United States of further Pacific naval bases. Much criticized by senior officers at the time, but a blessing nonetheless, this restriction forced the Navy to consider more closely the art of amphibious warfare conducted across the vast spaces of the Pacific. By 1933 a fleet marine force had been established; landing craft, supply problems, and joint action with the Army were all being considered. It was still only a small seed, but it was to grow into the vast and remarkable amphibious task forces and self-sustaining fleet trains of the Pacific war in the early 1940s.

"AS NAVAL PEOPLE . . ."

Although the Washington treaty provided for a U.S. Navy of roughly the same size as the Royal Navy—and two fifths larger than the Japanese Navy—the Americans possessed one marked advantage over their past and future allies, the British. The U.S. Navy was a classless service that had never been in need of the selection reforms introduced by Fisher and Churchill and others—none of which, incidentally, was wholly successful. Advancement on merit and merit alone was many times more effective in the U.S. Navy than in the Royal Navy. The U.S. Navy suffered none of the Royal Navy's Victorian-Edwardian class prejudice and lingering distaste towards brains and the lower orders, which kept down so many good men right up to the early years of the Second World War.

From the American Naval War College there emerged every year some seventy graduate senior officers. These were the men who fought and won the greatest naval war in history with extraordinarily low casualties.

The election of Franklin Roosevelt in November 1932 had an effect on the U.S. Navy similar to that which Churchill's arrival at the Admiralty would have on the Royal Navy seven years later. Everyone in the service knew how attached to the Navy was the onetime Assistant Secretary and now Commander in Chief. And like Churchill in 1940, Roosevelt appointed as Secretary of the Navy a man who would do his bidding. Senator Claude Swanson was "a benign old Virginian who wore high, wing collars and a frock coat," whose appointment "indicated that Roosevelt would be his own Secretary of the Navy."

Few of the fears of what would happen to the nation under Roosevelt percolated into the Navy. "I was just bustin' to see that smile in the White House and to shake your hand," wrote Captain Harold R. "Betty" Stark, a future chief of naval operations, "If I should try to say any or all that I feel, it could be but a poor attempt in the first place, and an inroad on your time in the second. I know you are too busy now . . . for social calls but some time . . . I just want to see you in those surroundings where we have so long wanted and needed you."

Three months later this same officer referred in a letter to the President to the new building program—"a veritable Godsend" he called it. "Few people realize how far below treaty strength and relative strength we have sunk, and also how badly, in some instances, we need replacements. . . ."

The new building program between 1933 and 1941 reflected more than the worsening of international relations. They reflected the urgency and determination with which Roosevelt tackled the neglect and inadequacies suffered by the Navy since he had ceased to be Assistant Secretary. In battleships alone the 1936 program included two, the 1938 program called for four more, and in 1940 eleven mastodons of forty-five thousand to fifty-eight thousand tons were ordered or projected, together with six battle cruisers, (America's first). This scale of rearmament made Britain's most extravagant program look puny indeed. (In fact a number of these ships were never completed.)

Naval aviation expansion was not so massive, and not massive enough to meet war needs as it turned out, but was still given great new impetus during Roosevelt's early years at the White House, two 20,000-ton carriers being laid down in 1934, and then others in increasing volume until some dozen were under construction by the time of Pearl Harbor. The same number of eight-inch-gunned cruisers was ordered between Roosevelt's inauguration and the end of 1941, and huge programs of light-cruiser, destroyer, and submarine construction were put in hand.

Scarcely a day passed when Roosevelt did not involve himself in some aspect or another of the workings of the Navy. Like Churchill, he had a steady preoccupation with the design of new men-of-war. In June 1934 we find Roosevelt proposing to Swanson the construction of "flying deck" cruisers, hybrids that combined the firepower of a heavy cruiser with flying-off and flying-on facilities, a configuration that the Russian Navy exploited fifty years later. The General Board in fact advised against these vessels. "As we already have three airplane carriers, flying deck cruisers are not needed at this time."

Recalling the desperate need for large numbers of anti-U-boat patrol vessels in the First World War, Roosevelt wrote to his naval aide in 1937 that plans should be prepared "for a wooden vessel which can be turned out in about six weeks and can be built by many shipyards throughout the country."

Roosevelt also prepared a memorandum suggesting the laying down of two 8,000-ton cruisers armed with four 11-inch guns "plus as many 5″ dual as possible." He wanted a ship with "a good chance of standing up against the German pocket battleship type." Like Kaiser Wilhelm II, Roosevelt designed ships in his sleep; and like that emperor's, many of his designs were sound and some prophetic.

The President and C in C took just as much interest in the minutiae of his Navy: in promotions, new training schemes, defense of bases, the performance of new Navy aircraft, the movements of ships. "I am inclined to agree with the recommendation," he wrote to Swanson on June 28, 1935, "that a heavy cruiser be kept as the flagship of the C-in-C Asiatic Fleet. Will you therefore either keep the *Augusta* on her present assignment, or relieve her with another heavy cruiser, preferably one of the older ships of this class. . . ." Hearing of German progress in alternative forms of marine engine, Roosevelt called for a paper on the merits and demerits of "dieselization." Then again he called for the most detailed intelligence available on the new Japanese battleships. Unfortunately Swanson replied, "I am satisfied that Japan will use 16″ guns," when to the dismay of the U.S Navy later they turned out to be of 18.2-inch caliber.

Roosevelt was never happier than with the fleet at sea and he made as many and as long visits as the responsibilities of the White House allowed. Personnel at all levels loved it. "Your visit to the Fleet has had a very stimulating influence upon its entire personnel," wrote Swanson (December 3, 1935).

Between 1938 and 1941 Roosevelt's wartime team was formed. Swanson died in July 1939. "Claude loved you more than anyone I knew," his widow wrote to Roosevelt. Frank Knox, a tough, shrewd Chicago newspaper publisher was appointed Secretary of the Navy to replace Swanson's successor, Charles Edison, in June 1940.

Harold Stark, now an admiral, was appointed Chief of Naval Operations in March 1939. "I do not have to tell you how much I appreciate your confidence," he wrote to Roosevelt, "nor that you will have all the loyalty and effort I can give; you know that. My hope is that my service to the Navy, where you are placing me, will measure up to what you expect and to the benefit of our seagoing forces which we both so love. I assure you I will do my very best."

THE GREATEST CRUSADE

Among others who were to figure so prominently in the U.S. Navy hierarchy during the coming war was James V. Forrestal, in the post Roosevelt had occupied as a young man; Forrestal would succeed Frank Knox as Secretary when Knox died in 1944. At sea there was Admiral Ernest King as C in C Naval Forces, later to replace Stark as Chief of Naval Operations after March 1942; the naval aviation wizards Vice Admiral William F. "Bull" Halsey and Vice Admiral Frank "Black Jack" Fletcher; Vice Admiral Raymond "Electric Brain" Spruance; and the future commander of the Eighth Fleet, Vice Admiral Henry Kent Hewitt. These senior officers, and so many others who were to become household names after Pearl Harbor, contributed to the quality of the U.S. Navy at war, composing without doubt the best team of leaders in any naval war in history.

Within a week of Churchill's assuming office again as First Lord of the Admiralty, Roosevelt wrote a letter to him that initiated a remarkable exchange of communications, by letter, telegraph, and telephone, which were to cover every aspect of the war until Roosevelt's death on the brink of Allied victory in April 1945. Read in sequence, these communications reflect in sharp detail the course of the war as seen from the White House and 10 Downing Street, from the time when Britain and the British Commonwealth and France declared war on Nazi Germany, through the cold, unreal winter of 1939–40, to the crushing blitz-kriegs of the spring and early summer of 1940 that left Britain alone and Italy a new enemy. Then the second and third phases: the spreading of the conflagration with the German attack on Russia, the Japanese attack on the United States, until every ocean and every continent except the Americas experienced the flames and suffering of war.

Roosevelt had frequently employed the informal approach of a personal letter in his conduct of diplomacy and foreign affairs. He had been advised, and had judged himself, that there was a strong likelihood that Churchill would before long become Prime Minister; and for the present, Churchill controlled the Navy, which traditionally secured the eastern flank of the Americas. However hostile United States public opinion might be towards involvement in another European war, the survival of Western democracy in Europe was of vital concern to the American government. And a quick totting up in *Jane's Fighting Ships* showed that the German Fleet, supported by the surrendered fleets of France and Britain, provided a force greatly superior to any that America could muster. It therefore seemed both natural and sensible to establish an informal line of communication with Churchill in London. The consequences of Roosevelt's wise step were incalculable.

"It is because you and I occupied similar positions in the World War," Roosevelt began, "that I want you to know how glad I am that you are back again in the Admiralty. Your problems are, I realize, complicated by new factors, but the essential is not very different. What I want you and the Prime Minister to know is that I shall at all times welcome it if you will keep me in touch personally with anything you want me to know about." Then, referring to Churchill's three-volume life of his ancestor the first duke of Marlborough, which Churchill had sent to him six years earlier, Roosevelt said how glad he was that Churchill had completed the work "before this thing started."

Churchill, after consulting the Prime Minister and members of the War Cabinet, drafted a reply to this welcome letter and dispatched it through the U.S. Embassy by diplomatic pouch. The subject of Churchill's letter was German surface raiders and the anxiety they were causing, just as if the two men had been corresponding twenty-five years earlier.

At an inter-American conference in Panama City on September 23 the delegates had adopted the so-called Declaration of Panama, designed to safeguard the republics of the Americas from the consequences of the European war. It was Roosevelt's idea, with domestic politics in mind, to create a deep zone extending from three hundred to one thousand miles out to sea, from the Canadian border to the Argentine, in which hostile acts by the belligerents would be prohibited. It was internationally illegal and impossible to enforce but it seemed to make everyone feel happier, including Churchill.

In his reply to Roosevelt's first letter, Churchill wrote (October 5, 1939) that the prohibited zone would make easier the tracking down of German surface raiders on the assumption that the zone would be properly policed by the U.S. Navy. "The more

American ships cruising along the South American coast the better, as you, sir, would no doubt hear what they saw or did not see. Raiders might then find American waters rather crowded, or may anyhow prefer to go on to sort of trade route where we are preparing." Churchill concluded his first message with his tongue firmly in his cheek: "We wish to help you in every way in keeping the war out of Americas."

The suggestion that American sighting of German raiders might benefit the Royal Navy in its searches was not presumptuous. Even before the Second World War, secret consultations had taken place in London between Royal Navy and U.S. Navy representatives concerned especially with the maintenance of security of the North Atlantic trade routes in time of war.

The first direct naval cooperation between Roosevelt and Churchill took place by transatlantic telephone even before Roosevelt received Churchill's reply. The subject was the sinking of the *Athenia*. Hitler was furious at this sinking by one of his U-boats. The very last thing he wanted to do at this stage was to arouse American anger as the sinking of the *Lusitania* in 1915 had done. He therefore ordered it to be made known that a bomb had been planted on the ship at Churchill's orders in order to cause an outcry in America. The statement was followed by a bogus inquiry by the German Navy, the outcome of which was made known to the American naval attaché in Berlin. On September 16 this officer noted in his diary that he had been summoned by Grand Admiral Erich Raeder, who told him that the previous night he had received negative reports from the last of the submarines that could possibly have torpedoed the *Athenia*. "He asked me to report the matter to my embassy, which I did."

To add verisimilitude to this story, Raeder gave out a warning over the German radio to America that a similar bomb had been planted in the American merchantman *Iroquois,* then in mid-Atlantic out of Cork, implying that German intelligence had got wind of Churchill's second plot. Roosevelt at once put through a call to Churchill in London.

Churchill was dining with naval company at the time and told the butler that he could not answer the telephone. But the butler pressed him to come and Churchill reluctantly did so, discovering that he was talking to the White House and that the subject was an urgent one. Roosevelt took Churchill's advice and had the ship thoroughly searched—nothing was found—and then publicized the whole plot, discrediting German intelligence and making plain to the world that the *Athenia* must indeed have been the victim of a U-boat. Direct cooperation between the President and future Prime Minister had started well.

The Royal Navy found the last of the big German raiders, the *Graf Spee,* unassisted by the patrols of the U.S. Navy, and Roosevelt—and the whole American people—followed the action and the aftermath with excitement and admiration. Knowing how interested the President would be in the technical and other details of the action, Churchill wrote on Christmas Day 1939 ("Sir, all the compliments of the season") to tell him that these would be coming at once by airmail. "Damage to *Exeter* from eleven-inch guns was most severe and ship must be largely rebuilt. Marvel is she stood up to it so well." It was an action such as this, with smaller cruisers attempting to tackle a German pocket battleship, that Roosevelt had had in mind when he proposed eleven-inch-gunned American heavy cruisers; and Roosevelt was grateful for the "tremendously interesting account of the extrordinarily well fought action of your three cruisers."

The naval battle of the river Plate had, however, led to protests to Britain from several South American states, claiming that the British warships had penetrated the noncombatant zone recently set up, and the United States felt obliged to add her voice. Churchill, in his Christmas Day message, regretted this and other incidents but pointed out that "as a result of action off Plate whole South Atlantic is now clear . . . of warlike operations. This must be a blessing to South American republics," Churchill's telegram continued, "whose trade was hampered by activities of raider. . . . In fact we have rescued all this vast area from war disturbances. . . . Trust matter can be allowed to die down and see no reason why any trouble should occur unless another raider is sent which is unlikely after fate of first. South American States should see in Plate action their deliverance perhaps indefinitely from all animosity."

Friction at sea continued, with the United States increasingly upset by Britain's search and detention of American ships suspected of carrying contraband to the enemy—shades of the War of 1812, when Britain and the United States had last fought one another! "At the time of dictating this [February 1, 1940]," Roosevelt wrote coolly, "I think our conversations in regard to search and detention of American ships is working out satisfactorily— but I would not be frank unless I told you that there has been much public criticism here. The general feeling is that the net benefit to your people and to France is hardly worth the definite annoyance caused to us."

"The United States was cooler than in any other period," Churchill wrote later on this unsatisfactory state of relations. "I persevered in my correspondence with the President, but with little response."

As the United States naval attaché in Berlin noted, "It appears that Great Britain is clamping on the blockade of Germany much more drastically than it did in 1914." The cause of American annoyance was British insistence on bringing American merchantmen into the danger zone drawn by the United States around British shores in order to ensure that they were not carrying contraband goods destined for Germany. This practice had ceased since a system had been devised for clearing these merchantmen before leaving American ports, and Churchill replied, firmly but courteously, that this was now operating satisfactorily—"no American ship has been brought by the navy into the danger zone"—but that one large American line was advertising that they didn't have to bother about these niceties. "You can imagine my embarrassment," Churchill remarked.

Roosevelt replied (March 5, 1940):

> To the Naval Person from the President
>   Upon my return to Washington, I received your message. I deeply appreciate your efforts. I am having the situation thoroughly studied and will communicate with you further as soon as possible.
>
>   Roosevelt

But the "search and detention" friction continued, arousing further anger in the United States and anxiety in Britain. Lord Lothian, British ambassador in Washington, wrote to Lady Astor, the American-born member of Parliament for Plymouth, "You will have seen from the papers that poor old Britain has had 'the heat turned on' against it recently by the State Department. It is a nuisance because, as you know well, once the American public begins to feel that Great Britain is treading on its corns, it gets easily inflamed because of old memories."

It was not until American sentiment towards Britain mellowed after Dunkirk and the Battle of Britain and the subsequent bombing of London and other cities that the blockade resentment diminished.

Criticism in America of the Royal Navy and Churchill was aroused on entirely different grounds in April and May 1940. Recalling how the many times larger German High Seas Fleet of 1914–18 had been unable to break British dominance of the North Sea, the U.S. naval attaché in Berlin wrote of the failure of the Royal Navy to halt the invasion of Norway, "The immediate reaction, among Americans and foreign naval attachés, was where in hell was the British Navy? They got caught flat-footed." Roosevelt was in despair. He had all his life admired the skill and prowess of the Royal Navy and he felt personally affronted that the Germans had been able to carry out this devastating operation seemingly without serious opposition. "The thing that has made me hopping mad," he was heard to remark, "is where was the British Fleet when the Germans went up to Bergen and Oslo? It is the most outrageous thing I have ever heard of."

No communication has been recorded between the President and Churchill during the difficult and anxious weeks after the Scandinavian invasion, except the dispatch to Washington by Churchill of the official account of the Battle of the River Plate. But by that time the Royal Navy had lost much of the kudos it had gained in that distant action.

The date of May 15, 1940, five days after Churchill took over the prime ministry, marks a fundamental change in the relationship and communications with Roosevelt. Churchill is sixty-five years old, Roosevelt fifty-eight. Churchill is leader of His Majesty's Government, Roosevelt as head of state and head of government combines the roles of sovereign and Prime Minister in Britain; Churchill at all times recognizes this distinction, as eyewitnesses will observe when he gives a little bow at their first meeting on board the *Augusta,* and it is evident in the frequent use of "Sir." On May 15 Churchill, in a long telegram becomes simply and appropriately "Former Naval Person," and signs himself "With all good wishes and respect." Since their earlier tiff about the British blockade, the European continent has shuddered under the shock waves of a massive blitzkrieg that has shattered the puny defenses of Denmark, Norway, Belgium, and Holland. The Wehrmacht has stormed into Luxembourg and France, crushing all before it. Open cities are being torn apart by high-level and screaming dive bombers. The warning signs from across the Channel are clear for all to see; and Churchill in this first telegram of the new era warns the President, "You may have a completely subjugated, Nazified Europe established with astonishing swiftness." Then, closer to home: "We expect to be attacked here ourselves, both from the air and by parachute and air borne troops in the near future. . . ."

This telegram reflects a view of Britain's position after the German breakthrough at Sedan and the swift retreat in the west very different from the robust and defiant tone of Churchill's radio broadcasts of this period. There is no hint of compromise or surrender to Germany—"we shall continue the war alone and we are not afraid of that"—but there is a note of urgency, of almost desperate urgency, that would have shocked the British people if this "most secret and personal" communication had been made public, especially the statement that "the weight may be more than we can bear." This was not a consideration at British breakfast tables at the time.

Churchill's first "shopping list" was a formidable one: the loan of forty or fifty destroyers, several hundred of the latest type of aircraft, anti-aircraft guns and ammunition, steel in unspecified quantity but sufficient to make up the loss of supplies from Sweden, Spain, and North Africa. More breathtaking was the suggestion that the United States should proclaim nonbelligerency in order that it could provide all help "short of actually engaging armed forces." And finally, Churchill while pledging to continue "paying dollars as long as we can" hoped that when they ran out "you will give us the stuff just the same."

At this time Roosevelt and his chiefs of staff had no conception of the danger and imminence of defeat in Europe. Military minds were still conditioned by the pace of military action of

1914–18, and there was a strong tendency to view Churchill's *cri de coeur* as false, political, or hysterical. Cry wolf! Roosevelt replied the next day but he offered little and did not comment on the extremely hot issue of a proclamation of nonbelligerency. It was far ahead of what he could even consider politically.

Churchill was already viewing with dismay the rapid disintegration of French resistance and endeavoring to put some steel into the heart of Britain's ally; he was facing the threatened entry of Italy into the war, and was deeply preoccupied with preparing the nation's defenses against invasion. Roosevelt's seeming procrastination was almost more than he could bear. In a brief telegram (May 18, 1940) he told Roosevelt that "we must expect . . . to be attacked here on the Dutch model [bombing and airborne troops] before very long" and "if American assistance is to play any part it must be available soon." Two days later, a second telegram presented in uncompromising terms what might happen if "the present administration were finished and others came in to parley amid the ruins." Who could blame a new government for temporizing and using the British Fleet as a bargaining counter to obtain "the best terms they could for the surviving inhabitants"? Of course Britain would fight on to the bitter end, Churchill stressed. And then: "Excuse me, Mr President, putting this nightmare bluntly." Was it a nightmare, or was it blackmail? Worse was to come.

Lord Lothian was making no better progress in Washington. "The truth about U.S.A. is that it is dominated by fear of war—which is exactly what Hitler wants. Oh for Theodore Roosevelt!!" he wrote to a friend. The ambassador expressed his exasperation to Lady Astor: "Your countrymen are very volatile. When the allies get a success they say, 'Well, that's fine. They can win without us.' When Hitler is winning they say, 'It's all over.' " Now, on the vexed and urgent question of the destroyers, he suggested to Churchill a formula that might produce results. This was to weaken American intransigence by offering certain rights on British-owned or -controlled territory that would further secure American defenses, for example leasing certain air and naval bases in Newfoundland, Trinidad, Bermuda, and the West Indies. America's appetite for bases was, he reckoned, limitless. Teddy Roosevelt would have approved!

Churchill opposed this suggestion unless something firm was

slapped down on the counter in exchange. He had been much offended when, months earlier while he was still at the Admiralty, American defense chiefs had turned down his suggestion that the British secret of asdic should be exchanged for the revolutionary American Norden bombsight. In fact the U.S. Navy officers were not too impressed by what they had heard of asdic, and agreed with the Germans, who "hold the British listening gear in contempt." He had also refused a U.S. Navy request to appoint observers in British men-of-war, and commented on proposed interchanges of technical information, "Generally speaking I am not in a hurry until the United States is much nearer to the war than she is now."

At a War Cabinet meeting (May 27) Churchill complained bitterly that the United States had "given us practically no help in the war." First America had thought Britain was presenting a false black picture, was Churchill's view; "and now they saw how great was the danger, their attitude was that they wanted to keep everything that would help in their own defence."

But it was Roosevelt's failure to respond to the appeal for destroyers that most infuriated Churchill. Even before the evacuation at Dunkirk, the Royal Navy had lost 30 percent of its destroyer strength. There were more than one hundred First World War flush-deckers laid up in east coast American yards, rusting, unwanted for two decades, and the President had the effrontery to write that America's own defense requirements precluded the Navy from disposing "even temporarily" of these destroyers. Furthermore, the authorization would, he said, require congressional approval (which it did not, as was later shown) and "I am not certain that it would be wise for that suggestion to be made to the Congress at this moment."

Roosevelt's difficult political and defense position was not a subject much in Churchill's mind during this supreme crisis. Only much later could he acknowledge the President's dilemma in facing broad isolationism throughout the land, and the defense staff's opposition to diverting supplies to a seemingly doomed belligerent when their own needs were so desperate. For example, General George V. Strong, chairman of the war plans division, advocated no further aid to Europe, as "a recognition of the early defeat of the Allies." Private manufacturers should be prohibited from accepting orders from Britain, and if necessary British and French possessions in the Western Hemisphere should be occupied to keep them out of German hands.

On behalf of the Army, General George Marshall, and Stark for the Navy, deprecated sending anything more to Europe. They were supported by the Senate Foreign Relations Committee, whose chairman, Key Pittman, replied to Churchill's renewed plea, as "a matter of life and death" (June 15), with a demand that Churchill should send the entire British Fleet to American waters immediately to preserve it from falling into German hands. "It is no secret that Great Britain is totally unprepared for defense and that nothing the United States has to give can do more than delay the result," reported the senator; and he hoped that the plan to transfer the British Fleet "will not be too long delayed by futile encouragement to fight on."

The voice of Henry Morgenthau, Secretary of the Treasury and close confidant of Roosevelt, was almost the only one, and unheard, advocating urgent aid. "Unless we do something to give the English additional destroyers, it seems to me it is absolutely hopeless to expect them to keep going."

American intervention to help Britain during and after Dunkirk and the fall of France was certainly not helped by the American contingent in London, with the exception of courageous newspapermen like Ed Murrow and Drew Middleton who sought to tell the truth about Britain's plight and needs. The ambassador, Joseph Kennedy, made clear that Britain had no chance of survival, even before the attack in the west, and persevered in his hostility until he quit some months later, when Roosevelt commented, "I never want to see that son of a bitch again as long as I live. Take his resignation and get him out of here." "It seems to me that if we had to fight to protect our lives we would do better fighting in our own backyard," Kennedy wrote in one dispatch to Roosevelt. And in another: "The United States will have plenty to worry about in their own country. The cry should be to prepare for anything right there."

On Joseph Kennedy as ambassador, on his alarmist, even hysterical tendencies and general unhelpfulness, Roosevelt and Churchill spoke with one voice—although strictly not aloud for the other to hear. Churchill's distrust of the man was total. "Joe always has been an appeaser and always will be an appeaser," Roosevelt complained to Morgenthau. "If Germany and Italy made a good peace offer tomorrow Joe would start working on the King and his friend, the Queen, and from there on down, to get everybody to accept. He's just a pain in the neck to me."

There is no telling how many lives were lost as a direct result of Kennedy's strong and persistent hostility to sending any American aid to Britain in 1940. Why Roosevelt tolerated him has never been satisfactorily explained. He attempted to justify Kennedy's retention by claiming that he at least "knew his man" and could discount much that was contained in his dispatches, an unconvincing and uncharacteristically negative policy. Or was Roosevelt politically afraid of his vast wealth and influence?

Another even more dangerous if covert American figure in London at this time was a code clerk in the American Embassy named Tyler G. Kent. He was so strongly opposed to any American aid for Britain that he copied and smuggled out of the embassy, for enemy eyes, Churchill-Roosevelt messages. He was arrested and spent the remainder of the war in a British jail.

Abroad, Joseph Kennedy was the most influential opponent to dispatching old American destroyers to Britain; at home in the United States, Admiral Stark's voice was loudest and most convincing in professional defense circles, in spite of his close affinity to Roosevelt, whom he knew to be, in principle and at a price, sympathetic to Britain. Stark not only believed, politically, that any deal over American destroyers would create outrage in Congress, but also that the mothballed ships would be vital for America's defense when France and Britain capitulated, which he believed to be inevitable and imminent.

The destroyers-for-Britain controversy labored on through the cataclysmic summer of 1940, the chief contestants being the two national leaders, their ambassadors, and their service chiefs. Around June 15, Churchill seems to have lost confidence in the personal approach and left Lothian and the War Cabinet to get on with the struggle. It was not until the last day of July that Churchill renewed his pleas. In emphasizing the need for destroyers among other urgent requirements, Churchill wrote, "The Germans have the whole French coast line from which to launch U-boats, dive-bomber attacks upon our trade and food, and in addition we must be constantly prepared to repel by sea action threatened invasion. . . ." He then gave the names of eleven more destroyers that had been sunk or knocked out in the past ten days. "Mr President, with great respect I must tell you that in the long history of the world, this is a thing to do now."

A few days earlier Roosevelt had told Secretary of the Navy Knox that Congress was in no mood to allow any form of sale. "You might, however, think over the possibility at a little later date of trying to get Congressional action to allow the sale of these destroyers to Canada on condition that they be used solely in American hemisphere defense." That represented the President's line of thinking on July 22. But this last Churchill appeal struck home, a bull's-eye. Immediately on receiving it, Roosevelt got onto Secretary Knox with instructions to see Lothian and put to him the proposal for a deal, a deal based on destroyers in ex-change for British bases. Lothian was "almost tearful in his pleas for help and help quickly," Knox reported later after putting the proposition to the British ambassador. As early as May 24, Loth-ian had put up the idea of a similar quid pro quo to Churchill, who had peremptorily dismissed it. Now, more than two months later, Churchill and the War Cabinet were prepared to be less fas-tidious. Churchill later justified the exchange of fifty "antiquated and inefficient craft" for an indefinite lease on a string of Atlantic and Caribbean bases by suggesting that "the strategic value of these islands counted only against the United States. They were, in the old days, the stepping-stone by which America could be at-tacked from Europe or England. Now, with air power, it was all the more important for American safety that they should be in friendly hands."

Through the first half of August, Roosevelt struggled to turn American opinion in favor of such a deal, rallying all the forces he could muster. These included the national hero of the First World War, General John J. Pershing, who made a radio appeal on be-half of Britain and of America's supporting her cause in any way possible—"We have an immense reservoir of destroyers left over from the other war. . . ." Progress remained slow, so slow that Roosevelt resorted to the law. Did he really have to get congres-sional approval? Did he not have the right to act on his own initiative? Lawyers of renown and distinction busied themselves in the library of the New York Bar Association; a prominent letter above the names of distinguished and nationally famous lawyers appeared in *The New York Times.*

Strengthened by the law, and by a rising chorus of voices in the nation calling for help for the beleaguered British, Roosevelt decided to act on his own. The decision to go ahead was communicated to Churchill on August 13, 1940. The Battle of Britain was at its height and the hard-pressed squadrons of Fighter Command were holding off the Luftwaffe challenge. The spirit of the British people had never been more unified and determined to survive. It was a beautiful, if deadly dangerous, summer.

"It is my belief," ran Roosevelt's message, "that it may be possible to furnish to the British Government as immediate assistance at least 50 destroyers. . . ." The bases to be leased were specified, and the earlier condition about the Royal Navy in the event of successful German invasion toned down at the insistence of Churchill. It now read: "Assurance on the part of the Prime Minister that in the event that the waters of Great Britain become untenable for British ships of war, the latter would not be turned over to the Germans or sunk, but would be sent to other parts of the Empire for continued defense of the Empire."

Roosevelt liked to use the expression "As naval people . . ." As naval people, the relief of Churchill and Roosevelt was mutual and heartfelt. "I need not tell you how cheered I am by your message," Churchill signaled Roosevelt, "nor how grateful I feel for your untiring efforts to give us all possible help." The fifty flush-deckers themselves—terrible sea boats, old, requiring extensive modification before being fit for duty, disliked by those who manned them—did fulfill some sort of role in due course. But to Churchill the material consequences of the American decision were far less important than the effect on enemy, and British, morale, and on neutral opinion. The deal was, Churchill informed the War Cabinet, "a long step towards [America's] coming into the war on our side."

Back in May, before France fell, Roosevelt had given the order that the Army should send to the French a number of fighter planes that were urgently required. The American Army would just have to wait. "After all," Roosevelt had told Morgenthau, "we will not be in for 60 or 90 days." Those ninety days had passed, and in spite of the destroyer deal and Churchill's optimism about an early American entry into the war, the bomb and torpedo explosions of Pearl Harbor were still more than a year away.

But Roosevelt's Columbus Day message for 1940 was a stirring one. As bombs fell on a dozen darkened British cities, he told his audience, "The men and women of Britain have shown how a free people defend what they know to be right. Their heroic defense will be recorded for all time. . . . Our course is clear. Our decison is made. We will continue to pile up our defense and our armaments. We will continue to help those who resist aggression far from our shores."

On August 2, 1940, the interventionist American Secretary of the Interior, Harold L. Ickes, wrote to Roosevelt, favoring the destroyers-for-bases deal, and at the same time planting in Roosevelt's mind a fanciful parallel that would justify to the American public a radical idea that the President was brooding over. Britain was, quite simply, going broke. Her industry had already turned over to war production on a far more comprehensive scale than German industry, which was still manufacturing, for export and home consumption, goods that had long since ceased to be produced in British factories. Under the American Neutrality Law, war matériel could only be supplied on a "cash-and-carry basis" and the cash had all but ran out. At the same time the American administration now recognized that Britain intended to fight it out to the end and that the defeat of Britain would leave the United States in a grave situation. "Never before since Jamestown and Plymouth Rock has our American civilization been in such danger as now," Roosevelt warned in his "fireside chat" over the radio on December 29, 1940.

"It seems to me," wrote Ickes, "we Americans are like the householder who refused to lend or sell his fire extinguishers to help put out the fire in the house that is right next door although that house is all ablaze and the wind is blowing from that direction." This provided the kernel for Roosevelt's later "lending the garden hose" phrase, the analogy being just right for the American people.

While cruising in the U.S.S. *Tuscaloosa* in early December

1940, Roosevelt had received the longest telegram—over four thousand words—from Churchill. It summarized the war situation and prospects for the future. Following a list of the dangers the nation faced, Churchill wrote, "In the face of these dangers, we must try to use the year 1941 to build up such a supply of weapons, particularly aircraft, both by increased output at home in spite of bombardment, and through ocean-going supplies, as will lay the foundation of victory." The outstanding orders for war matériel from the U.S. were already worth four and half billion dollars. How was this bill to be met? It was far beyond the resources of the customer.

Far back in time, Roosevelt could recall, when he had been a youthful, bustling assistant secretary of the Navy, in order to evade rather than break the law, he had proposed that American merchantmen should be armed with guns "loaned" from the Navy Department. Now the idea began to form in his mind of using this principle, on a vastly greater scale and seemingly without long-term cost to the nation, in order to solve Britain's payment problem. It was at least better than building up an unrepayable loan of the kind that had bedeviled Anglo-American relations since the First World War.

At a press conference at the end of his winter cruise, Roosevelt, after telling his audience that "there was no particular news," presented the notion that the immense orders from Britain were great for America. They were, he said, "a tremendous asset to American national defense, because they create, automatically, additional facilities. I am talking selfishly, from the American point of view—nothing else." What he was trying to do was "to eliminate the dollar sign." Lending money to Britain was "banal."

This was the moment he chose to bring in the hose-and-neighbor analogy. "I don't say . . . 'Neighbor, my garden hose cost me 15 dollars; you have got to pay me 15 dollars for it.' I don't want 15 dollars—I want my garden hose back after the fire is over. . . ."

In short, Roosevelt told his riveted audience of hard newspapermen, America would take over British orders and lease them to Britain "on the general theory that the best defense of Great Britain is the best defense of the United States."

"AS NAVAL PEOPLE..."

Thus was born "lend-lease"—"the most unsordid act in the history of any nation" as Churchill later described it, a startling and momentous blend of altruism and realism that was to solve the worst of Britain's financial problems and that Britain was later to apply to war matériel for Russia on a similar giant scale. There was a long, bloody fight ahead before Roosevelt got the approval of Congress, but, together with the recently concluded destroyer deal, it marked the end of a brief and distant friendship between the President and the Former Naval Person and the beginning of a courtship that would culminate in the ceremonial in Placentia Bay eight months hence.

The threat of the French Fleet was a subject that worried and preoccupied Roosevelt almost as much as it did Churchill, and within the limits imposed upon him, he supported all the British steps to neutralize the great number of powerful vessels remaining in French and French colonial ports after the defeat and surrender of June 1940. In the first days of July, Churchill, the War Cabinet, and the Admiralty jointly ageed that firm steps had to be taken to deal with the most powerful concentration of French warships, at Oran in North Africa. "Force H," consisting of the battle cruiser *Hood*—the biggest warship in the world—two battleships, a modern carrier, two cruisers, and supporting craft, was ordered to head for the port and deliver an ultimatum to the French authorities.

The entire French force, of roughly the same strength, was instructed to either join the British force and "continue to fight for victory," sail to a British port with a promise that the crews could be repatriated, or sail to a French port in the West Indies, or to an American port, to be demilitarized. After prolonged negotiations the French rejected all these alternatives. There was then applied what Churchill referred to as "the deadly stroke," with aerial attacks and a ten-minute bombardment by Force H. One of the French heavy ships escaped but the remainder were crippled or blown up, with grievous loss of life.

It was a hateful task but absolutely necessary. Other benefits accrued. "Here was this Britain," as Churchill wrote, "which so many had counted down and out, which strangers had supposed to be quivering on the brink of surrender to the mighty power arrayed against her, striking ruthlessly at her dearest friends of yesterday and securing for a while to herself the undisputed command of the sea."

Roosevelt's reaction, conveyed through Lord Lothian, was wholly favorable, and American public opinion was impressed. In due course, the United States succeeded in neutralizing, without resorting to violence, French men-of-war stationed in the West Indies. The two most deadly thorns in Britain's flesh were the new and immensely powerful fifteen-inch-gunned French battleships *Jean Bart* and *Richelieu;* the former lay in Casablanca harbor, without her main armament, at the time of the fall of France, while the *Richelieu* was operational and had now reached Dakar on the West African coast.

Eary in November Churchill learned that the French government planned to bring these two ships to Toulon. "It is difficult to exaggerate the potential if this were to happen," Churchill notified Roosevelt (November 10, 1940), "and so open the way for these ships to fall under German control." Roosevelt reacted swiftly and firmly, and informed Churchill that the American chargé d'affaires in Vichy, seat of Marshal Pétain's puppet French government, was seeking confirmation of this report. If it was confirmed, "the Chargé d'Affaires has been instructed to convey to Marshal Pétain an expression of the grave concern of the Government and to point out that the Government of the United States ... believes that if it is necessary ... to move the units in question the French authorities will not transfer them to any port inconsistent with the ultimate interests of the United States." Roosevelt added that he had told the French that he would gladly buy the battleships "if they will dispose of them to us." Churchill said that he was "deeply obliged for the promptness of your action."

The American offer was not taken up by the French authorities—they would have been prohibited from doing so by their masters in any case—and the *Richelieu* at Dakar remained a serious threat. Towards the end of September, Lothian informed Roosevelt that Churchill was planning a naval attack on Dakar in order to land a force of General Charles de Gaulle's Free French and take over the town and port, and the *Richelieu,* which had been disabled by an aerial torpedo attack from a carrier. This would have the further advantage of denying the strategically important port to the Germans as a future U-boat base.

When Lothian told London of Roosevelt's approval, Churchill telegraphed (September 24) his appreciation and, ever anxious to persuade the United States Navy into a demonstration of unified action, suggested Roosevelt might care to send men-of-war to nearby West African ports, so that the ships could then call at Dakar when the port was captured. Roosevelt was given no time to respond to this idea for the very next day Churchill signaled Washington that "I must regret we had to abandon Dakar enterprise." The French defenders, not for the first or last time, had demonstrated against their fellow countrymen and recent allies a will to fight that had not been consistently evident during the German attack on the homeland. They defended the port and town so effectively, and with the declared intention to continue to do so to the last man, that the operation was called off. One of the main reasons for the French success was the *Richelieu,* which used her fifteen-inch guns to great effect but was herself damaged.

Roosevelt much regretted this setback but did not in any way blame the Royal Navy as he had done over Norway. Meanwhile, he gave comfort to the Former Naval Person by continuing to apply pressure on Vichy France through the ambassador in Washington. "The fact that a government is a prisoner of war of another power does not justify such a prisoner in serving its conqueror in operations against its former ally," he told the ambassador firmly, and reported this to Churchill (October 24). Roosevelt added a thrust to the heart by hinting that "when the appropriate time came" the United States would see to it that France would not recover her old overseas possessions.

In site of the Dakar failure, and the presence of powerful French men-of-war in Vichy-controlled Toulon, Churchill felt that the damage done to the *Richelieu* removed her as a threat. With the neutralization of other French units caught at Alexandria, he was now easy in his mind about the future of the French Fleet.

For the present the threat of the German surface fleet, savaged in the Norwegian campaign, was restricted to the battle cruisers *Scharnhorst* and *Gneisenau,* the pocket battleship *Scheer,* and one or two heavy cruisers whose condition was uncertain. There was no reason for any complacency but the Admiralty was confident that superior forces could rapidly be brought to bear if any of these men-of-war came out to attack North Atlantic shipping.

With the entry of Italy into the war and the elimination of the French Fleet, Britain was faced with massive new naval considerations in the Mediterranean. Churchill despised Mussolini and his government, their bombast and sycophancy towards Hitler. "People who go to Italy to look at ruins won't have to go so far as Naples and Pompeii again," he muttered threateningly to his secretary early on the morning of June 10. Nor did he have a high regard for them militarily. As for their fleet . . .

The Italians had for long been regarded as better builders of ships than sailors. In 1940 the Italian Fleet was of about the same strength as the scattered or defunct French Fleet had been. The ships were certainly the most beautiful and the swiftest in the world. A number of Italian cruisers could make over forty knots and could comfortably outpace the standard British biplane torpedo bomber when steaming into a stiff wind. It had mockingly been said before the war that the Italians needed this speed to run from the enemy, and this proved to be the case.

This Italian Fleet remained a menace, however, and was dealt with severely and swiftly on the night of November 11, 1940. Twenty lumbering Swordfish biplanes, guided by flares, made a low-level torpedo-dropping attack on the Italian Fleet in Taranto harbor and knocked out three of the six battleships there in a miniature prototype of Pearl Harbor a year later. With the loss of two planes in all, it was the most cost-effective operation of the war, and its success was closely noted by the Japanese. Reconnaissance was provided by a squadron of American-built planes operating from Malta, a point that Churchill did not miss in his report to Roosevelt.

With the virtual elimination of the French Fleet and the temporary crippling of the Italian Fleet, Churchill was relieved of two grave anxieties. By contrast, the future of the United States Fleet occupied his thoughts and entered into his calculations every day. A vast amount of time was spent in working out ways of involving units of the American Atlantic Fleet in the shooting war—the never-ending war of the U-boats and German bombers whose toll of shipping was developing into as critical a danger as in 1916–17. Between May and December 1940, a total of 3,239,190 tons of British, Allied, and neutral shipping had been lost due to enemy action. By contrast with the First World War, when bases on the west and southwest coasts of Ireland had been available, Britain was deprived of these and also of the use of French Atlantic ports, which were now "a nest of hornets," and which saved the U-boats the long passage round Scotland or the dangerous passage through the English Channel.

Admiral Karl Doenitz, C in C of the German U-boat fleet for the entire duration of the war, established his headquarters in France and his still-small, highly efficient force operated mainly from Saint-Nazaire, Lorient, La Pallice, and Brest. New techniques included night attack and, later, "wolf-pack" tactics, which had been tried out in 1918. The Royal Navy found difficulty in countering them. Between ten and twenty U-boats operated together under shore command, at first fanning out until a convoy was located, when it was shadowed usually by a single U-boat during daylight. The wolf pack then came under local command for a tightly organized series of night attacks, made on the surface before submerging to avoid counteraction. The same procedure would be followed the next night, and again, for perhaps three or four nights running.

"You will have seen what very heavy losses we have suffered . . . to our last two convoys," Churchill signaled Roosevelt on Trafalgar Day (October 21) 1940. ". . . We are passing through an anxious and critical period." A week later Churchill referred again to "the U-boat and air attacks upon our only remaining life line, the north-western approach." In his long telegram on December 7, 1940, Churchill listed the additional difficulties in the fight against the U-boats the Royal Navy now faced, lacking "the assistance of the French Navy, the Italian Navy and the Japanese Navy, and above all," he added pointedly, "the United States Navy, which was of such vital help during the culminating years."

Except that this time there had been preliminary discussions on joint action in the Atlantic between the U.S. Navy Department and the Admiralty in London, the situation in 1940 was very similar to that facing Roosevelt in 1916. As Assistant Secretary of the Navy, Roosevelt's methods had been as relatively insensitive as his own power of influence had been relatively puny in the First World War. In place of Wilson, Daniels, and the isolationists of 1916, Roosevelt in 1940 faced the influential America First semifascist brigade led by the spoiled, naïve, onetime hero Charles Lindbergh, the hard-line Republicans who saw political advantage in the "keep our boys at home" theme, and the ubiquitous isolationists.

It was all very familiar. But Roosevelt faced the situation resolutely, confident in his own unsurpassed political skill and sensitivity to the beat of the public pulse. No one in the nation recognized the danger as clearly as he did. As Sam Morison has written, "President Roosevelt, considerably in advance of public opinion, apprehended the threat to American security contained in the German seizure of the Atlantic Coast of France, and the strong possibility of a German invasion of Great Britain. For three centuries the British Navy could always be depended upon to prevent any power dominant on the European Continent from obtaining control of the Western Ocean sea lanes. In expectation that Britain could do it again, the United States Navy since 1922 had been largely concentrated in the Pacific, to watch Japan. Now we were faced with a possible pincer movement from across both oceans."

In addition to the informal talks between the two navies that had been taking place for some time, in July 1940 Roosevelt asked Stark to select a naval delegate for a three-man defense team to fact-find in London. Stark selected Rear Admiral Robert L. Ghormley. As "special naval observer" he matched the success of Admiral Sims in London in 1917. From the start, Churchill was determined to give the team priority attention and a warm welcome, and ensure that frankness was the keynote of the conversations. "What arrangements are being made to receive this important United States mission?" he demanded. "I should see them almost as soon as they come, and I could give them a dinner at No. 10."

Ghormley's impressive and favorable reports led to a highly important memorandum of defense policy that Stark drew up and handed to Secretary Knox on November 12, 1940, a time of savage shipping losses in the Atlantic. Stark's document had historical importance because for the first time it stated baldly that the U.S. Navy might have to involve itself in combined operations with the Royal Navy in the Atlantic. It was also many months ahead of any seriously considered defense policy in envisaging that eventually the United States would have to "send large air and land forces to Europe or Africa, or both, and to participate strongly in this land offensive. The naval task of transporting any army abroad would be large."

Although by the end of 1940 Roosevelt was reconciled to the eventual American involvement at Britain's side, he still believed that it might be restricted to air and sea support—perhaps on a massive scale, but without the necessity of sending great armies across the seas. Six months later, with the German attack on Russia, he was confirmed in his view that "it will mean the liberation of Europe from Nazi domination."

Meanwhile the wheels had been set in swift motion to bring the U.S. Navy into direct involvement in the Battle of the Atlantic. At the end of January 1941 secret staff conversations began in Washington among American, Canadian, and British delegations from the three services, Admiral Ghormley, recently returned from London, leading for the U.S. Navy. Rear Admiral Roger Bellairs, who had been on Jellicoe's staff when Churchill was First Sea Lord in 1914, and Rear Admiral Victor Danckwerts, who in the same year, serving on the *Kent,* had taken part in the destruction of two of Spee's cruisers, the *Nürnberg* and *Dresden,* represented the Royal Navy. As a symbolic gesture of unity, on the day the talks began in the United States, in Britain Roosevelt's recent political opponent, Wendell Willkie, handed to Churchill an affectionate letter from Roosevelt. It included the Longfellow verse "Sail on, O Ship of State/Sail on, O Union, strong and great! . . ." Churchill telegraphed that he was deeply moved and that he was going "to have it framed as a souvenir of these tremendous days, and as a mark of our friendly relations."

It was an auspicious start to the Washington negotiations, which resulted in a number of historic decisions and principles. These included the decision, in a shooting war, to beat Germany first "as the predominant member of the Axis powers" and also because of the fear that German scientists might invent new and terrible secret weapons, unlikely to emerge from Japan. The Atlantic Ocean and Europe were defined as the decisive theater. In the event of America's entering the war, a supreme war council would be formed (it was, as the Joint Chiefs of Staff); and meanwhile staff conversations would be continued, the blockade of Germany rigorously enforced, Italy knocked out of the war by a concentration of naval power in the Mediterranean, and American and British troops concentrated in Britain to prepare for an invasion of the Continent.

This time, the delegates determined, there would be none of the chaos and lack of coordination that had delayed the effect of America's entry into a European war, and had cost numberless lives, in 1917 and 1918.

But of more immediate moment was the agreement that "the United States Navy would take over the prime responsibility for protecting transatlantic merchant convoys, as soon as the Atlantic Fleet was in a position to do so." This was the second stage in the unstated American "short of war" policy, and a much more effective and important stage than the destroyer deal. This American Support Force, as it was termed, would be made up from parts of the Atlantic Fleet and would initially consist of three destroyer squadrons and a dozen long-range flying boats.

Initially, the U.S. Navy provided convoy escort from the Argentia, Newfoundland, base already under urgent construction, to Iceland, which had been occupied peacefully during the Battle of France by British forces. The relief of pressure on the Royal Navy was valuable. It was hoped that soon further American involvement in the desperate struggle with the U-boats and bombers would tip the scales more heavily in favor of eventual victory. This was to happen, but it was going to take more than two years, and full American participation, before the U-boat was mastered.

While these profitable talks were proceeding in Washington, Harry Hopkins was in England, seeing a great deal of Churchill, forming an imperishable new friendship with the Prime Minister, and writing to his old friend at the White House with vivid descriptions of life in Britain and with lists of urgent needs for survival. One evening at Chequers, the Prime Minister's country residence, after a strenuous day inspecting bomb damage in the West Country with Churchill, Hopkins produced a box of gramophone records. They were, Churchill's principal private secretary recalled, "all American tunes with an Anglo-American significance. We had these until well after midnight, the P.M. walking about, sometimes dancing a pas-seul, in time with the music. We all got a bit sentimental & Anglo-American under the influence of the good dinner & the music."

With down-to-earth Anglo-American military and naval talks in Washington proceeding swiftly and amicably, and sentimental Anglo-American dancing at Chequers in England, how was it possible that the final sealing of the bonds be long delayed, or that they should be divisible?

No one in Washington, and no one in London, enjoyed a good naval battle more than the nations' two leaders. In May 1941, while U.S. Navy convoy work was building up, a new threat to Atlantic trade was developing, and this time no number of American destroyers, or ex-American destroyers, could help very much.

At the beginning of the war, the German Navy had under construction two formidable battleships, each more powerful than any battleship the Royal Navy could muster. The *Tirpitz* and *Bismarck* were to be over forty-five thousand tons and armed with eight 15-inch guns. Like the German dreadnought battleships that had opposed the Grand Fleet at Jutland, they were so strongly protected and built that they were virtually unsinkable by gunfire alone. Their completion was awaited anxiously by Churchill and the Admiralty. The first to go into service was the *Bismarck,* and this giant battleship was known to have left the Norwegian port of Bergen on May 21 or 22, 1941, in company with a heavy cruiser, the *Prinz Eugen,* herself a match for any cruiser in the Navy. It was evident that the two ships intended to engage in raids on North Atlantic convoys, with French Atlantic ports as bases upon which eventually to fall back, and reinforce the battle cruisers *Scharnhorst* and *Gneisenau* and the heavy cruiser *Hipper,* which were already at Brest. There were no fewer than eleven convoys at sea or about to sail, including a pricelessly valuable troop convoy from Canada, and a large convoy out of Liverpool for the Middle East. The German surface fleet had suddenly become menacing again.

When the news of this breakout arrived at Chequers, Averell Harriman was Churchill's guest, on a fact-finding mission as Roosevelt's special envoy. He became deeply involved in the pursuit and engagements that followed. In Washington, Roosevelt was kept almost as well informed, and in equal suspense, from the moment the telegram arrived from Churchill: "We have reason to believe that a formidable Atlantic raid is intended." In recounting what steps the Royal Navy was taking to answer this threat, Churchill added, "Should we fail to catch them going out your Navy should surely be able to mark them down for us. . . . Give the news and we will finish them off."

Churchill and his guests stayed up until 2:30 A.M. on the morning of Saturday, May 24, in the hope of news. The old battle cruiser *Hood* and the new battleship *Prince of Wales,* so new as to be imperfect in any action, supported by heavy cruisers, were in full pursuit, guided by radar.

At seven o'clock the next morning Harriman was awoken by the presence of Churchill at his bedside, dressed in a short nightshirt and yellow sweater. "Hell of a battle going on," announced the Prime Minister. "The *Hood* is sunk. Hell of a battle." Harriman asked about the *Prince of Wales*. "She's still at her," he was told cheerfully, leading Churchill later to remark that "it costs nothing to grin." Churchill then returned to his room, and to sleep, to be awoken by his principal private secretary, John Martin, at half past eight. "Have we got her?" Churchill asked him. Martin answered, "No, and the *Prince of Wales* has broken off the action."

"This was a sharp disappointment," Churchill wrote later. "Had then the *Bismarck* turned north and gone home?" It would have been the German ship's best course, returning home in triumph after destroying Britain's greatest warship, especially as the smaller and outgunned *Prince of Wales* had scored several hits with fourteen-inch shells, one of which had pierced a fuel tank. This injury led to a continuous and serious loss of oil and, equally serious, to an indelible stain to mark the *Bismarck*'s track as she sped southwest towards the convoy routes.

Churchill may have spared a grin for Averell Harriman but his mood at Chequers that weekend was grim and he was led to remark that the past three days "had been the worst yet." He was furious that the *Prince of Wales* had broken off action and, according to one of his secretaries, he "keeps saying it is the worst thing since Troubridge turned away from the *Goeben* in 1914." The Navy was having a bad time of it in the Mediterranean at this time, too, where the Army had been driven out of Greece and was about to be driven out of Crete as well. Churchill did not have a good word for anyone—the faithful Dudley Pound in the Admiralty or Admiral Andrew Cunningham, the C in C in the Mediterranean ("He must be made to take every risk").

After the shadowing cruisers lost contact with the *Bismarck,* the pursuit turned into a nightmare—a nightmare suffered in four nations: in Canada, where it was known that thousands of her troops were now at grave risk en route to Britain; in the United States and Britain, now jointly responsible for the defense of countless ships and men in the Atlantic; and in Germany, where the Admiralty knew of the *Bismarck*'s damage and that the raid had now become a race for survival with the French port of Brest as the haven.

It was a near million-to-one chance and dramatically appropriate that the quarry was at length spotted by an American-built plane manned by an Anglo-American crew. The long-range Consolidated PBY amphibian, named Catalina by the R.A.F., had only recently been delivered to Britain in small numbers and was already proving valuable to Coastal Command for U-boat hunting. It had an enormous range and carried depth charges as well as defensive machine guns. The U.S. Navy had, only weeks earlier, decided to send some seventeen experienced Catalina pilots to Britain to teach the R.A.F. how to fly them, and to learn in exchange how Coastal Command was operating in the Battle of the Atlantic. One of those who volunteered was Ensign Leonard "Tuck" Smith, a farmer's son from Higginsville, Missouri, aged twenty-six. He had been assigned to Catalina Z of 209 Squadron based on Oban on the west coast of Scotland, as copilot with Flying Officer Dennis Briggs, R.A.F.

The crew of Catalina Z were aroused at 2 A.M. on May 26, 1941, and ordered out to search for the escaped battleship. They had been in the air for over six hours when, flying at five hundred feet below low cloud, Smith suddenly caught sight of a distant dark shape on the sea. Briggs, who had just taken over the controls, climbed into cloud and emerged again directly over the ship. It was enormous, and it was without doubt the *Bismarck,* ablaze from end to end—or so it seemed—with the flash of anti-aircraft guns. The Catalina's radio operator managed to transmit their position as the big amphibian was thrown about the sky evasively. And the pursuit was on again, with the odds in favor of the *Bismarck*'s making it safely to France.

But air power did for the *Bismarck* in the end, as air reconnaissance had found her. A single torpedo from an eighty-knot torpedo biplane costing a few thousand pounds caught the *Bismarck* in extreme stern, jamming her rudders. And then, with awesome inevitability, the armada of battleships, battle cruisers, and heavy cruisers dispatched to run down the enemy closed round the hapless giant, fourteen- and sixteen-inch shells tearing to pieces her upper works and hull at point-blank range, just as Beatty's battle cruisers had shattered the *Blücher* twenty-six years earlier, with the coup de grâce delivered by torpedoes.

Churchill was able to announce the dramatic news of the end of the *Bismarck* in mid-speech in the House of Commons on May 27. The news was at once flashed to Washington, and on the following day Churchill promised to send Roosevelt "the inside story of the fighting with the *Bismarck.*" The *Bismarck* had been, he added, "a terrific ship and a masterpiece of naval construction. . . . The effect upon the Japanese will be highly beneficial," Churchill surmised. "I expect they are doing all their sums again." No one mentioned, until long after the end of the war, that it had been an American on combat patrol in an American warplane who had found the *Bismarck*. The American Neutrality Act had been flagrantly violated, and the whole affair was "a very hot political potato," at home and abroad.

The rest of the naval news in that summer of 1941 was less palatable, and Churchill had little of a favorable nature to report to Roosevelt. The losses in the eastern Mediterranean, especially of destroyers and cruisers, were very serious. In the Battle of the Atlantic, the loss of around half a million tons of shipping monthly in the early summer fell in July and August but later rose again to unacceptable levels in spite of greater American intervention.

The German attack on Russia on June 22, which Churchill

believed would lead to a speedy triumph for Germany while Roosevelt held the opposite view, certainly offered no relief for the hard-pressed Royal Navy. On the contrary, the support of Russia by every means, which became Churchill's instant policy, must lead to further stretching of naval resources with convoys to Murmansk via the Arctic and within range of German bombers as well as U-boats from Norway.

Churchill would have valued highly some spectacular piece of good news to mark the meeting with Roosevelt in August at Placentia Bay. Nothing occurred to lighten the darkness. But it was one of Churchill's great qualities that he could recover himself and rise above the worst news. He was difficult, even dangerous, company at Chequers during the awful weekend of uncertainty over the *Bismarck* and the fate of Crete. But by the following Tuesday, in the makeshift premises to which the House of Commons had had to retreat when the chamber was bombed into uninhabitability, Churchill was speaking with buoyancy and optimism even before the news was passed to him that the threat was over and the giant battleship was at the bottom of the Atlantic.

On July 25, Churchill signaled Roosevelt, "Am looking forward enormously to our talks, which may be service to the future." Roosevelt was equally excited and was already relishing the cloak-and-dagger deception he was about to practice. He was also deeply curious to meet the war leader he had admired since he became Assistant Secretary of the Navy almost thirty years ago. Roosevelt was suspicious of Churchill's imperial attitudes, hostile to his nineteenth-century views on colonialism and especially India. But how could he fail to be impressed by the manner in which Churchill had held his country together and inspired its martial spirit in spite of a series of stunning blows? Without Churchill's leadership, Roosevelt recognized, Britain might have lain down what few arms that were left to her and given in as rapidly and cravenly as had France little more than a year earlier.

Many facets of Churchill's character, judged from afar, still remained a mystery to the President, and he would have benefited greatly if an assessment by one of Churchill's closest and cleverest lieutenants had been available in the White House as it was at Chequers on the weekend before Churchill sailed. General Sir Claude Auchinleck, the commander in the Middle East, was at Chequers then, and was going to be relentlessly grilled by Churchill in connection with his offensive plans in the western desert. "The Auk" was unfamiliar with Churchill's methods and provocative style of dealing with his commanders. It was of inestimable value, therefore, that Major General Hastings "Pug" Ismay, as Chief of Staff to the War Cabinet closer to Churchill than almost anyone, was also at Chequers that weekend. Ismay was an old friend of Auckinleck's and was therefore anxious to brief him and make him aware of what sort of man his host and political boss was.

Ismay later wrote down "the gist of what I said" in his memoirs:

> Churchill could not be judged by ordinary standards; he was different from anyone we had ever met before, or were ever likely to meet again. As a war leader, he was head and shoulders above anyone that the British or any other nation could produce. He was indispensable and completely irreplaceable. The idea that he was rude, arrogant and self-seeking was entirely wrong. . . . He was certainly frank in speech and writing, but he expected others to be equally frank with him. . . . He was a child of nature. He venerated tradition, but ridiculed convention. When the occasion demanded, he could be the personification of dignity; when the spirit moved him, he could be a *gamin*. His courage, enthusiasm and industry were boundless, and his loyalty was absolute. No commander who engaged the enemy need ever fear that he would not be supported. . . . He was not a gambler, but never shrank from taking a calculated risk. His whole heart and soul were in the battle, and he was an apostle of the offensive.

When Churchill stepped on board the *Prince of Wales* at Scapa Flow on the morning of August 4, 1941, he knew that he had much to learn about the President he was to meet. Since the overture he had received from Roosevelt almost two years earlier, he had pondered on the nature and policies of the American leader. Churchill understood American politics infinitely better than Roosevelt understood the British parliamentary system and the convoluted processes that had caused it to work since 1688. He admired the style and subtlety—to say nothing of the immense courage—that had taken this dreadfully disabled man to the White House and had kept him there for almost nine years. He admired his ruthlessness and was comforted by the certain knowledge that they possessed in common a charm of manner and quality of patrician leadership that would make communication straightforward.

Churchill had admired Roosevelt's New Deal and the way he had dragged the United States out of the terrible Depression following the stock market crash of 1929. He had admired his radical politics at home, but was puzzled by the naïveté of Roosevelt's radical foreign policy. For a man who had approved so wholeheartedly of America's colonial exploits at the turn of the century, and after, as conducted chiefly by his kinsman Teddy Roosevelt, the President's antipathy for British and French colonialism appeared ridiculously inconsistent.

Churchill understood better American mercenary tendencies, which he had inherited himself through his mother, and was less outraged than some of his Cabinet members by the cash-on-the-nail attitude towards arms supplies when France fell and the survival of democracy in western Europe rested on a small British air force and a much battered navy. In December 1940, when London was suffering some of its worst bombing raids, Washington was pressing for Britain's gold reserves in South Africa to be released and dispatched to America pending approval of the proposed Lend-Lease Act by Congress. There was even the suggestion that the U.S. Navy might be used as mailman.

On December 28, Churchill drafted a telegram addressed to Roosevelt that began, "We are very anxious to tide over the interval of payments until you have declared policy of United States to Congress. But I am much puzzled and even perturbed by the proposal now made to send a United States battleship to collect whatever gold there may be in Cape Town. . . . It is not fitting," he continued, "that any nation should put itself wholly in the hands of another, least of all a nation which is fighting under increasingly severe conditions for what is proclaimed to be a cause of general concern . . . I should not be discharging my responsibilities to the people of the British Empire if, without the slightest indication of how our fate was to be settled in Washington, I were to part with this last reserve from which alone we might buy a few months' food."

These were the strongest and certainly the bitterest words every written by Churchill to the President. But Roosevelt never read them. Time and again Churchill gained much needed relief in putting to paper his thoughts on the crisis of the day, modifying them repeatedly, and then either dispatching the final draft in a more considered or milder form or thrusting the paper aside, for good. On this occasion sound judgment told him that he should await Roosevelt's next broadcast to the nation, the end-of-the-year fireside chat. In the event, this presidential message proved to be the most outspoken warning to the need of the American people to guard against the danger they faced: "Never before since Jamestown . . ." and the clarion cry, "We must be the great arsenal of democracy."

Ever since the fall of France, Churchill had accepted that Britain's will and means to prevail depended, more than any other factor, on the cultivation of close relations with Roosevelt until—as day follows night—the United States was drawn into the conflict. On the Atlantic voyage, between and during the games of backgammon with Harry Hopkins, Churchill learned more about the man who regarded Hopkins as his closest confederate. Churchill increasingly liked what he heard, and even accepted with good grace that it would be fruitless and unwise to press the President about American intentions to become involved militarily in the war.

With the warm handshake between the two leaders on the deck of the *Augusta*, a new phase in the relationship between the Former Naval Person and the C in C of the United States Navy opened. It was a brief phase, more an overture to the Wagnerian crash of bombs and torpedoes at Pearl Harbor and in the South China Sea four months later. These catastrophes marked the beginning of a new era of joint command and total cooperation—inhibitions, reservations, domestic political considerations, all sunk along with the battleships both nations lost in those early days of December 1941.

SEVEN

Day of Infamy

Harry Hopkins lunched with Roosevelt in the Oval Office of the White House on Sunday, December 7, 1941. "We were talking about things far removed from the war," Hopkins recalled later, when the telephone rang. It was Secretary of the Navy Knox on the line. He informed the President that an air raid was taking place on Pearl Harbor, according to a broadcast from Honolulu. No, it was not an exercise—"no drill." Hopkins thought that there must be some mistake; he could not conceive that the Japanese could be so foolish. But the President "thought the report was probably true and thought it was just the kind of unexpected thing the Japanese would do"—breaking up a peace discussion with a surprise all-out attack.

Two Japanese diplomats were at that time in Washington, Kichisaburo Nomura and Saburo Kurusu, ostensibly to preserve the peace with the United States by negotiation of differences. They were due shortly at a further meeting with Secretary of State Cordell Hull. Roosevelt now called up Hull, told him the news, and asked him to hold the meeting, "to receive their reply formally and coolly and bow them out." It was heard later that the Secretary of State added a touch of rich language to his formal statement to the diplomats. Admiral Stark then called up from the Navy Department to confirm the news from Hawaii and inform the President that there had been damage and loss of life.

In England, Churchill had two Americans as guests for the weekend at Chequers, the ambassador, John Winant, and Averell Harriman. Churchill was low and depressed at dinner, almost as if he was on the verge of a "black dog," one of the occasional moods that had assailed him since his early political days. Shortly after nine o'clock he switched on the little American portable radio Hopkins had once given him. The news bulletin had already begun, and at the end of a number of items about the fighting in North Africa and Russia, there was a brief mention of reported Japanese attacks on American shipping at Hawaii and British shipping in the Dutch East Indies.

The potential enormity of the news had not yet sunk in when Churchill's butler entered. He had listened earlier and more attentively to the news and confirmed the report of these Japanese attacks.

"We looked at one another incredulously," Winant recounted later. "Then Churchill jumped to his feet and started for the door with the announcement, 'We shall declare war on Japan.' There is nothing half-hearted or unpositive about Churchill—certainly not when he is on the move."

And "on the move" Churchill certainly was. Within minutes he was talking to Roosevelt at the White House. "Mr President, what's this about Japan?"

"It's quite true. They have attacked us at Pearl Harbor. We're all in the same boat now," Roosevelt replied, and then told Churchill that on the following day he intended to go to Congress "to declare a state of open hostility.

"This certainly simplifies things," said Churchill before handing the telephone over to Winant. "God be with you."

Winant and Harriman, according to Churchill, "took the shock with admirable fortitude," while Churchill did his best to hide his elation. War between Germany and the United States, too, was now inevitable. Everything towards which Churchill as Prime Minister had been working for eighteen difficult and dangerous months had now, suddenly and spectacularly, taken place. From that moment he knew that the sinister and evil empires of Japan and Germany, as well as Mussolini's seedy regime, were doomed. There could be only one result now; the imponderables were: How long? And at what cost? "No American," wrote Churchill, "will think it wrong of me if I proclaim that to have the United States at our side was to me the greatest joy. . . . So we had won after all!"

The reaction in the White House to the news was mixed and more complicated. The pain and the tumult from which Roosevelt was suffering were evident to Cabinet members who entered the Oval Office, urgently summoned for conversations. There were three chief emotions at play, and at conflict, in the President's mind: shame for the Navy, which was almost a part of his being and on which he had lavished such pride for all his conscious life; anguish and pity for those who had already suffered and would suffer in such numbers in the future; and relief that the uncertainty that had hung ever more heavily over the considerations and debates of the past months was at last over.

Now the decisions would be clear-cut, pragmatic, military. The leader of the nervous, squabbling mob was now the commander on the parade ground barking orders to the disciplined ranks. But for this instant there was the pain of disillusionment, of that there was no doubt. What had the Navy been doing to be unprepared when so many warnings had been issued and war was clearly so imminent? In one hour, it was now clear, Japanese planes had crippled the U.S. Pacific Fleet, the battleships neatly berthed in a row like fairground targets.

The Secretary of Labor recalled the scene in the Oval Office as Roosevelt spoke. "His pride in the Navy was so terrific that he was having actual physical difficulty in getting out the words that put him on record as knowing that the Navy was caught unawares, that bombs dropped on ships that were not in fighting shape and not prepared to move, but were just tied up."

All that would have to be investigated. For the present the anguish must be overcome. For, just as—in Roosevelt's coined phrase—this had been a day of infamy, so also was it a day of destiny for the man who ruled the most powerful nation on earth. In spite of the rain of blows that had fallen upon his country, and would continue to fall for certain, Roosevelt had supreme confidence in America's strength as soon it was mobilized. For, if the Japanese had surprised the Navy with the speed and effectiveness of the Pearl Harbor operation, this was no greater that the surprise experienced in Washington at the diplomatic ineptitude of the Japanese military leadership. The Japanese, with their reputation for guile and craftiness, had opened hostilities in a manner guaranteed to unite the enemy instantly and inspire it with a will and determination that could have been achieved in no other way.

There must, in the end, be victory in the Pacific. And as for Germany, inevitably—well, she might be a more difficult nut to crack. But here again there was no lack of confidence in the President's mind. What had Stark told him recently? Colonel Etherton, a close friend of the Chief of Naval Operations, who had been educated in Germany and knew Hitler well, recalled Hitler saying, "There is only one man in the world whose picture when I look at it, makes me think he would be a pretty tough opponent, and that is President Roosevelt."

Hitler, was, indeed, the first enemy, as had already been agreed with Britain, and only three days were to pass before Germany and Italy declared war. But for the present and without neglecting the needs of the bitter and everlasting Battle of the Atlantic, it was the naval situation in the Pacific that had to be corrected. There were only two battleships out of eight fit for action at Pearl Harbor after the Japanese attack, and there were, proportionately, as few planes left fit to fly. All over the Pacific, from Malaya to Timor, from Wake Island to Hawaii to Guam to the Solomon Islands, the Japanese crack task forces of battleships, carriers, and cruisers were on the attack.

On the credit side, however, the most important relief was that not a single carrier had been at Pearl Harbor at the time of the attack. By great good fortune all were absent on various duties, and as the Imperial Japanese Navy had just demonstrated, the capital ship of the future *was* the carrier, its armament not the fourteen-inch guns of the *Oklahoma,* lying capsized at the bottom of the harbor, but bombing and torpedo aircraft with a range far beyond that of any gun and with an accuracy only a gun at point-blank range could match. It was also noteworthy that none of the sunk battleships was less than twenty years old. There were more than that number, modern, brand-new, already completed or completing in home shipyards. The Japanese, then, had

aroused the fury and fire of the United States by destroying an obsolete battle fleet made up of an obsolete type of man-of-war. They had not even killed many people—not many more than were killed on a bad night in the bombing blitz on Britain.

Unharmed at the end of this day of infamy were the considerable carrier and submarine forces of the U.S. Navy, and these were the ships that would win the war in the Pacific. On every count except proof of the effectiveness of the Japanese air arm, Pearl Harbor was a Japanese disaster. This judgment has the advantage of hindsight. At the time there was, understandably, grave anxiety. It was undeniable that Japanese skill and weaponry had been gravely underestimated. This was confirmed by the Japanese victory in the South China Sea three days later. In a remarkble feat of arms, Japanese planes operating at an unprecedented range, and armed with torpedoes of unprecedented destructive power, sank the British battleship *Prince of Wales* and the battle cruiser *Repulse* in short order while at sea. Both ships were equipped with what was considered adequate anti-aircraft protection but lacked the fighter aircraft cover now recognized as essential.

Inevitably, heads rolled for the Pearl Harbor fiasco. Admiral Kimmel, C in C Pacific Fleet, was first for the guillotine, although "responsibility for the debacle was in fact spread so widely through governmental and service organizations that individual error other than excusable human fallibility was not pinpointed." He was relieved of his command on December 17 and at once applied for retirement. To Roosevelt's sorrow and chagrin, Stark had to go, too, after criticism at the inquiry that he had not kept Kimmel sufficiently informed of the imminent danger to the base. Stark was, however, merely transferred, and in March 1942 was made C in C U.S. Naval Forces in the European theater of operations. He remained a close friend and confidant of the President to the end.

Stark had served in the Navy Department in Washington for many years, latterly as chief of the Bureau of Ordnance. The officer, who once had resisted Roosevelt's plea to take the wheel of his destroyer, was preeminently a desk admiral. He was, in the eyes of Robert E. Sherwood, "able to consider the political as well as purely military aspects of the global situation. . . . He had exceptional qualities as a staff officer, but lacked the quickness and the ruthlessness of a decision required in wartime . . . his contribution to the formation of Grand Strategy was immeasurable."

Stark's successor, Ernest J. King, was a very different man, with none of Stark's refinements of diplomacy, "a stern sailor of commanding presence, vast sea-knowlege and keen strategic sense." At first judgment he appeared as a dour, uncompromising figure, and very often at second judgment, too. He never ceased to want the Pacific war to take priority and preference, was deeply suspicious of Britain as an ally, was dubious about the quality of the Royal Navy, and fought off for as long as he could any British or other Allied support in the Pacific war. Between the wars he had been much concerned with the development of naval aviation and commanded a carrier for two years before taking a Naval War College course. At the time of Pearl Harbor, after gaining his wings at the age of forty-nine, he was the only American officer of high rank with specialized experience and knowledge of undersea, surface, and air warfare.

Ernie King was in command of the Atlantic Patrol Force before coming to Washington. He was, it has been said, "a man of strong will and hot temper: but he also possessed an innate sense of justice which allowed him to pardon failure in those whom he knew to have done their best." On his appointment as C in C U.S. Fleet and Chief of Naval Operations, he stated as his policy, "It is time to toss defensive talking and thinking overboard. Our days of victories are in the making—we will win this war." His determination to make the U.S. Fleet win the war in the Pacific unaided was caused, it was said, "by the need he felt for wiping out the memory of the disaster at Pearl Harbor."

Ernest King was vindictive, irascible, overbearing, hated and feared. He had no time for his comtemporaries, regarding General Marshall as stupid, General "Hap" Arnold as Marshall's yes-man and Admiral Leahy as a fixer. On the British side, he liked Pound and admired Portal, but mistrusted Churchill and loathed Alan Brooke.

King drank too much, seduced his fellow officers' wives, was a poor sport. So how did it come about that Roosevelt, who knew about the drink problem, appointed him to supreme command when King was 63 and already reconciled to going "to the scrap heap"? Only a part of the answer can be found in the fact that he was by chance in Washington at the time of Pearl Harbor when everyone was in a state of panic and became convinced that the tall, handsome, stern King would sort things out.

King himself, with engaging frankness, explained his appointment: "When they get into trouble they send for the sons of bitches."

On the Joint Chiefs of Staff Committee, sat up to plan and supervise the direction of the war, Admiral King was regarded as difficult, and sometimes quite intractible, "a tough sixty-three-year-old salt of strong views and uncompromising temper who had grown up with the American Navy and was intensely jealous of its independence."

Churchill found King trying for his obstinacy and inflexible views. In the closing stages of the war when Churchill, far ahead of the American administration, sought to limit Russian intransigence and penetration into eastern Europe and the Balkans, King lined up with the radical and suspicious American view of British motives. Better a Communist revolution, and a Communist regime in Greece, for example, than give assistance to Churchill and the Greek government. King refused the use of American ships to help transport the British division ordered there by Churchill. Roosevelt was prevailed upon to cancel King's order but only after much acrimony.

As the catastrophe of Pearl Harbor brought King to Washington to replace Stark, Nimitz owed his position as C in C Pacific for almost the entire war to the judged failure of Admiral Kimmel to prepare that base for the attack. Chester Nimitz was more agreeable company than King. "Nimitz won the respect and affection of sailors of all nationalities who came under his command," *The Times* of London stated on his death. "He was that rare person in any fighting service—a leader of exceptional presence who was yet naturally and entirely modest." It was also stated that "whenever a British ship called at Pearl Harbor he found time to board her and . . . would walk round the decks informally, chatting to officers and men in the most winning and intimate manner." Referring to King, but without naming him,

THE GREATEST CRUSADE

Admiral Bruce Fraser, C in C British Pacific Fleet, once re-marked, "The warmth of Nimitz's welcome was in marked contrast to the attitude of those American naval men who had not wished to see the English return to the Pacific." Morison's considered judgment was that "Nimitz probably inspired a greater personal loyalty than did any other admiral in the war"—and it is hard to beat that compliment.

Roosevelt probably felt closer to Chester Nimitz than any other of his admirals. At the height of the Pacific war, the President and his C in C Pacific continued to exchange personal notes.

15 October 1943

Dear Chester:—

That is a delicious jam and I have been eating it for breakfast. Many thanks for sending it to me.... I hope so much that one of these days, when you go to meet Ernie [King] in San Francisco you will keep on to Washington so that I can have a good talk to you.

My best wishes,
Always sincerely,
Franklin D. Roosevelt

Their "good talk" had to wait until the following July when Roosevelt embarked in the U.S.S. *Baltimore* for Pearl Harbor to confer with Nimitz and General Douglas MacArthur. It was the President's last visit to the fleet, and towards the end of it, he wrote to thank his friend and admiral for all he had done—"the arrangements you have made and the efficient manner in which they have been carried out ... I now feel I have a first hand understanding of some of the problems of the Pacific."

As the fighting crept close to the Japanese homeland and the U.S. Marines captured the key island of Iwo Jima against fanatical resistance, Roosevelt received from Nimitz a copy of a triumphant photograph that was to become famous. Roosevelt thanked him for "that very fine picture of the Flag being raised on Mount Suribachi by the Marines. I am delighted to have it for my collection." It was signed by Nimitz, Admirals Turner and Spruance, and the marines' General Holland Smith.

Admiral Richmond Kelly Turner had by this time become

"the leading practitioner of amphibious warfare in the Pacific," a fine officer who had recovered from an early setback and a near-deadly dose of malaria to form an imperishable partnership with Raymond Spruance.

Admiral Spruance personified the whole philosophy of conduct of the gigantic Pacific campaign, which rested upon caution and steadiness, minute planning, and a proper traditional regard for full backup and consolidation of supplies before a further advance with the minimum losses of men and matériel. His nickname Electric Brain derived less from his early specialist training in electrical engineering than from his quick thinking in a crisis. Most authorities agree that he possessed the best tactical mind of any naval commander in the Pacific; and Morison has commented that he was "a happy choice indeed" for command at the Battle of Midway, "for Spruance was not merely competent; he had the level head and cool judgment that would be required to deal with new contingencies and a fluid situation: a man secure within."

Spruance was, it has been said, "a man of quiet and modest personality but possessed of great powers of orgnization and outstanding resolution in moments of crisis . . . a master of the complexities and uncertainties of large-scale amphibious warfare. If it was Nimitz who created the supremely successful Pacific strategy, it was Spruance and Halsey who translated the energy into action."

William F. Halsey was a strongly contrasting character to Spruance, a flamboyant fire-eater and probably the commander most popular with the lower deck in the Pacific Fleet. Halsey proved the exception to the rule of caution that generally governed the naval war in the Pacific, and on several occasions paid a heavy price for the risks he took, but he was a brilliant director of naval aviation. Halsey, according to Morison, will "always remain a controversial figure, but none can deny that he was a great leader, one with the 'Nelson touch.' His appointment as Commander South Pacific Force at the darkest moment of the Guadalcanal campaign lifted the hearts of every officer and bluejacket. He hated the enemy with an unholy wrath and turned that feeling into a grim determination by all hands to hit hard, again and again, and win."

THE GREATEST CRUSADE

Halsey, from long association with Roosevelt in the admiral's destroyer days, was very close to the President, too. But by Roosevelt's nature, his feeling for the sea, and his lifelong love for the American Navy, he possessed an affection for all his admirals. Besides King, Stark, Nimitz, Turner, Spruance, and Halsey, Roosevelt felt an all-embracing affinity with Admirals Daniel Barbey and Theodore Wilkinson, Admirals Wilson Brown and Frederick Sherman, Admirals Richard Conolly, Thomas Hart, Thomas Kinkaid, Marc Mitscher, and many others.

From the outset of the Pacific war Roosevelt was blessed with an exceptional secretary of the Navy, a very different man from Josephus Daniels of the First World War, and by no means the cipher whom Churchill had chosen as First Lord when he became Prime Minister. William Franklin Knox was a Bostonian with a fine fighting record as a younger man. He had been born in 1874 and fought in the Rough Riders in the Spanish-American War and as a colonel of field artillery in France in 1918. His careers between the wars were newspaperman first and Republican politician a close second. By 1936 he was nominated for Vice-President on the Republican ticket, and was publisher of the *Chicago Daily News*. Roosevelt brought him into his administration in July 1940 during the infiltration exercise of his opponents before the 1940 presidential election. Knox was not known for any special interest in the Navy but he was a first-rate administrator, and tough besides. He needed all his strength to deal with Admiral King, who loathed and despised him and came close to reorganizing the administrative structure of the Navy in 1942 in order to strip to almost nothing the civilian influence in naval affairs. It took Roosevelt's intervention to prevent this step towards a total King dictatorship.

For his part, Knox was always trying to get King out of Washington and into the Pacific and a seagoing command. He never succeeded. And the incessant sniping from King certainly contributed to Secretary Knox's premature death on April 28, 1944. On hearing of Knox's death—from a heart attack—Churchill signaled, "His Majesty's Government and especially the Admiralty feel his loss acutely, for no one could have been more forthcoming and helpful in all our difficult times than was this distinguished American statesman and War Administrator."

DAY OF INFAMY

The excellent and efficient Knox was succeeded by James V. Forrestal, Knox's number two, who had done much useful liaison work in Britain before Pearl Harbor. Roosevelt admired him as much as he had admired the dogged Knox. Again far too much of the Secretary's time was taken up dealing with King and his temperament. Forrestal was cooler with him than Knox had been. "Forrestal's temperament seemed to have been more annoying to King than the admiral's mannerisms were to Forrestal," Forrestal's biographer suggested.

With both his secretaries of the Navy, Roosevelt maintained smooth-running relations, but they were political relations that lacked the special quota of warmth he reserved for his admirals— even for King, to whom he showed a tolerance far beyond what this irascible and uncooperative admiral deserved.

Roosevelt had a close, almost paternal affection for his naval aide for much of the war, John L. McCrea. When Roosevelt created the new and highly important post of chief of staff to the President, who would also preside over the Joint Chiefs of Staff, he selected an admiral, William Leahy, who had served for forty-six years before being sent as ambassador to Vichy after the fall of France. The naval element was always there, in the Oval Office, in conferences, and wherever Roosevelt traveled nationally and internationally. The kinship was total, the affection heartwarming. It survived the shame of Pearl Harbor as an affectionate father forgives a lapse in behavior of a favorite son. Admiral Kimmel had to go if only for maintaining "an unwarranted feeling of immunity from attack" at the base in spite of "purple" warnings from Washington of a likely Japanese attack. However, his enforced retirement deeply grieved Roosevelt.

In Roosevelt's philosophy you did not cast bricks at admirals: They were your friends. When he learned that Rear Admiral William H. Allen, commandant of Charleston Navy Yard, was having a lot of political trouble with the city's mayor, and when he learned that this Republican officer had proclaimed that the city was the worst this side of Singapore, that at a ship's launch he had invited three hundred Republicans and six Democrats, Roosevelt merely asked when he was due to retire. Told that Admiral Allen would retire in five months, he took no further action. Roosevelt could not bear rows with sailors, and that was that.

*   *   *

And now, what of the Pacific fleets, Japanese and American, and the course of the mighty and long-drawn-out campaign, for America tribulation "mid toil and tumult of her war . . . "? With the elimination of the American battle fleet at Pearl Harbor and, three days later, the *Prince of Wales* and *Repulse* off Singapore, the Imperial Japanese Navy could lay claim to control of the central and western Pacific Ocean. All that remained to the west was the weak American Asiatic Fleet under the command of Admiral Thomas C. Hart, and a mixed force of American, Dutch, and British cruisers and destroyers under the command of the Dutch Rear Admiral Karel Doorman based on Surabaja. The Japanese had been disappointed to find no carriers at Pearl Harbor but were confident in their own superiority in skill and matériel if the American carriers should ever emerge to challenge them.

The Imperial Japanese Navy was a superbly efficient fighting machine, highly professional, dedicated, and skillful. Their ships and equipment were first class. Their two newest battleships dwarfed even the German *Bismarck*, their 18.1-inch guns the biggest ever fitted to a man-of-war, their carriers fast and efficient, and the planes they carried, supported by a fine shore-based maritime air force, superior to anything the Americans possessed. Their Long Lance 24-inch torpedoes were propelled by liquid oxygen, which gave them unprecedented speed and range. Torpedoes carried by carrier planes could be dropped from a height that amazed the men of the *Prince of Wales*. Although they had no radar, their night-fighting methods had been taken to a peak of efficiency, aided by enormous night binoculars—which had deceived prewar pundits into the comforting illusion that they were confirmation of Oriental myopia.

The C in C of the Combined Fleets, Isoroku Yamamato, had justifiable confidence in the superiority of Japanese arms at the end of 1941. He had also voiced his belief that victory must come to Japan within one year, or it would never come. He was aware of the vastly greater industrial capacity of the United States when it was switched to war production, enlarged, and speeded up. On the evidence of the first few months, it did look as if Yamamoto's time limit for America's defeat would be met.

The U.S. Navy deserved Roosevelt's pride and admiration.

The hard-core professionals were a fine body of sailors, but with the accelerating growth of the fleet they were relatively few in number and the called-up reservists and new recruits required to man the new ships coming from the yards lacked the experience of the peacetime men. The carrier aircrews and the submariners in particular were outstanding in their specialist trades. The newer ships, too, were first class. The sixteen-inch-gunned new generation of battleships now joining the fleet were as stoutly protected and built as their German counterparts, could make thirty knots, and could take massive punishment. Not one was to be lost in almost four years of war in the Pacific.

The greatest equipment weakness was in the Navy's torpedoes, which were slow and unreliable and not in the same class as Japanese torpedoes. Time and again in those early months of war, destroyers and submarines were courageously brought within close striking range of the enemy only to be frustrated by inefficient torpedoes. Inadequate anti-aircraft protection bedeviled the ships of every fleet in the world, none more so than the British and American. Many months passed and many ships were damaged or sunk by bomb or torpedo before sufficient anti-aircraft batteries were fitted. Then the screen of metal and high explosive made penetration to the target almost impossible, even by *kamikaze* suicide pilots.

But it is quality of personnel that counts in the end as much as quality and output of matériel. The Japanese professionals of 1941 were unsurpassed in any navy. But as the war took its toll, and Yamamoto's first year passed without a conclusion, hastily trained replacements were no match for the old professionals. American training facilities were many times greater than the enemy's and with every passing month the tens of thousands and finally hundreds of thousands of civilian sailors became more accomplished, learning as fast as Americans always have learned. By 1945, when the carrier fleet had increased from five to over ninety, new battleship construction had replaced the Pearl Harbor losses many times over, and cruisers, destroyers, auxiliaries, transports, and landing craft numbered many hundreds, the U.S. Navy was not only the biggest fleet the world had ever seen but its skill and efficiency were remarkable by any standards.

But while the U.S. Navy recruiting-office queues were still

forming in the early weeks of 1942, the Japanese task forces and invasion forces ranged far and wide and almost unopposed. Doorman's international heterogeneous force was destroyed piecemeal in the Java Sea. Vice Admiral Chuichi Nagumo's First Air Fleet, exultant after Pearl Harbor, swept west and south, smashing into submission Wake Island, Rabaul, and Amboina, bringing war to Australia for the first time by devastating Darwin and its shipping. Then west into the Indian Ocean, challenging British control of these waters and the small mixed fleet of Admiral Sir James Somerville. Two heavy cruisers, a carrier, and her escort were all sent to the bottom by dive bombers, and Colombo and the British naval base of Trincomalee at Ceylon were given the same treatment as Darwin.

The task force returned home on April 18, 1942. It had been an amazing cruise across a third of the world, triumphing from Pearl Harbor to Ceylon, 157 degrees west to 80 degrees east. They had all but destroyed the American battle fleet, crippled the British Eastern Fleet, and caused devastation wherever they steamed. If ever there has been an invincible fleet, this was it—five carriers against the two most powerful navies in the world. And not one of the carriers had been attacked, let alone damaged.

How could the Japanese high command succeed in the equally difficult next task: to restrain themselves and their admirals from overconfidence and ambitions beyond the bounds of wisdom? Malaya, Singapore, the whole Malay barrier were safely in their hands; the Philippines and Borneo would soon be theirs, and Burma, with India directly threatened. To the north, part of the long string of the Aleutians was soon to be under their control, threatening the west coast of Canada and the United States.

Succumbing to what came to be known as the "victory disease," voices in the high command demanded an acceleration of the long-laid plans for total victory in the Pacific, with surrender of their enemies—Australia and New Zealand in the south, India in the west, China (almost accomplished), and finally the North American nations, when war-weariness and disillusionment led Canada and the United States to seek terms.

Under the heady fumes of sakè toasts, it all seemed not only possible but inevitable. The contemptible Americans had revealed the hollowness of their past claims of invincibility; the

British had sent their best battleship and, like their much vaunted eastern base of Singapore, it had succumbed at once. Now, disregarding the age-old military adage of securing your supplies and supply lines before further advance, the Imperial Japanese Navy thrust for Midway, from which they could assault and capture the Hawaiian Islands; strike south towards the New Hebrides, the Fiji Islands, and the Solomons to cut U.S. communications with Australia; and attack New Guinea on the northern doorstep of Australia. It was a breathtaking program of conquest for a nation that had emerged from secretive isolation only eighty years earlier.

Six months to the day after the Pearl Harbor attack, the invincibility of the Japanese at sea was put to its first full test, almost on Australia's doorstep, in the Coral Sea. It was an operation like none other before it in the history of sea warfare, in which electronics and aviation played the major roles and the ships' roles were limited to search and the carriage of aircraft. In the course of the two-day battle on May 7–8, 1942, no ship on either side sighted the enemy, and the presence of a battleship would have been a hindrance rather than an advantage.

The battle taught both sides lessons that were applied in all subsequent operations in the Pacific war. Commanders learned that pilots tended to exaggerate the size of enemy ships and claims of damage inflicted on them; they learned to keep back some fighters for the protection of their carriers when dispatching an attacking force; they learned to resist laying on an attack until certain of the enemy's position. Scouting and reporting by destroyer and by aircraft were unsatisfactory; and for the Americans radar played a significant part for the first time. American intelligence also benefited greatly from its code-breaking ability, which was a heavy advantage through all the Pacific operations. This was supplemented by the valiant work of so-called coast-watchers, the Allied spies who operated with shortwave radios from concealed observation points on Japanese-held islands.

Coral Sea was a long-drawn-out and indecisive engagement during which the Japanese lost a small carrier and Admiral Fletcher one of his large carriers. But for the Australians and Americans it was an encouraging and exhilarating experience that proved that the Japanese could be halted, on this occasion frustrated in their amphibious attack on Port Moresby in New Guinea. Also for the first time, the Japanese planes proved relatively vulnerable, and the American fighter pilots in particular shot down with consummate skill enemy bombers in considerable numbers.

Weather, radar, deception, initiative, luck, all played their part in this fascinating contest. The long revered art of gunnery was practiced only by the men manning the anti-aircraft guns, who were to prove key figures in the campaigns ahead, and the fighter pilots.

Superior intelligence played a vital role in the next Japanese move. Foiled in the southward offensive, Admiral Yamamoto now thrust east again, hell-bent on the capture of Midway, the key to the door to the Hawaiian Islands and the eastern Pacific. The Japanese C in C knew that he was engaged in a logistical race as well as the widest-ranging naval campaign in history. He knew that before the end of 1942 the American Pacific Fleet would have been reinforced with the men-of-war being rushed to completion in American yards. He must attack now, without delay, shrugging off the setback at Coral Sea, ignoring the evidence of American and Australian will to fight.

By May 10, Admiral Nimitz at Pearl Harbor had every reason to believe that his opponent would be attacking Midway within fourteen days. And he possessed only two operational carriers. Admiral Nagumo alone had twice this force of these new capital ships. In the Pearl Harbor dockyard men worked round the clock to repair a third carrier, the *Yorktown,* badly damaged at Coral Sea.

While the code breakers worked their magic skills, providing Nimitz with a clear picture of Japanese plans, even, finally, the precise date of the attack, he dispatched his only two carriers, under the command of Admiral Spruance, to intercept Nagumo's carriers as they advanced, strongly supported by a battleship task force, from the northwest. By prodigies of industry, the *Yorktown* was repaired in three days, emerged from dry dock, and was at once on her way to join Spruance's two carriers at a rendezvous on the ocean cheerfully code named Point Luck. Admiral Fletcher flew his flag in the *Yorktown* and was in overall command.

DAY OF INFAMY

The Japanese pilots were bursting with self-confidence, the fresh replacement pilots as buoyed up by the record of this task force at Pearl Harbor and off Ceylon. "We were so sure of our own strength that we thought we could smash the enemy fleet single-handed, even if the battleship groups did nothing to support us," Commander Fuchida boasted. Admiral Nagumo, ever the realist, was not so sure. He had no idea of the whereabouts of the American carriers. If he had possessed the detailed knowledge vouchsafed to Fletcher and Spruance, this critically important operation might well have led to a Japanese victory.

If Coral Sea was the overture to a new age of sea warfare, Midway confirmed this historical fact. Many Japanese and American airmen died in the air and on the ocean on that fourth day of June 1942. Several squadrons were decimated by fighter and anti-aircraft fire. American torpedoes were as ineffective as they had been earlier, Japanese torpedoes as effective. Attacks by torpedo bombers and dive bombers that should have been synchronized were hopelessly uncoordinated. But at the end of the two days, all four Japanese carriers were at the bottom of the sea or fatally damaged while only one American carrier succumbed to the furious Japanese assault.

Besides 4 carriers and a heavy cruiser, the Japanese lost around 250 naval aircraft and their aircrews—most of them the irreplacable, highly trained professionals of the Pearl Harbor triumph. The Imperial Japanese Navy was still by no means crippled but it was never to regain the ascendancy of earlier days. In the fierce fighting around the Solomon Islands that followed Midway, the Japanese showed themselves superior in night fighting and the Americans and Australians suffered heavy losses, this time mainly in gun duels and destroyer torpedo attacks. The Battle of Savo Island was a clear Japanese victory, and at Santa Cruz Islands in October 1942, the Japanese committed more damage than they received and won a tactical victory.

But within a year of Pearl Harbor and the termination of Yamamoto's time limit for Japanese victory, the Japanese were not only being held on every quarter but the United States Navy had become a many-headed hydra and the most Herculean efforts by the Japanese could no longer prevail. The whole Bismarck Archipelago was under American control, and General MacArthur could start on the long and bloody route back to the Philippine Islands, from which he had been ejected in the early typhoonlike Japanese offensives.

The Pacific war in 1943 and 1944 resolved itself into attacks on Japanese island bases in the central and western Pacific by task forces of carriers, like queen bees, protected by battleships, cruisers, destroyers, and submarines. Japanese positions would be bombarded by surface ships and bombarded from the air before assault forces went ashore and secured possession. The U.S. Fifth Fleet, under the overall command of Admiral Spruance, was made up of a number of these task forces, supported by fleet trains of transports and landing craft, by mid-1943 an armada, consisting of over two hundred ships and some fifteen hundred aircraft.

Admiral Nimitz's overall plan, worked out at his Pearl Harbor headquarters and in conjunction with Admiral King and the Joint Chiefs of Staff, was to repossess the Pacific islands methodically to a set timetable and at a cost of as few lives as possible. While facing ever-weakening relative Japanese material resources, the strength of determination of the enemy appeared to increase with every island-hopping step towards the Japanese mainland. Japanese occupying troops fought to the last man without air support or hope of reinforcement. As the last Japanese carriers were sent to the bottom under the impact of enormous American air fleets, *kamikaze* suicide pilots, mere boys who could scarcely take off on their one-way missions, hurled their bombers at American men-of-war. Even the battleship *Yamato,* largest in the world, was reduced to committing a form of naval *harakiri* by steaming to her inevitable end at the hands of hundreds of American torpedo and dive bombers.

In the Battle of Leyte Gulf on October 25, 1944, the Japanese Navy was virtually wiped out, and little defense was left to the crushed and constricted empire that had sought to conquer half the world. After Midway, the outcome was inevitable, given a continuing American will to win and the vast industrial resources at her command. The first credit for eventual victory must go to the officers and men who outfought, often against odds, the Japanese in the first year of the Pacific war. It was men like Admirals Spruance and Fletcher, Halsey and Kinkaid, Turner and Aubrey Fitch, under the overall command of Nimitz (CINCPAC, as his title was compounded), who took the first waves of the storm and held steady, who were the first heroes of the Pacific war. It is quite wrong to suggest, however, as some historians have done, that the later victories were straightforward and inevitable. They were nothing of the kind. The Japanese sailor remained a formidable foe to the end, and it is a sound commander who takes the fewest risks and prevails with the fewest possible casualties and smallest losses of matériel.

There has been no more decisive victory at sea than that created by the U.S. Navy (latterly assisted by Allied navies) 1941–45. The atom bomb may have saved millions of Japanese lives, and many thousands of Allied lives, and it is one of God's mercies that it did so. But in terms of naval warfare the fight was over by then, and all that remained was to secure a bloody hold on the Japanese islands and crush the last life out of the wretched, misled nation.

Today there are a number of older people who can recall Roosevelt on naval business in his last years. They will all testify to the enthusiasm, interest, and affection he always demonstrated, at sea or in the White House or Hyde Park. Just as Peter Kemp believes that Churchill would have made a superb fighting admiral if he had spent his life in the Navy, no one can doubt that Roosevelt would have enjoyed a career at sea and been a supremely good captain of a ship, and fleet commander.

One naval officer, Admiral McCrea, recalled Roosevelt observantly and with affection in the White House and aboard a battleship. As Captain McCrea he had been naval aide to Roosevelt in the early part of the war and was responsible for setting up his map room. The film actor Robert Montgomery had driven ambulances in France early in the war, and later as a U.S. Navy lieutenant in London had become familiar with Churchill's map room, based originally on the map room Churchill had devised when First Lord in 1914. On his return to Washington, Montgomery told McCrea of its details and usefulness. "I want you to draw up a plan for an installation of the same sort here," McCrea instructed him. And this was done.

The White House map room, which later incorporated an Army map room as well, was based on the maps and charts secured to the walls, the Atlantic and Pacific oceans dominating two walls, with more charts of Southeast Asia, Indonesia, the Mediterranean, and the Indian Ocean. Movements of ships and convoys, the position of enemy ships or task forces, Japanese submarines and German U-boats, statistics of losses and projections, a file of the latest messages between the war leaders were always available. It was a veritable storehouse of information. "McCrea," Admiral Leahy once told him, "I think there is more information about the war concentrated in your Map Room than there is in any other place in Washington."

McCrea later recalled how Roosevelt "would wander in and out at all times of the day and night," and frequently displayed to his aide his "amazing knowledge of geography" partly acquired through his longtime hobby of stamp collecting.

From time to time Roosevelt would reminisce about the days "when I was in the Navy." "The President liked to discuss individuals," McCrea recalled. "When he was 'in the Navy,' King, Nimitz, Halsey and many others were 'on their way up.' He knew them personally and expressed much interest in their careers. 'What have they done in the recent past?' he would say. . . . When he was 'in the Navy' he was exceedingly popular with the younger officers. He was lighthearted and gay—had none of the stiffness about him which the young were inclined to associate with the Secretary level. . . . Many of the bureaus would hold in abeyance mail which they thought they would have trouble in getting the Secretary's signature and wait until the Secretary was out of town and then present such mail to the Assistant Secretary for his signature, which they invariably got."

There came a time when McCrea felt that he ought to leave Washington and get closer to the fighting war. It was a Sunday in late October 1942. "I maneuvered the President into the matter of leaving. We had been talking about odds and ends and I sensed my moment. I told him that I was not insensible to the honor of being the Naval Aide to the President in time of war and while I realized that much of importance with reference to the war was taking place in Washington, nevertheless I felt that I should be out there somewhere in a ship . . . after all, Mr. President, I must live with my conscience and I really think I ought to go. 'All right, John, all right, I'll let you go at the end of the year.' "

DAY OF INFAMY

McCrea's departure was postponed and he expressed his anxiety about losing the ship he had been promised. Roosevelt's reply, "gently, ever so gently and with a smile, [was] 'Why, John, under the circumstances I don't think they would take the ship away from you.'"

The ship assigned to McCrea was the new battleship *Iowa*,* a giant of over forty-five thousand tons with nine 16-inch guns, well-nigh impenetrable armor, and a speed of thirty-three knots. She was commissioned on February 24, 1943, and was based in the North Atlantic for a while in case the *Tirpitz* came out. In the autumn she was assigned to take Roosevelt to Oran en route to the Teheran conference with Churchill and Stalin.

Roosevelt boarded—or rather was hoisted into her—at the mouth of the Potomac River, greeted by his old naval aide. On the second day out the battleship suddenly took violent evading action at high speed, heeling over at an acute angle. "It's the real thing! It's the real thing!" a voice cried out, and another voice on the public address system yelled, "Torpedo defense! This is not a drill!" Then there was a massive explosion in the wake of the ship. An escorting destroyer had discharged a live torpedo by accident.

Admiral King wanted the captain to be relieved of his command instantly. "But Roosevelt would have none of it, doubtless proceeding on the theory that it would be punishment enough for the poor wretch when he had discovered he had almost torpedoed five admirals."

"All our crowd are getting a real rest . . . " Roosevelt wrote to his wife. The episode and the conclusion were typical of the man—of his invariable good sense, his cheerfulness, his affection for his Navy, and his matter-of-fact, wryly amused attitude towards a crisis.

*Recently reactivated yet again.

EIGHT

Prime Minister's Team

Churchill's naval team after he became Prime Minister was of much higher quality than any he could have mustered in the First World War. As Prime Minister and Minister of Defense, he had no intention of having a powerful or independent-minded civil head of the Navy in succession to himself. He intended to run the war and all three services at the highest level through the chiefs of staff, and the office of First Lord of the Admiralty was to be demoted almost to extinction.

With the fall of Chamberlain as Prime Minister, the government that Churchill now led (May 10, 1940) was a coalition one, with Labour party members in the Offices of Labour and Economic Warfare, a Liberal as Secretary of State for Air, the leader of the Labour party, Clement Attlee, as Lord Privy Seal. After consultations with Attlee, Churchill offered the post of First Lord of the Admiralty to the Labour member A. V. Alexander.

No one could have made a stronger contrast in the Admiralty with Churchill himself, his predecessor. Albert Victor Alexander had been First Lord in Ramsay MacDonald's 1929 Labour administration, which Churchill regarded as sufficient reason for putting him back into the Admiralty. He was "a thick-set, chunky man with a square face and looked rougher and tougher than he really was." He got through paperwork well and was well liked. Guy Grantham found him "a pompous little man" and Peter Kemp says "he was nothing more than a cipher really. But he was a very nice, simple man who was brought up in the cooperative movement. Whenever he came to see me after the war he always took his hat off when we passed the local co-op shop."

Anything of a highly confidential nature was kept from A.V.A., as he was called, or Wide Mouth for his indiscretions. In October 1940 Churchill, who was almost obsessively security-minded, gave instructions that Alexander's name should be added to the circulation list of Enigma decrypts (intercepted and decoded German signals), for he "of course must know everything known to his subordinates." But the instruction was never carried out, and Alexander went through the entire war largely ignorant of the pricelessly valuable work done at Bletchley by "Ultra," the collective code word for decrypts obtained by the Enigma code-breaking machine. Dramatic events were therefore constantly surprising Alexander, like the resighting of the *Bismarck,* but he never seemed to take offense. A.V.A. was a splendid orator, and Sir Clifford Jarrett, his principal private secretary for four years, regards his speechmaking up and down the land on behalf of the Navy as his greatest war contribution.

With Churchill's promotion, Dudley Pound's power and responsibility increased greatly, although Churchill was never distant from his shoulder. Pound was sixty-two years old, unimpressive in manner, wholly dedicated to the service, and without much sense of humor—in fact not unlike Sir Arthur Wilson, Churchill's first First Sea Lord. But Pound had a shrewder and more flexible mind than Tug Wilson. "I've never seen anyone who worked so hard," says Admiral Grantham, his former naval assistant. "He was at work at 6:30 A.M. I was always bad in the morning. When I reported before breakfast I always gave the wrong answers, which had to be corrected later in the day. At length, Pound said to me, 'You don't seem to be very good before breakfast.'" In fact, Pound soon acquired the reputation for being a sleeper at meetings and people said that he ought not to start work before dawn. Churchill noticed this quite early on in their relationship; he also observed that if any subject relating to the Navy came up, he would not only at once be alert but appeared not to have missed a single word of the proceedings. "Nothing slipped past his vigilant ear, or his comprehending mind," Churchill recalled. In fact, Pound was never out of pain from an arthritic hip, and later from the tumor that killed him.

Pound was half American, on his mother's side, and J. P. Morgan was his uncle. Morgan wanted Pound to join the bank, but there was never any possibility of that in Pound's mind. Apart from his shooting, the Navy was his whole life.

Recalling his relationship with earlier first sea lords, Churchill had at first contemplated the prospect of Dudley Pound as his partner with some reservations. "I had strongly condemned in Parliament the dispositions of the Mediterranean Fleet when he commanded it in 1939 at the moment of the Italian descent upon Albania," Churchill wrote. "Now we met as colleagues upon whose intimate relations and fundamental agreement the smooth working of the vast Admiralty machine would depend. We eyed each other amicably if doubtfully. But from the earliest days our friendship and mutual confidence grew and ripened."

Guy Grantham can all too clearly remember Pound's working routine after the too early start, the first part of the afternoon at the Admiralty again, then a chiefs-of-staff meeting that would go on until dinner. Grantham would then have all the dockets ready for his return around midnight, when they would go through them, and the brief his assistant had prepared, until about 1:15 A.M. "I slept in my office at this time," Grantham recalls, "and one night when Pound had not returned at 1 A.M. I turned in, to be awoken sharply by the message that the First Sea Lord wished to see me. There he was, at his desk. 'Come on,' he said, 'get down to it. And never do that again.' "

Arthur Marder perceived the real qualities of Pound—unlike Captain Roskill, whose misjudgment and prejudice in his official history of the war at sea have led to a grave miscarriage of historical justice.

> In a short time [Marder has written], Churchill formed a close attachment to, and trust in, Pound. He was impressed with the admiral's energy, keen intellect and analytical mind, and mastery of his profession. He respected this officer of unimpeachable character who was able to state his case to

ministers in a dry and factual manner and without ever losing his temper, and to stand up firmly when necessary to the prodding of the arch-prodder. Pound feared neither God, man, nor Winston Churchill. Churchill had no great opinion of the planners ("masters of negation" he once called them), but he was ready and willing to accept Pound's judgement, which he trusted. On his part, Pound recognized that Churchill's qualities of leadership were so exceptional as to justify extraordinary effort to co-operate with him and to support him. He accordingly quickly developed an intense loyalty towards Churchill. He was never heard to criticize him or to complain about him. "I have the greatest admiration for W. C., and his good qualities are such and his desire to hit the enemy so overwhelming, that I feel one must hesitate in turning down any of his proposals."

Like Jellicoe, Pound's one great weakness was an inability to depute. He wanted to be in on everything, and Churchill was not in a position to correct this fault. The one massive blunder for which Pound must be held responsible was the near destruction of the massive PQ17 convoy of war materials to Russia in the summer of 1942. Fearing attack from a powerful German force of armored ships, Pound ordered the convoy to scatter, depriving it of almost all its escort vessels and leaving the merchantmen the helpless victims of bombers and U-boats. Only eleven of the thirty-five ships that had sailed reached their destination.

"Dudley Pound should never have intervened—you can't run a battle from the Admiralty," asserts Admiral Grantham. "Like Churchill, he felt that in any operation that was taking place he should have his say." On the other hand, Pound's great asset was that he could and did stand up to Churchill when it was important to do so. Churchill "had a deep respect for Pound and his judgment and for all naval wisdom," and when his health started to fail in August 1943 Churchill expressed deep concern. Pound suffered a stroke later that month while in Washington, was brought back home and died, appropriately, on Trafalgar Day, October 21. "A very gallant man who literally went on working until he dropped," Field Marshal Alanbrooke, his brilliant opposite number at the War Office, wrote in his diary. "He was a grand colleague to work with."

PRIME MINISTER'S TEAM

Roosevelt agreed and on Pound's death telegraphed his ambassador in London, "U.S. joins with Great Britain in mourning the death of the former First Sea Lord who directed the operations of the fleet through four critical years and whose sagacity and wide experience made him a pillar of strength. . . . I was privileged to count Sir Dudley Pound among my friends and his passing brings a deep sense of personal loss."

In the early stages of the war, the officer who had even more influence on Churchill was Admiral Sir Tom Phillips, the Vice Chief of Naval Staff. Like Sturdee in the First World War, Tom Phillips was regarded as an intellectual with a rapid and astute mind. This view was better justified in the case of Phillips. "He was a very clever man," says Admiral Grantham, who knew him well at the Admiralty, "but a traditionalist."

Shortly before Pearl Harbor, and against the strong advice of Dudley Pound, when Churchill determined to dispatch two powerful capital ships out to the Far East in the belief that they would act as a deterrent to Japanese ambitions, it was Tom Phillips who was selected to command this "Force Z." It was a curious choice. "It shook me when Tom Phillips was chosen," Admiral Grantham recalls. "It is terrible to send a staff officer to sea when the war has been going on for a long time; he has got out of touch with what it is like. For instance, Phillips was a two-watch man [watch on, watch off, as opposed to the less taxing three-watch], which was too much for men month after month. Sitting in the Admiralty he had not learned that sort of thing."

As all the world was soon to learn, the dispatch of Force Z led to a major disaster. Churchill wrote of it later:

> I was opening my boxes on the 10th [December 1941] when the telephone at my bedside rang. It was the First Sea Lord. His voice sounded odd. He gave a sort of cough, and at first I could not hear quite clearly. "Prime Minister, I have to report to you that the *Prince of Wales* and the *Repulse* have both been sunk by the Japanese—we think by aircraft. Tom Phillips is drowned." "Are you sure it's true?" "There is no doubt at all." So I put the telephone down. I was thankful to be alone. In all the war I never received a more direct shock. . . . As I turned over and twisted in bed the full horror of the news sank in upon me.

THE GREATEST CRUSADE

It is far easier to get a critical view of British admirals of the Second World War through Churchill's eyes than one of American admirals through Roosevelt's eyes. The reason for this lies in Churchill's distrust of the breed of admirals in general, by contrast with Roosevelt's tendency to relate with his admirals. It is not that the President took a bland or uncritical view of the senior officers of his service. On the contrary, he followed their progress keenly and endeavored as far as was possible to see that the right men were installed in the right commands. In this he was much more successful than Churchill. Once they were there, Roosevelt let them get on with the job, confident in his own judgment and the judgment of his chiefs of staff. Here was evidence, if such were needed, of his self-confidence, steadiness, and sense of security.

Churchill was not only fundamentally insecure—and remained so even when acknowledged as the greatest public hero since Wellington and Nelson, and recognized even by his closest friends as a victim of megalomania—he distrusted admirals from his experiences with them from 1911 to May 1915. With a few exceptions he regarded the professional hierarchy of the Royal Navy of the First World War as tradition bound, unadventurous, and underendowed with initiative and intelligence. Some he believed quite simply lacked courage. He judged Cradock to be insubordinate, stupid, and rash; Milne and Troubridge stupid and cowardly; Carden craven and weak; De Robeck little better; even Jellicoe lacking in positivism.

It is easy to see the origins of Churchill's overregard for aggression in his admirals. The experiences in the Mediterranean, when the *Goeben* had escaped as a result of timorousness and ineptitude, and later with Carden and De Robeck at the Dardanelles, and then the demonstrations of negativism and stupidity at the Battle of Dogger Bank (which should have been a major, not minor, victory) and, after Churchill had left the Admiralty, at Jutland, confirmed his belief that the Nelson spirit was all but extinguished. It was kept flickering only by the younger generation represented by, for example, Commodores Tyrwhitt, Goodenough, and Alexander-Sinclair, by Keyes, and by Beatty.

Of these go-getters, Roger Keyes had remained a friend and supporter during all the years between the wars, an officer in whom "all the old offensive spirit of the Navy was personified." In 1924, when Churchill was not only out of office but out of Parliament, Keyes had tipped him off about a safe and promising seat where he might be welcome, warned him unsuccessfully of the Japanese threat the following year, cruised with him in the Mediterranean. As a member of Parliament from 1934, Keyes was a keen supporter of Churchill in the wilderness, pushing for him to be Minister of Defense in 1936 and First Lord again in 1937 and 1938.

Keyes was not terribly bright, but he was as brave as a lion and loyal as a gundog. When Churchill became Prime Minister he made Keyes head of a new fighting branch, Combined Operations. In this capacity, after service in Norway and elsewhere, Keyes had many sparring matches with other services and with politicians. Recalling his skill and gallantry at Zeebrugge, Belgium, in the First World War, Churchill backed Keyes in his proposal to attack the small Italian island of Pantelleria in December 1940. It came to nothing, opposed by steadier calculations.

"Churchill was personally fond of Keyes, whose courage at Zeebrugge he admired," Sir John Colville has written recently, "but this fondness was not shared either by Churchill's colleagues, or by the Chiefs of Staff or by General Ismay, who found his demands to be Chairman of the Chiefs of Staff Committee and even, at one stage, Deputy Prime Minister, wholly ridiculous." "Keyes was the Fisher of World War II," comments Captain John Litchfield. "He was brought back when he was past it." Still determined to be in the thick of action after his retirement if he ever got a chance, Keyes became an unofficial observer with the U.S. Fleet. At the Battle of Leyte Gulf while he was flying too high without oxygen after being gassed by a toxic smoke screen, his heart was so strained that he died soon after, a very decent and very gallant naval officer.

Keyes's appointment in 1940 reflects Churchill's inordinate regard for admirals of action. Admiral Harwood was another example. He had fought gallantly against odds at the Battle of the River Plate and brought the Navy great kudos. "So Churchill made him C in C Mediterranean," Peter Kemp recalls, "a very different job. He was a failure and never recovered from it. Harwood was a good fighting admiral with very little stuff up top. He was an example of Churchill's overadmiration of the positive in commanders."

If Harwood at the river Plate battle demonstrated to Churchill that the fighting spirit of the Navy was more Nelsonian in 1939 than in 1914, Admiral Sir Dudley North gave evidence a few months later of the old sloppiness and lack of grit that had (in Churchill's judgment) broken the Dardanelles offensive. North was Flag Officer Commanding North Atlantic Station at Gibraltar at the time of the ill-fated Dakar expedition in 1940. Like Admiral Milne in 1914, North was considered in the service as "a courtier sailor," a favorite of the palace, full of Royal Yacht service and periods as senior equerry, and highly conscious of the honors that had been heaped upon him.

North had taken up this shore-based "safe" appointment when he was fifty-nine years old, chiefly because, considering his royal connections, he had to be given something to do and he could not do too much harm there—at least in the context of November 1939. But by the summer of 1940, with the fall of France and the fate of the French Fleet and French colonies in the balance, FOCNA assumed vastly greater responsibilities, for which he was to prove himself unfit.

"I have a distinct recollection," wrote Sir Clifford Jarrett, "that people at the top in the Admiralty were becoming fed up . . . with the readiness which he appeared to find reasons for inaction or delay." His inaction on September 9 proved fatal to his career, and of serious consequence to the Anglo-French force ordered to establish the Free French in Dakar in West Africa. On that day North learned from a reliable French intelligence source that a powerful Vichy French force of three cruisers and three *contre-torpilleurs* (exceptionally powerful destroyers) might leave Toulon and force the passage of the Strait of Gibraltar. North did nothing and, although there were redeeming facts in the admiral's favor, the consequence was that the men-of-war passed through into the Atlantic at high speed without interference, and headed for Dakar, where their presence was of great comfort to the Vichy French and great influence in the disastrous outcome of the expedition for the Allies.

The Dudley North affair became a naval *cause célèbre.* Except for Dudley Pound, who sacked him, there was scarcely an admiral who did not consider that this likable flag officer had been made a scapegoat by Churchill for the failure of the whole expedition. Churchill always had to have a scapegoat for his disasters, so ran senior naval opinion. Look how he had blamed the French for the failure at Antwerp in 1914, and everyone but himself for the Dardanelles! In fact, as Peter Kemp confirms today, "This was very much an Admiralty business and nothing to do with Churchill." But the Navy's admirals had not forgotten Churchill as First Lord in 1914–15 any more than he had forgotten them, and this stigma stuck right up to North's death in 1961, when *The Times* of London wrote ridiculously of him as the Admiral Byng of World War II.

Without doubt the greatest British seagoing admiral of World War II, and of the twentieth century, was Andrew Browne Cunningham, known as A.B.C. His performance in the Mediterranean, sometimes against what seemed to be hopeless odds, and against the full might of the Luftwaffe when he had virtually no air power of his own and quite inadequate anti-aircraft defenses, was a lesson in cool judgment, fine example, imperishable courage, and masterly handling of his fleet. "A.B.C. was absolutely superb," Peter Kemp affirms today, "despite the losses he suffered." He had a terrible time in the eastern Mediterranean during the Greek and Crete evacuations, and took some heavy criticism for losing so many ships. But the wonder was that he did not lose the lot under the circumstances, and the Navy's success in keeping all but airborne troops out of Crete led to the permanent crippling of Germany's airborne forces as a result of their savage losses.

Cunningham, writes Kemp, "was the epitome of the fighting admiral. Not a great deal of 'brain' but one of the few admirals who chose a good staff and used it intelligently and to the full. He loathed 'yes-men', got rid of them as quickly as he could, and expected his staff to stand up to him if their opinions differed from his."

With the death of Dudley Pound, Cunningham was brought home as First Sea Lord, which he did not enjoy. Nor at first did Churchill much enjoy his company: He had wanted another, more pliable, admiral. "In this role A.B.C. was fortunate in following Pound who bequeathed him an Admiralty which was working like a well-oiled and remarkably efficient machine. So it didn't matter that he was a bit out of his depth." Churchill had sometimes shown exasperation and impatience with Cunningham the fighting admiral, particularly if he was not showing bared-teeth aggression. In Whitehall, paradoxically, he was later immensely kind and patient with him "and eased him through the political difficulties of trying to stand up to the other (very strong) Chiefs of Staff."

"Andrew Cunningham's arrival in the C.O.S.," wrote Alan Brooke in his diary, "was indeed a happy event for me. I found in him first and foremost one of the most attractive of friends, a charming associate to work with and the staunchest of companions when it came to supporting a policy agreed to amongst ourselves, no matter what inclement winds might blow. I carry away with me nothing but the very happiest recollections of all my dealings with him. His personality, charming smile and heart warming laugh were enough to dispense at once those miasmas of gloom and despondency which occasionally swamped the C.O.S."

A.B.C. never failed to give credit for the great debt Britain owed to the United States, and to Roosevelt in particular, in the two and a quarter critical years before Pearl Harbor:

> I find it difficult to see how Britain could have survived without assistance from the other side of the Atlantic before the formal entry of the United States into the war after the Japanese attack upon Pearl Harbor on December 7th, 1941. Indeed, we have so much for which to be everlastingly grateful to the United States of America that it cannot be expressed in words. Much of that gratitude is due to Franklin Delano Roosevelt and his advisers for their wisdom and foresight in bringing home to the mass of their countrymen that after the fall of France, Britain, bleeding, and impoverished, stood alone as a buttress against the Nazi domination of the civilized world.
>
> I knew nothing of President Roosevelt as a politician. To me he was a man of great wisdom, charm of manner, humanity and simple kindness. He took a profound interest in the Navy, and in the days of his affliction collected stamps as a hobby and a relaxation. His quiet, unforgettable voice in those 'fireside talks' over the radio must have lifted the hearts of millions all over Britain and the Empire just as they did in America. I think it is right to say that our admiration and affection for the President of the United States of America were

second only to the feelings we treasured for our own great leader, Mr. Churchill.

Cunningham, the Nimitz of the Mediterranean and immensely popular with the fleet, was "a man of florid and smiling countenance with the blue eyes of the born sailor and the genial manner of one whose naval career had been passed chiefly in small ships."

The other admiral who also performed wonders, in his case with the Home Fleet, was Bruce Fraser. From May 1943 he carried the responsibilities of protecting the Russian convoys and of keeping the Atlantic free from the German surface raiders (appropriately sinking the *Scharnhorst* in the Navy's last classic big-gun action), and then took over in the Pacific. He remained a popular bachelor totally dedicated to the service. "Everyone liked Fraser and admired him," says Admiral Grantham. Equally important, he stood up to Churchill when it was necessary to do so. He feared nobody.

Admiral John Tovey, Fraser's predecessor as C in C Home Fleet, also had a mixed relationship with Churchill, and held his own against him with equal resolution. He was the admiral with the most celebrated World War I record, having performed with great gallantry in his destroyer *Onslow* at the Jutland battle. Until July 1943 he led a life of anxiety and action, as demanding as Cunningham's in the Mediterranean—the *Bismarck* chase and destruction, the PQ17 convoy disaster (in which he was fatally overruled by Dudley Pound), the worst U-boat convoy battles—all these occurred during his time.

Admiral Grantham describes Tovey as a "tall, impressive man, always immaculately dressed, a strong character and a committed churchman [he became a church commissioner]. He had a strong sense of discipline and was a fine example to all serving him. At the same time, he seemed rather remote to all those who did not know him well."

Admiral Philip Vian was the flag officer most decorated for bravery and most admired by Churchill for his superaggression, from the boarding in real Nelsonian style of the German ship *Altmark* to the *Bismarck* business, when he commanded the harassing destroyers, to the beating off of an immensely superior Italian force in the Mediterranean, including a modern battleship and heavy cruisers, at the Second Battle of Sirte. Churchill loved him. During the Normandy invasion in 1944, Vian commanded the naval forces covering the British landings. After Churchill visited the front line in Normandy on June 10, he embarked in Vian's destroyer *Kelvin*. It had been a surprisingly quiet day and Churchill suggested a bombardment to wake things up.

" 'Since we are so near, why shouldn't we have a plug at them ourselves before we go home?' He said, 'Certainly,' and in a minute or two all our guns fired on the silent coast. We were of course well within the range of their artillery, and the moment we had fired Vian made the destroyer turn about and depart at the highest speed. . . ."

If Vian saw the most action, Admiral Sir James Somerville was the most intelligent flag officer of the war, and he, too, was enormously popular. Somerville also possessed an ingenious scientific mind, had invented a form of ship sounding gear, the predecessor of sonar, and had been De Robeck's fleet wireless officer at the Dardanelles. Due to a wrong diagnosis of an illness by naval doctors, he had been retired before the Second World War, but bullied his way back in again and was in the last ship to clear Calais during the Dunkirk evacuation. It fell upon Somerville, as Flag Officer Force H, to bombard and cripple the French Fleet at Oran. He never really forgave Churchill for making him carry out this distasteful task, but his war career prospered.

"Perhaps the most remarkable of his successes," writes Peter Kemp, "came after the Singapore disaster when he was made C-in-C East Indies with a scratch fleet made up in the main of the old R-class battleships. Morale was at a very low ebb after the loss of the *Prince of Wales* and *Repulse,* and this was a scratch fleet which must have known it was completely outclassed by the Japanese. Yet by the time he got it out into the Indian Ocean, he had built it up to a state of extraordinarily high morale. He was that kind of man."

When Churchill made Lord Louis Mountbatten, Keyes's successor at Combined Operations, Supreme Commander in Southeast East in 1943, the first question Mountbatten asked Dudley Pound (according to Mountbatten) was whether he was allowed to sack Somerville, twenty-three years his senior, for whom he had conceived a powerful dislike. Once out in the East, Mountbatten found it difficult to find an excuse for ridding himself of such an efficient and liked flag officer. However, at a fleet inspection Mountbatten considered that he had been treated with a lack of respect appropriate to his rank, and that was the end of the sea-going career, in August 1944, of one of the finest fighting admirals of the war.

Churchill's attitude towards the admirals who served the Royal Navy in his time was mercurial—"excellent—when he thought they were shooting!"; appalling when he perceived pro-crastination or plodding. We can see why Mountbatten was selected in 1941 and can follow the pattern of his progress with a fair measure of accuracy. Cunningham had no use for him as a leader. Churchill had promoted his father, Prince Louis of Battenberg, to the Navy's top job because he had the valuable advantage of access to the palace, was satisfactory to work with, and was a good, brainy administrator. Mountbatten was a cousin of the King, too, was personable, had shown his qualities in peacetime, and had supported Churchill during the wilderness years when Mountbatten was a mere captain in his thirties. Now, in war as a destroyer flotilla commander, he rapidly showed a degree of aggression and positivism to satisfy even Churchill's highest standards. The beam of favor settled upon this already privileged and boundlessly ambitious young officer, and in view of his dash nothing now could halt the speed of his progress. When Mountbatten succeeded in safely bringing home his destroyer, which had been damaged, not for the first or last time, Churchill said that he ought to get a Distinguished Service Order. "Dudley Pound said, 'Not yet, it is too early.' But Churchill insisted, and that was that." By early October 1943, Mountbatten, a favorite of Roosevelt, too, was on to higher things, appointed Supreme Commander in Southeast Asia: ". . . to feel that it had fallen upon me to be the outward and visible symbol of the British Empire's intention to return to the attack in Asia."

Captain Roskill has written of Churchill's love-hate relationship with his admirals. There is a deeper measure of truth in this than is at first apparent. He was indeed in love with the Navy but, like an aspiring member of a club who knows he will never be nominated for membership, Churchill was always jealous of the committee members—the admirals—who were there in power. He resented their skills and ability to command and maneuver great fleets and perhaps change the destiny of a nation with massive broadsides from their guns. The romance of sea power never faded and this was why he was at heart a traditionalist, like so many of the admirals who served under him. At the same time, and in apparent contradiction, he was an innovationist, welcoming new brains and new ideas, and propounding a good many—sometimes too many—himself. Such a lot of contradictions!

The Royal Navy was outmaneuvered and outwitted in April 1940 at the time of the Norwegian invasion because Admiralty thinking, and Churchill's thinking, were still conditioned by a past age of naval warfare. When it was learned that the German Fleet was out, it might have been the Grand Fleet leaving Scapa Flow to meet the High Seas Fleet. Heavy German units, according to Admiralty reckoning, were about to attempt the breakthrough into the Atlantic to prey on British shipping—"a purely naval affair," as Sir Ian Jacob of the War Cabinet Secretariat described it. Troops already embarked in British men-of-war, themselves destined for an intervention at Stavanger and Bergen, were put back ashore, without informing anyone in Whitehall, and the ships put to sea only to learn too late that it was a full-scale German invasion.

But now Churchill reacted with speed and decision to correct the sorry miscalculation, and although the situation was never recovered at least the German surface fleet lost heavily and was temporarily crippled. Churchill, who for years had been warning Britain of the growing strength of the Luftwaffe, had at the same time misunderstood the deadly effect it would have on naval operations unsupported by air power. To be both a traditionalist and an innovator did lead sometimes to confused thinking, and to tragedy. The Force Z affair—the dispatch of the *Prince of Wales* and *Repulse* to the Far East—was a prime example of muddled conception. A carrier was to accompany them to provide air cover, but when this was not forthcoming, against all Admiralty advice he ordered them to carry on alone, confident in their ability to defend themselves against air attack. But if Admiral Phillips, once at Singapore, had not sought to attack the Japanese invasion fleet, which was his undoing, he would have been a prime target of Churchill's abuse.

It was as well that the really "big" British admirals—notably Andrew Cunningham, Bruce Fraser, and James Somerville, and of course Dudley Pound in the Admiralty—were capable of withstanding the quaint, puzzling, misguided, hectoring, and sometimes abusive messages dispatched to them. They knew their man, overcame their resentment, and got on with the job. When Cunningham was at the most delicate stage of his negotiations with the French admiral commanding the French fleet in Alexandria after the fall of France, Churchill dispatched impatient and critical signals: "Do not, repeat NOT, fail." There was only one place for this sort of rubbish, and in it went, without acknowledgment.

Lacking Roosevelt's trust and confidence in his admirals, Churchill had his antennae forever extended, sensitive to the slightest hint of his admirals' failure to live up to his exacting standards of forcefulness and offensive-mindedness; and was at the same time highly resentful of any tendency towards counter-criticism. Once, when Secretary Knox was complaining of an American admiral's decision to turn back from an offensive operation in the Pacific and asked Churchill's advice—"What would you do with your Admiral in a case like this?"—Churchill replied with, one imagines, a shrug of resignation, "It is dangerous to meddle with Admirals when they say they can't do things. They have always got the weather or fuel or something to argue about."

Martin Gilbert has said, "Churchill felt closer to people than they felt to him." This shrewd, simple generalization can be applied to his admirals. The trouble was that if they did not come up to the mark (in his judgment) he felt all the worse about it and overreacted accordingly, almost as if slighted.

All said and done, it was an odd relationship but it did not work too badly, thanks on the one side to Churchill's unsurpassed image of bulldog heroism and national reputation as Britain's savior, which few senior naval officers doubted, and on the other side by the general good-humored tolerance, sense, and resilience of the admirals who served him. The proof is to be found in what they achieved together, not in the price paid by their mistakes.

NINE

"A True Affection"

With the entry of the United States into the war on December 7, 1941, there opened a new phase in the relations between Churchill and Roosevelt, bringing them together into an unique personal alliance. In December 1941 Britain was like a hardened, veteran warrior, blessedly thankful for the support of this new ally, sympathetic to this ally's early setbacks, eager to pass on the lessons he has learned. The language of this time reflected the authority of Britain, no longer wheedling, no longer begging; instead now laying down policies and practices. It was the "we must" period—"we must be ready to send considerable forces"; "we must face here the usual clash"; "we have, therefore, to prepare for the liberation." Brisk and firm.

As a British chiefs-of-staff meeting was told when a member presumed that the "softly-softly" treatment of America would continue, "Oh! that is the way we talked to her while we were wooing her; now that she is in the harem, we talk to her quite differently."

But not for long. By 1943 American industry and American military effort were into their stride. Britain, and Churchill, were having to yield points on a host of subjects—the nomination of commanders, priority of supplies, and so on. Old suspicions and prejudices reemerged, not only as married relations tend to become more friable in easier times, but because dominance, and with it influence, had switched to the younger member of the team. Even in an alliance of friendship, an alliance of survival, the weight of argument is measured in metal and explosive.

In one respect relations between Roosevelt and Churchill became less intense after Pearl Harbor. Until America came into the war, the Former Naval Person and the C in C of the U.S. Navy were deeply and more or less continuously concerned with naval matters because the cooperation was closer and more overt than with the other two arms. Since the beginning of 1941 the two navies had been working together, with increasing intimacy. In 1942 cooperation was total for all three services; and therefore, just as Churchill's day-to-day involvement in the Royal Navy was diluted after he became Prime Minister, so the American and British navies now became one item in a worldwide agenda involving every item concerned with the conduct of the war.

However, minutes of the meetings of the chiefs of staff, official reports and histories, published and unpublished memoirs, and above all the direct exchanges between President and Prime Minister all confirm their undiminished interest in naval affairs.

Less than a week after Pearl Harbor, Churchill was hurrying across the Atlantic again, this time in the *Prince of Wales*'s sister ship the *Duke of York*. On this passage there were fewer films and no backgammon. As Roosevelt had telegraphed on the day the *Prince of Wales* and *Repulse* went down, "Naval situation and other matters of strategy require discussion." It was a businesslike crossing just as it was a businesslike meeting. En route Churchill drew up a long memorandum on the state of the war and plans for 1942.

Then to the White House, arriving in Washington by air on the evening of December 22, 1941, to find Roosevelt awaiting Churchill. "There was the President waiting in his car. I clasped his strong hand with comfort and pleasure," Churchill wrote of the occasion. "I formed a very strong affection, which grew with our years of comradeship, for this formidable politician who had imposed his will for nearly ten years upon the American scene, and whose heart seemed to respond to many of the impulses that stirred my own."

"A TRUE AFFECTION"

The formal discussions and private conversations in the evenings at the White House ranged widely over the naval scene. Coral Sea and Midway had still to be fought, and neither of the war leaders, nor their staffs for that matter, had any conception of the revolution that was taking place in sea fighting. While Admiral Nagumo's all-conquering carriers, unaccompanied by a single battleship, ranged freely across the Pacific and Indian oceans, naval strategy in Washington was still built about the battle fleet. "The Allies will not have for some time the power to fight a general fleet engagement. . . ." The last general fleet engagement had been fought at Jutland in 1916, and even those proceedings had been dominated by fear of the destroyers' torpedoes.

Following his three-weeks-long stay in the United States and Canada, Churchill returned to face the multitude of troubles created by Japanese advances on every front. The fate of Singapore was only one of the agonies. But on February 12, 1942, three days before the city fell, the Royal Navy suffered another humiliation as close to home as the English Channel when the repaired battle cruisers *Scharnhorst* and *Gneisenau*, with the heavy cruiser *Prinz Eugen*, raced home from France. "We are out after them with everything we have," Churchill signaled Roosevelt. But it was not enough, and with the umbrella assistance of a strong fighter force they got through the Strait of Dover and made their way home, although both big ships were damaged by mines.

When Roosevelt learned that the three German men-of-war had passed through the Channel without being sunk, he characteristically dispatched a telegram of cheer—"I hope you will be of good heart"—and judged that in fact it had been a British tactical victory: "I am more and more convinced that the location of all the German ships in Germany makes our joint North Atlantic naval problem more simple."

In order to help the Royal Navy to contain the substantial German force of surface raiders now that they were concentrated, Roosevelt proposed to send two new battleships to reinforce the British Home Fleet. Back in 1917 Roosevelt had given a similar order to Admiral Rodman to reinforce the British Grand Fleet at Scapa Flow with three battleships. This time they were more urgently required, although in the event only one battleship, a carrier, and two heavy cruisers were finally sent.

But it was the U-boat and its remorseless and unremitting war on Atlantic shipping that concerned the two war leaders more than any other subject in their communications. In March 1942 Roosevelt asked if the R.A.F. could concentrate some of its resources on bombing U-boat bases and building and repair yards, and within a few days Churchill was able to report that 250 bombers had attacked "U-boat nests" at Lübeck—"Results are said to be the best ever." (In fact no concrete U-boat shelter was ever penetrated by a bomb.)

In March and April 1942 the subject of Malta was a prime consideration of the two war leaders. The Germans and Italians had unleashed an unprecedented air assault on the island, where a surviving force of twenty-five fighters faced an enemy force of some six hundred fighters and bombers. Churchill proposed the use of the American carrier *Wasp* for taking fighter reinforcements to within six hundred miles of the island, and flying them off. Would Roosevelt agree to this dangerous mission? Admiral King, as usual, was suspicious of British motives. He worked out that H.M.S. *Furious,* once a Fisher-inspired eighteen-inch gunned battle cruiser now converted into a carrier, had the capacity for the job and thought that Churchill was again trying to commit American ships to do the work the British could do themselves. Roosevelt overruled King and made the *Wasp* available. With further fighters aboard the British carrier *Eagle,* this desperately needed supply probably saved the island, which was at its last gasp. The *Wasp* made a second delivery of some fifty fighters and Churchill telegraphed Roosevelt his thanks "for allowing *Wasp* to have another good sting"; and to the captain of the carrier: "Who said a wasp couldn't sting twice."

If King failed to deprive Churchill of this carrier for the Mediterranean for the succor of Malta, he succeeded in torpedoing Churchill's plans for American reinforcement on the other side of the world. April 1942 was the month when Admiral Nagumo was creating havoc in the Indian Ocean and Churchill begged for a modern battleship and carrier from the U.S. Pacific Fleet to reinforce British forces, already badly hammered in that area. "It is my personal thought," Roosevelt concluded a long message (April 16, 1942), "that your Fleet in Indian Ocean can well be safeguarded during next few weeks without fighting major engagement. . . ."

"A TRUE AFFECTION"

In the midst of all these naval crises, in the Mediterranean and Indian Ocean, General MacArthur, C in C Far East, asked the British directly for a carrier and more shipping to support his operations. Where did he think this was to be found? The only British carrier in Indian waters, the little *Hermes*, had just been sent to the bottom. Churchill was stupefied: "I should be glad to know whether these requirements have been approved by you," he asked the President, ". . . and whether General MacArthur has any authority from the United States for taking such a line." They had not been so approved.

In the early summer of 1942 the naval situation was as critical in the far Arctic north as in the mellow Mediterranean and tropical Indian Ocean. Here the Murmansk-Archangel convoys were suffering acute and finally unacceptable losses, assailed by destroyers, torpedo and bombing planes, and U-boats, while the giant battleship *Tirpitz* lay in its Norwegian lair, threatening to strike at any time. The two leaders agreed on the political as well as military necessity of getting supplies to Russia, but it was Britain that was bearing the main burden of the losses. Roosevelt suggested that convoy escorts in the Atlantic should be diverted to the Murmansk run. Churchill replied (May 1, 1942), "With very great respect what you suggest is beyond our power to fulfill . . . difficulty of Russian convoys cannot be solved merely by anti-submarine craft. Enemy heavy ships and destroyers may at any time strike." Churchill then listed recent losses. "I beg you not to press us beyond our judgement in this operation which we have studied most intently. . . . I can assure [you] Mr President we are absolutely extended. . . ."

Appealed to in these terms, Roosevelt always accepted Churchill's judgment, and as a compromise suggested that supplies to Russia should be cut and that Stalin should be told that the reason for this was that the war supplies and the shipping were needed for the invasion of the Continent—in the event, still more than two years away.

This desolate picture from every naval quarter was at last relieved by the news of Admirals Spruance and Fletcher's dramatic victory at the Battle of Midway. "Delighted to hear your good news . . . " Churchill signaled.

The high summer weeks of 1942 marked the U-boats' "happy days" (as the crews called them) in the Caribbean and along the east coast of the United States, too, when shipping sailed un-escorted and the U-boats worked with the added advantage of un-blacked-out American cities as silhouette illumination. It was like a turkey shoot. The reversal of roles allowed Churchill to pay back some of the assistance generously given by the U.S. Navy a year earlier. Now he proposed that the numerous patrol craft being built in American yards for Britain should be placed in a common pool and drawn upon by the U.S. Navy as well as the Royal Navy as required.

Two flotillas of British antisubmarine escorts were sent to strengthen the American escorts and instruct them in the tactics of convoy protection. Closer collaboration could hardly be imag-ined: This was total unity of action. Roosevelt agreed at once (July 24, 1942) and suggested that the allocation of patrol craft should be decided by the Combined Chiefs of Staff.

While the Battle of the Atlantic continued to rage at high in-tensity through that summer of 1942—almost a million tons of shipping lost in May—the Allies were completing their prepara-tions for their first major offensive in the west. This was Operation Torch, the invasion of North Africa following upon a major at-tack from Egypt. Torch required the closest Anglo-American naval cooperation and this worked so smoothly and cordially that the two leaders were rarely brought into the details of arrange-ments. Meanwhile, Eleanor Roosevelt made her first wartime visit to Britain and correspondence was for a while on a mutually affectionate domestic note.

At the turn of the year 1942–43 the Churchill-Roosevelt naval alliance was put under strain again as a result of interservice dis-cord. Admiral King had always wanted to fight the Pacific war first, contrary to the Allied commitment that Hitler must be beaten as first priority, and relentlessly tried to reverse this deci-sion. As well, King wanted to beat the Japanese Navy without British support; he would have preferred to dispense with Austra-lian support, too, but this was clearly impossible. General Mar-shall on the other hand was in favor of attacking Germany as soon as practicable and with an invasion of the mainland of Europe.

But after a year of war in the South Pacific, King was down to a single, and damaged, carrier and was obliged to sink his pride and ask for a loan from the Royal Navy. Churchill offered to send two fast, modern fleet carriers in exchange for a small American carrier to support the Home Fleet. This conformed with the principle of integration so abhorred by Admiral King. "I am much in favour of sending you two carriers rather than one if this can be managed," Churchill suggested to Roosevelt, "as this will not only give you increased strength but would allow the two ships to work as a tactical unit. . . ." Such a force would also demonstrate to Australia and New Zealand that the Mother Country was deeply concerned for their safety and that it was not only America upon whom they were dependent. King disliked what he regarded as a gesture of imperialism as much as he disliked the idea of a separate British task force working with the Pacific Fleet rather than a single carrier being absorbed into Admiral Nimitz's command. There was for a time a good deal of unpleasantness at command level. But the two leaders damped down the fires, and the fast armored carrier *Victorious* was sent to Pearl Harbor, to be warmly welcomed by Admiral Nimitz.

Once again, in March 1943, the burning topic between the two leaders was the U-boat menace. "I am extremely anxious about shipping situation," Churchill signaled on March 24, and wrote in detail of "its extreme gravity." For Germany and Italy the shipping problem scarcely existed—North Africa was the only front supplied by sea—but for the Allies the shipping burden was almost crushingly heavy and must, so it seemed, increase with the buildup towards the invasion of Europe.

The Battle of the Atlantic, then, remained the key contest, cruel, unremitting, stretching to the utmost both the science of destruction and human indomitability. No single weapon of war brought Churchill closer to despair than the German submarine. Its final defeat was brought about by a combination of weapons. As in the Pacific, the code breakers played a critical part, and by 1943 the Enigma code-breaking machine was reading virtually all the signals between U-boats and orders from headquarters.

Because full knowledge of Enigma has become available only in the past decade, perhaps too much emphasis has recently been placed on the near-magical wonders of the Bletchley code-breaking organization and its machines, tremendous though these were. Peter Kemp, who worked in the Admiralty Intelligence Centre throughout the war, believes today that the battle against the U-boat would have been won in the end anyway. "It would have taken a little longer. The crucial things were centimetric radar, shipborne HFDF [high-frequency detecting and finding], and continuous air cover—they would have beaten them without Enigma, and we were very conscious that if we overplayed Enigma they would know and change the whole damn lot [of codes]."

Of all the changes of fortune in the Battle of the Atlantic, none was clearer than that brought about by "closing the gap" in air cover in May 1943, which brought about round-the-clock air surveillance over the entire Atlantic only weeks after Churchill's *cri de coeur*. While Churchill and Roosevelt were in session together at the Trident Conference in Washington (May 12–25, 1943), crews of long-range aircraft, sailors of escort vessels, and the Bletchley code breakers were turning the tide at last. From almost seven-hundred thousand tons of shipping losses in March, these combined forces brought the figure down to less than half this frightening total in May, and except for July 1943 kept the figure below one hundred-sixty thousand tons for the remainder of the year. For the Allied Powers, including Russia, it was as great a victory as Stalingrad. Admiral King refrained from offering congratulations, and instead asked Roosevelt to question Royal Navy figures of successful attacks on U-boats. Were they too good to be true? In some embarrassment, Roosevelt did as he was asked. Yes, they were all confirmed, proven "kills," he was told.

The Trident Conference was the third meeting between the leaders and had become essential to settle future strategy following the winter successes in North Africa and the Mediterranean. Churchill sailed for America in the *Queen Mary,* again along with a large party, and five hundred German prisoners of war as a token of success on the field of battle. The security surrounding this voyage was even more elaborate than that for the original "fishing party," and included the setting up of ramps all over the ship to indicate falsely that Roosevelt would be sailing back to Britain to continue the conference. For the last leg of the voyage a strong presence of American men-of-war closed about the liner. "Since yesterday we have been surrounded by U.S. Navy and we all greatly appreciate high value you evidently set upon our continued survival," Churchill signaled his host.

"A TRUE AFFECTION"

Churchill crossed the (now much safer) Atlantic yet again in August 1943—"a most swift and agreeable journey"—in the *Queen Mary*, the first meeting this time at Quebec. The agenda included the invasion of Europe, Operation Overlord, in approximately nine months' time, the greatest amphibious operation in history and thus by definition the greatest naval operation in history. Conference agendas this time were concerned almost entirely with offensives—counterattacks in Russia, new advances in the Pacific, the invasion and defeat of Italy, the destruction of U-boats (one a day on average over the past few months), mighty Anglo-American bombing offensives over Germany. And finally, and in the deepest confidence, the most epochal offensive subject of all—"tube alloys," the euphemism for atomic energy research, which was the subject of a joint agreement of the highest importance.

Churchill returned to Britain on September 19, 1943, to be met by renewed demands from Russia to reinstitute the Arctic supply convoys that had proved so crushingly expensive in the past. One of the threats to these convoys was temporarily removed by a daring attack on the *Tirpitz* in her elaborately protected Norwegian anchorage. For security reasons, Churchill confined his message reporting this success to "We believe we have damaged the *Tirpitz* and that she will have to go back to Germany for docking." In fact a force of miniature submarines had succeeded in penetrating the defenses surrounding the giant battleship and two 2-ton bombs had been detonated beneath her hull. The resulting explosions put all her engines out of action and damaged her steering gear. Although it could not be known at the time, she was never to be made operational again. Now Admiral Fraser could face passing through the Russian convoys that winter with greater equanimity. Better still, not only did the supply armadas get through almost without loss, but when threatened by Germany's only surviving operational heavy ship, the *Scharnhorst*, Bruce Fraser sank her. For Churchill it was a Christmas evening tonic. "The sinking of the *Scharnhorst* has been great news to us all," signaled Roosevelt.

Naval communications between the two leaders during the winter of 1943–44 were mostly concerned with the buildup to D Day, interspersed with vehement complaints from Churchill on the offensive and uncooperative attitude of Russia, and less vehement complaints from Roosevelt, who increasingly saw himself as peacemaker between the socialist Stalin and the imperialist Churchill. In spite of the growing suspicion between Britain and Russia, Churchill never allowed this to affect his original pledge that he would do all in his power to support the Russian cause, and even agreed to lend the Russian Navy a battleship and a cruiser. It offended against his deepest instincts to do so, especially as the battleship was one that he had laid down during his first term of office as First Lord and carried the kingly name *Royal Sovereign.*

Russia was also fed more frequently than ever with convoys during the spring of 1944, with negligible losses and heavy destruction of U-boats. "You will be glad to hear," Churchill signaled (March 9, 1944), "that the latest Russian convoy has now got safe home, and that four U-boats out of the pack that attacked were certainly sunk. . . ." Since Admiral King's earlier doubts, Churchill had found it necessary to add the confirmatory "certainly."

It was in this same month of March 1944 that the subject of British participation on a relatively large scale in the Pacific came up again for discussion, this time on a more urgent and pressing basis. After the invasion of France in June—the date was now set—and with the surrender of the Italian Fleet and elimination of Germany's surface fleet, the Royal Navy would have a surplus of strength, especially of fleet carriers, battleships, and cruisers.

After the Combined Chiefs of Staff had approved in principle of the presence of a British fleet in the Pacific at the end of 1943, Admiral King had reluctantly agreed to accept a British and Commonwealth task force but would not put a date to it. "I am, in the upshot, left in doubt whether we are really needed this year," Churchill telegraphed with just a trace of asperity, on March 10, 1944. He continued, "Accordingly I should be very grateful if you could let me know whether there is any specific American operation in the Pacific (A) Before the end of 1944 or (B) Before the summer of 1945 which would be hindered or prevented by the absence of a British Fleet Detachment."

A British naval mission had been in Washington since February in order to study the logistics of American task forces, with their huge fleet trains, and reached the conclusion that any future British fleet must follow the American organization, which had proved so successful. The British Pacific Fleet came into formal being on November 22, 1944, consisting of 2 fast modern battleships, 4 fleet carriers with a total complement of about 250 aircraft, 5 cruisers, and 11 destroyers. Admiral Fraser was the C in C, and its base was Sydney, Australia.

Although it was largely a political force—the Americans had quite adequate forces of their own to deal the final blows at Japan, just as the British Grand Fleet had had sufficient strength to cope with the German Fleet in 1917—Admiral Fraser brought the fleet to a high pitch of efficiency, and the American command was much impressed. The British carriers had stoutly armored flight decks, and withstood bombing much better than their American counterparts.

Admiral King had determined that this fleet should not operate with Admiral Nimitz's main, central Pacific thrust but instead attach itself to General MacArthur's American-Australian command and assist in the recapture of the Straits of Malacca and Singapore. But Churchill would have none of this. He wanted the fleet to be in the main front line, and in at the eventual and inevitable surrender of Japan. Roosevelt agreed and told King to make the necessary arrangements.

Admiral Nimitz warmly welcomed Task Force 57, as the British fleet had now become. "The British force will greatly increase our striking power and demonstrate our unity of purpose against Japan," he signaled. "The United States Pacific Fleet welcomes you."

Churchill had always been most punctilious in sending commiserations or congratulations to Roosevelt on events in the Pacific war. "I was delighted to read of your success" and "Your operations in the Pacific assume every day a more vehement and compulsive course" were typical. After the six-day Leyte Gulf battle, which cost the Japanese Navy twenty-four warships, including four carriers and three battleships, Churchill signaled, "Pray accept my most sincere congratulations which I tender on behalf of His Majesty's Government on the brilliant and massive victory gained by the sea and air forces of the United States over the Japanese in the recent heavy battles.

"We are very glad to know that one of His Majesty's Austra-

237

lian cruiser squadrons had the honour of sharing in this memorable event."

In his turn, Roosevelt was quick to congratulate Churchill on the bombing of the *Tirpitz:* "The end of the *Tirpitz* is great news," adding with a typical waggish touch, "We must help the Germans by never letting them build anything like it again, thus putting the German Treasury on its feet."

With the military advance across France and Belgium in the summer of 1944 and the even swifter progress of the American naval forces in the Pacific, exchanges between Prime Minister and President became more and more concerned with grand strategy during the closing stages of hostilities and the worldwide political problems that were already beginning to loom—sometimes ominously—through the fog of war.

At the end of 1944, as Churchill was to write, "The whole shape and structure of postwar Europe clamoured for review. When the Nazis were beaten how was Germany to be treated? What aid could we expect from the Soviet Union in the final overthrow of Japan? And once military aims were achieved what measures and what organization could the three great Allies provide for the future peace and good governance of the world?" Above all, the fate of the Polish people, which had triggered this second great German war, was again causing as much anxiety as it had five years earlier, even if the grasping fists reached out this time from the east and from an ally.

It was hoped in Washington that, to spare Roosevelt, this proposed new meeting of the "Big Three" war leaders could take place somewhere halfway to Moscow. But Stalin would not leave the borders of his country for health reasons, he said, and Yalta on the Black Sea was eventually fixed as the meeting place.

The travel arrangements involved many internaval exchanges, including the decision to send warships to stand off Yalta as a floating headquarters and in case of need of accommodation. Churchill was anxious to rendezvous with Roosevelt at Malta for preliminary conversations and in order that "our military men should get together for a few days before we arrive at Yalta." But Roosevelt was anxious not to give the ever suspicious Russians the impression that there was preconference collusion between the Western allies, and to present the United States in neutral guise for the delicate and complex negotiations that lay ahead.

Roosevelt could not refuse all discussion in view of the rendezvous, but he arranged his itinerary so that there would be time for only the briefest meeting. He therefore crossed the Atlantic in the 13,600-ton heavy cruiser *Quincy,* arriving in Valetta harbor, with all its evidence of the long siege and savage bombing, less than 24 hours before the outward journey to Russia.

Roosevelt was a sick man. Normally, such was his love for the sea and for sailing with his Navy that "no matter how tired and worn he might appear when he started off on a cruise, he emerged from it looking healthy and hearty and acting that way." But when Admiral King went on board the cruiser to greet his President, "he was alarmed by the state of his health," noting deterioration rather than improvement.

Churchill had already arrived by air direct from Britain in one of three aircraft accommodating his party. One of the planes crashed en route, with few survivors—"such are the strange ways of fate," as he commented.

The U.S.S. *Quincy* arrived under a cloudless blue sky on the morning of February 2, 1945. It was just three and a half years since the leaders' first wartime meeting. Now it was like the Newfoundland "fishing party" in reverse, Churchill the host on the deck of the cruiser H.M.S. *Orion:* two elderly men who had led the free Western world to the brink of victory in the greatest war in history.

"As the American cruiser steamed slowly past us towards her berth alongside the quay wall," Churchill later recalled, "I could see the figure of the President seated on the bridge, and we waved to each other. With the escort of Spitfires overhead [at Placentia Bay it had been seaplanes], the salutes, and the bands of the ships' companies in the harbour playing 'The Star-spangled Banner' it was a splendid scene."

Churchill transferred to the *Quincy* for lunch, and the leaders were able to hold one brief meeting that evening with their staffs. Then, all through that night, members of the aerial armada carrying the total entourage of some seven hundred people took off at ten-minute intervals for the grueling, and cold, flight of fourteen hundred miles.

THE GREATEST CRUSADE

Churchill was asleep when the big Globemaster plane flew over the Dardanelles, the scene of the disasters of exactly thirty years earlier that had crippled, and almost destroyed, his political career. Then the intention had been to support and open up communications with the hard-pressed Russian armies, which had eventually succumbed in 1917 in the face of the German onslaught. Now everywhere the Germans were in retreat on the Russian fronts, in spite of the Dardanelles remaining closed.

Under international treaty no warships could pass through the Dardanelles and the Sea of Marmara without prior permission of the Turkish government. Although the Turks had been mainly sympathetic to the German cause—if nonbelligerent—in this war, there was no need for a bombardment before sending through the men-of-war, past the once blood-stained Gallipoli shores, over the sunken wrecks of 1915.

"Should we not tell President Inonu [of Turkey] about them at the latest possible moment," Churchill suggested to Roosevelt, "for his own strictly personal information, and ask him to give all the orders necessary to ensure that the ships shall pass through unquestioned except by formality?" This time the Turks were in no position to bar the way, but there was an element of irony in the fact that Churchill thought it diplomatic to make the request at all.

After Yalta, Roosevelt flew to Egypt and returned home in the *Quincy,* through the Mediterranean, to Newport News, Virginia, arriving on March 27, 1945. "It is good to be home," Roosevelt was telling the cheering House of Representatives two days later. "It has been a long journey." Everyone could see the price that Roosevelt had paid, and his speech was slurred in delivery and often repetitious, the vintage rhetoric faded.

Far away in the Pacific, Roosevelt's Navy was still heavily in action. Admiral Spruance led a carrier task force to within twenty minutes' flying from Tokyo and launched a scorching bomber attack on the Japanese capital. Seven battleships with cruisers and destroyers in support opened a bombardment of twenty-two thousand rounds of shells on the small but strategically vital island of Iwo Jima—an assault of high explosive that made the Dardanelles bombardment in 1915 seem like a volley from an air rifle. Carrier bombing planes followed this assault.

"A TRUE AFFECTION"

In four months' time, Roosevelt was informed, the first atomic bomb would be tested.

From the haven of Warm Springs, Georgia, in early 1945 Roosevelt wrote to Josephus Daniels, urging that the Philippines should be given their independence at the earliest possible time after complete liberation. It might cause "Uncle Ted" to turn in his grave, it might run counter to Roosevelt's own boyhood delight when the United States annexed the islands; but it conformed with his more recent principle of anticolonialism, and would give a good example to the imperialist British, French, and Dutch, who gave every sign of wanting to hold onto *their* old possessions.

"I do wish you could have been in my office the other day," Roosevelt added in his letter to Daniels, referring to the inauguration of Daniels's son Jonathan as the President's press secretary. "He is a grand person. . . ."

It was Roosevelt's last letter to his onetime chief. A few days later, on April 12, 1945, he died swiftly and without warning.

> When I received these tidings early in the morning of Friday, the 13th, I felt as if I had been struck a physical blow [Churchill wrote]. My relations with this shining personality had played so large a part in the long, terrible years we had worked together. Now they had come to an end, and I was overpowered by a sense of deep and irreparable loss. I went down to the House of Commons, which met at 11 o'clock, and in a few sentences proposed that we should pay our respects to the memory of our great friend by immediately adjourning. This unprecedented step on the occasion of the death of the head of a foreign State was in accordance with the unanimous wish of the Members, who filed slowly out of the chamber after a sitting which had lasted only eight minutes.

Later that day Churchill composed a letter to the man who, more than anyone else, had brought into being this unique personal alliance, and held it tight for three and a half tumultous years, Harry Hopkins: "I understand how deep your feelings of grief must be. I feel with you that we have lost one of our greatest friends and one of the most valiant champions of the causes for

241

which we fight. I feel a very painful personal loss, quite apart from the ties of public action which bound us so closely together. I had a true affection for Franklin."

Roosevelt fully understood the nature of Churchill's relations with the Royal Navy and recognized the sharp difference with his own less mercurial and interventionist policy. The President's admiration for what Churchill had done for the Royal Navy when Roosevelt was a young assistant secretary remained unchanged, and if he was critical of the Royal Navy's performance from time to time, notably off Norway in 1940, he was as worried as Churchill about the fate of the French Fleet in 1940. And he did not add his voice to the critics of Churchill's decision to intervene in Greece in 1941. On the contrary, while he deplored the savage naval losses at the hands of the Luftwaffe, he greatly admired Churchill's courage and principle in going to the rescue of an ally in distress, and many people believe that it led Roosevelt to put pressure on Congress to legislate lend-lease.

In their wartime relationship there were many points of dispute, sometimes serious and prolonged dispute, between the Prime Minister and the President. Roosevelt was high-handed about the disposal of the Italian Fleet, about certain military appointments, and about his relations with the Soviet Union. The Yalta Conference, in which Churchill's voice was perforce muted, was in its consequences for the Western world an utter and irretrievable disaster, with "the fast-failing President" coming to the meeting "determined to establish a world republic of independent liberal nations and [believing] that, unlike Churchill and the British 'colonialists', Stalin was ready to underwrite such a world. . . ." On the other hand Churchill *was* excessively imperial-minded in 1944–45 and had no intention of advancing the Indian cause for independence after the fighting was over. They even quarreled about the Argentine, Roosevelt wanting Britain to cut off diplomatic relations because of that republic's pro-Nazi intransigence, while Churchill knew Britain needed the meat.

But personal relations never seriously suffered and to talk of a crumbling alliance in personal terms is the height of nonsense. The deep attachment formed in 1941 matured into friendship unprecedented between two leaders in a conflict of prolonged ferocity and unequaled complexity.

"A TRUE AFFECTION"

No two people had better opportunity for observing the two war leaders together, nor better qualifications for making a judgment on the relationship, than Robert E. Sherwood and General Ismay, two of the small group of lieutenants at the top who ran the war and made the alliance work. Sherwood, Roosevelt's speech writer, noted:

> It is a matter of sacred tradition that when an American statesman and a British statesman meet the former will be plain, blunt, down-to-earth, ingenuous to a fault, while the latter will be sly, subtle, devious, and eventually triumphant. In the cases of Roosevelt and Churchill this formula became somewhat confused. If either of them could be called a student of Machiavelli, it was Roosevelt; if either was a bull in a china shop, it was Churchill. The Prime Minister quickly learned that he confronted in the President a man of infinite subtlety and obscurity—an artful dodger who could not readily be pinned down on specific points, nor hustled or wheedled into definite commitments against his judgment or his will or his instinct. And Roosevelt soon learned how pertinacious the Prime Minister could be in pursuance of a purpose. Churchill's admirers could call him "tenacious, indomitable," and his detractors could describe him as "obstinate, obdurate, dogged, mulish, pigheaded." Probably both factions could agree on the word "stubborn," which may be flattering or derogatory. In any case, it was this quality which at times made him extremely tiresome to deal with and at other times—and especially times of most awful adversity—made him great.
>
> Roosevelt and Churchill certainly had the capacity to annoy each other, but the record of their tremendous association with one another contains a minimum of evidences of waspishness or indeed of anything less than the most amiable and most courteous consideration. For they had a large and wonderful capacity to stimulate and refresh each other. In one of the darkest hours of the war Roosevelt concluded a long, serious cable to Churchill with the words: "It is fun to be in the same decade with you."

General Ismay, as Churchill's Chief of Staff, privy to every detail and every nuance of the relationship and present at all but the most private tête-à-têtes, chose "a remarkable episode" in Washington after the first Quebec Conference in 1943 to signify the depth of affection and confidence between the two men:

> The President had to go to Hyde Park before Churchill had finished all that he wanted to do. On leaving, he said, in so many words, 'Winston, please treat the White House as your home. Invite anyone you like to any meals, and do not hesitate to summon any of my advisers with whom you wish to confer at any time you wish. Please break your journey to Halifax at Hyde Park and tell me about it.' Churchill took advantage of this offer, and presided over a top level meeting on 11 September. The Americans were represented by Admiral Leahy, General Marshall, Admiral King, General Arnold, Mr Harry Hopkins, Mr Averell Harriman and Mr Lewis Douglas. On the British side there were Field Marshal Dill, Admiral Noble, Air Marshal Sir William Welsh, Lieutenant-General Macready and myself. It was like a family gathering, and every sort of problem was discussed with complete frankness. I wonder if, in all history, there has ever existed between the war leaders of two allied nations, a relationship so intimate as that revealed by this episode. The affection and trust which Churchill had inspired in Roosevelt was not the least of his service to the Allied cause.

The same must be said of the war-winning value of the affection and trust inspired in Churchill by Franklin Roosevelt. It is hard to believe that the Grand Alliance—the special relationship—that destroyed tyranny in 1945 could have endured through eight subsequent presidents and nine prime ministers and preserved the world from nuclear conflict if the foundations had not been laid with such precision and strength almost half a century ago.

APPENDIX A

Correspondence

Letter from King George VI to President Roosevelt delivered by Churchill's hand, Placentia Bay, Newfoundland, August 9, 1941:

> My dear President Roosevelt,
> This is just a note to bring you my best wishes, and to say how glad I am that you have an opportunity at last of getting to know my Prime Minister. I am sure that you will agree that he is a very remarkable man, and I have no doubt that your meeting will prove of great benefit to our two countries in the pursuit of our common goal.
>
> Yours sincerely,
> George R. I.

Longhand letter from President Roosevelt to King George VI dated August 11, 1941:

> ABOARD U.S.S. *Augusta*
>
> My dear King George:
> We are at anchor in this Newfoundland harbor close to H.M.S. *Prince of Wales* and I have had three delightful and useful days with Mr. Churchill and the heads of your three services. It has been a privilege to come to know Mr. Churchill in this way and I am very confident that our minds travel together, and that our talks are bearing practical fruit for both nations.
> I wish that you could have been with us at Divine Service yesterday on the quarterdeck of your latest battleship. I shall never forget it. Your officers and men were mingled with about three hundred of ours, spread over the turrets and superstructure—I hope you will see the movies of it.
> Will you be good enough to tell the Queen that her radio address yesterday was really perfect in every way and that it will do a great amount of good.
> We think of you both often and wish we could be of more

APPENDIX A

help—But we are daily gaining in confidence in the outcome—We know you will keep up the good work.

With my very warm regards,

Sincerely yours,
Franklin D. Roosevelt

APPENDIX B

The Atlantic Charter

THE PRESIDENT of the United States (of America) and the Prime Minister, Mr. Churchill, representing His Majesty's Government in the United Kingdom, being met together, deem it right to make known certain common principles in the national policies of their respective countries on which they base their hopes for a better future for the world.

FIRST, their countries seek no aggrandizement, territorial or other.

SECOND, they desire to see no territorial changes that do not accord with the freely expressed wishes of the people concerned.

THIRD, they respect the right of all people to choose the form of government under which they will live; and they wish to see sovereign rights and self-government restored to those who have been forcibly deprived of them.

FOURTH, they will endeavor, with due respect for their existing obligations, to further enjoyment of all States, great or small, victor or vanquished, of access, on equal terms, to the trade and to the raw materials of the world which are needed for their economic prosperity.

FIFTH, they desire to bring about the fullest collaboration between all nations in the economic field, with the object of securing for all improved labor standards, economic advancement, and social security.

SIXTH, after the final destruction of (the) Nazi tyranny, they hope to see established a peace which will afford to all nations the means of dwelling in safety within their own boundaries, and which will afford assurance that all the men in all the lands may live out their lives in freedom from fear and want.

APPENDIX B

SEVENTH, such a peace should enable all men to traverse the high seas and oceans without hindrance.

EIGHTH, they believe (that) all of the nations of the world, for realistic as well as spiritual reasons, must come to the abandonment of the use of force. Since no further peace can be maintained if land, sea or air armaments continue to be employed by nations which threaten, or may threaten, aggression outside of their frontiers, they believe, pending the establishment of a wider and permanent system of general security, that the disarmament of such nations is essential. They will likewise aid and encourage all other practicable measures which will lighten for peace-loving peoples the crushing burden of armaments.

Source References

A full entry is given at the first reference to a book's title; subsequent references are abbreviated: e.g., A. J. Marder, *The Dreadnought to Scapa Flow,* Vol. 1 (1960), p. 96, becomes Marder, *Dreadnought,* 1, p. 96.

The Churchill titles most frequently quoted are, first, the official biography in (so far) six volumes, the first two by his son, Randolph Churchill, the remaining by Martin Gilbert. All but Volume VI have accompanying companion volumes of related papers, which are abbreviated thus: *Churchill,* II, *Companion,* III, p. 1875. Second, Churchill's own history of the First World War, *The World Crisis,* in seven volumes; and lastly, Churchill's own history of the Second World War in six volumes. The references to these are abbreviated thus: WSC, *World Crisis,* III, p. 29 and WSC, *Second World War,* I, p. 343.

Acknowledgments are due to Curtis Brown Ltd. on behalf of C. and T. Publications for the use of extracts from the official biography of Winston Churchill by Randolph Churchill and Martin Gilbert; and for the use of extracts from Churchill's *The Second World War;* to the Oxford University Press for extracts from *H. H. Asquith: Letters to Venetia Stanley,* selected and edited by Michael and Eleanor Brock; and to Messrs. Charles Scribner's for the use of extracts from Churchill's *The World Crisis,* copyright 1923, 1927 Charles Scribner's Sons; copyright renewed 1951, © 1955 Winston S. Churchill. Reprinted with the permission of Charles Scribner's Sons; and Winston S. Churchill, excerpted from *My Early Life,* copyright 1930 Charles Scribner's Sons; copyright renewed © 1958 Winston S. Churchill. Reprinted with the permission of Charles Scribner's Sons.

THE GREATEST CRUSADE

Page Line
11   17   M. Gilbert, *Finest Hour: Winston S. Churchill 1939–41,* Vol. VI (1983), p. 1155.

13   36   H. V. Morton, *Atlantic Meeting* (1943), p. 83.

14   9   S. E. Morison, *The European Discovery of America: The Northern Voyages* (1971), p. 181.

14   25   Morton, p. 84.

14   35   J. P. Lash, *Roosevelt & Churchill 1939–41* (1977), p. 393.

16   4   *Time* magazine, August 11, 1941.

16   28   Franklin D. Roosevelt Library (FDRL), OF 200-J-R.

19   4   A. Averell Harriman and Elie Abel, *Special Envoy to Churchill and Stalin 1941–46* (1975), p. 75.

19   26   A. Cadogan, *Diaries* (1972), 398.

19   30   E. Roosevelt, *As He Saw It* (1946), p. 29.

20   13   S. E. Morison, *History of U.S. Naval Operations in World War II,* Vol. 1 (1948), p. 70n.

20   38   W. S. Churchill, *The Second World War,* Vol. III, *The Grand Alliance* (1950), p. 384.

21   8   R. E. Sherwood, *The White House Papers of Harry L. Hopkins,* Vol. 1 (1948), p. 354.

21   14   WSC, *Second World War,* III, p. 385.

22   34   *Time* magazine, August 25, 1941.

22   37   *New York Times,* August 18, 1941.

23   19   Morton, p. 125.

23   27   B. Brooke, *Alarm Starboard* (1982), p. 85.

26   12   R. S. Churchill, *Winston S. Churchill,* Vol. 1 (1966), p. 362.

26   14   Ibid., p. 363.

26   29   Ibid., p. 43.

28   11   W. S. Churchill, *My Early Life* (1930), p. 28.

28   30   *Churchill,* I, *Companion,* II, p. 896.

29   39   *My Early Life,* p. 161.

30   27   *Churchill,* I, p. 407.

31   3   *My Early Life,* p. 191.

31   25   *Churchill,* I, p. 415.

32   4   Ibid., p. 424.

32   29   *Churchill,* II, *Companion,* I, p. 445n.

33   24   T. Morgan, *Churchill, 1874–1915* (1983), p. 278.

33   32   Quoted in E. Longford, *A Pilgrimage of Passion* (1979), p. 388.

SOURCE REFERENCES

Page	Line	
34	5	To his wife, July 28, 1914.
35	5	A. J. Marder, *From Dreadnought to Scapa Flow,* Vol. 1 (1961), p. 253.
35	27	*Spectator,* October 28, 1911.
36	4	WSC, *World Crisis,* I, pp. 118–19.
37	8	R. S. Churchill, *Churchill,* II, p. 629.
38	29	R. Bacon, *The Life of John Rushworth, Earl Jellicoe* (1936), pp. 181–82.
40	9	J. A. Fisher, *Records* (1919), p. 184.
40	17	Kilverstone papers.
40	38	*Churchill,* II, *Companion,* III, p. 1875.
41	8	Foreign Office mss., 800/87.
41	26	*Churchill,* II, *Companion,* III, p. 1492.
45	2	F. Freidel, *F.D.R.: The Apprenticeship* (1952), p. 28.
45	11	*Philadelphia Record,* April 6, 1913, quoted in Freidel, p. 28.
45	13	J. MacGregor Burns, *Roosevelt: The Lion and the Fox* (1957), p. 19.
46	17	N. Miller, *The U.S. Navy* (1977), pp. 239–40.
47	4	*The Roosevelt Letters,* Vol. II, E. Roosevelt ed. (1948), p. 136.
47	15	Quoted in Ibid., p. 143.
47	30	J. P. Lash, *Roosevelt and Churchill 1939–41* (1977), p. 39.
47	34	FDRL HPP Box 93, February 23, 1913.
47	35	London *Times,* April 14, 1945.
48	3	J. Daniels, *The Wilson Era: Years of Peace 1910–17* (1944), p. 124.
48	11	Ibid., p. 125.
48	18	FDRL HPP Box 93, July 1, 1915.
48	27	Ibid., January 28, 1914.
48	36	Freidel, p. 157.
49	2	Burns, p. 51.
49	31	Freidel, p. 192.
50	21	FDRL, HPP Box 93, April 30, 1913.
50	33	FDR *Letters,* II, p. 219.
51	18	*New York Sun,* March 19, 1913, quoted in Freidel, p. 158.
53	5	Freidel, p. 249.
53	28	*Roosevelt and Daniels: A Friendship in Politics,* C. Patrick ed. (1952), p. 27.

THE GREATEST CRUSADE

Page Line
53   32   FDRL Box 93, August 21, 1916.
53   39   FDR *Letters,* II, p. 179.
56   11   Quoted in Freidel, pp. 244–45.
60   7   WSC, *World Crisis,* I, p. 189.
61   13   *Churchill,* II, *Companion,* III, pp. 1987–88.
62   14   WSC, *World Crisis,* I, p. 197.
62   39   R. Hough, *Louis and Victoria* (1974), p. 281.
63   7   WSC, *World Crisis,* I, p. 198.
65   13   *H. H. Asquith Letters to Venetia Stanley,* M. and E. Brock eds.
            (1982), pp. 150–51.
66   33   R. Hough, *The Great War at Sea 1914–18* (1983), p. 195.
66   37   Jellicoe mss. (British Library), September 30, 1914.
67   36   *Asquith-Stanley Letters,* p. 260.
68   6   M. Gilbert, *Churchill,* Vol. III (1971), p. 109.
68   25   Ibid., p. 113.
68   31   *Asquith-Stanley Letters,* p. 260.
68   35   *Morning Post,* October 19, 1914.
69   7   *Churchill,* III, p. 133.
69   7   Ibid.
70   12   *Churchill,* III, *Companion,* I, p. 250.
70   35   *Asquith-Stanley Letters,* p. 290.
71   6   Hough, *Louis and Victoria,* p. 305.
71   18   WSC, *World Crisis,* I, p. 401.
72   2   Marder papers, May 1, 1916.
72   12   Marder, *Dreadnought,* Vol. II (1965), p. 91.
73   12   WSC, *World Crisis,* I, p. 452.
74   15   *The Times,* January 25, 1915.
75   14   *Churchill,* II, p. 526.
75   32   A. Balfour to E. Marsh, September 8, 1911, Balfour mss.
            (British Library).
76   14   R. Bacon, *Lord Fisher,* Vol. II (1929), p. 181.
76   31   *Churchill,* III, *Companion,* I, pp. 45–46.
76   39   Hough, *Great War at Sea,* p. 148.
78   21   *Churchill,* II, p. 95.
79   23   *Churchill,* III, p. 35.
79   26   Ibid., p. 36.

SOURCE REFERENCES

Page	Line	
79	36	Ibid., p. 61.
80	12	Ibid., p. 92.
80	34	*Churchill*, III, p. 165.
81	11	*Asquith-Stanley Letters*, p. 329.
81	17	*Churchill as I Knew Him*, p. 270.
81	23	*Churchill*, III, p. 165.
81	34	Ibid., p. 166.
82	20	*Churchill*, III, *Companion*, I, p. 315.
82	29	Ibid., p. 841.
82	29	*Churchill*, III, p. 167.
83	30	*Churchill*, III, *Companion*, I, pp. 367–68.
84	22	Churchill to Fisher, December 23, 1914, Kilverstone papers.
85	16	*Churchill*, III, p. 260.
85	37	*Churchill*, III, *Companion*, I, p. 471.
86	23	*Churchill*, III, p. 290.
87	22	WSC, *World Crisis*, II, p. 184.
87	31	Asquith, *Memories*, p. 64.
88	5	*Churchill*, III, *Companion*, I, p. 586.
88	15	Ibid., p. 587.
88	27	Asquith, *Memories*, p. 96.
89	6	A. J. P. Taylor, *The First World War* (1963), p. 61.
89	23	WSC, *World Crisis*, II, p. 182.
89	38	Marder, *Dreadnought*, II, p. 236.
90	9	Taylor, p. 61.
92	16	WSC, *World Crisis*, II, pp. 374–75.
92	24	Longford, *Pilgrimage of Passion*, p. 409.
93	1	*Churchill*, III, p. 472.
93	18	Ibid., p. 473.
93	22	Marder, *Dreadnought*, II, p. 289.
94	17	*Portrait of an Admiral*, p. 203.
94	33	*Churchill*, III, *Companion*, I, p. 284.
97	19	FDR *Letters*, II, p. 199.
98	3	Freidel, II, p. 237.
98	7	FDR *Letters*, II, p. 199.
98	13	Ibid., p. 202.

Page	Line	
98	38	FDR private letters, pp. 256–57.
99	9	Ibid., p. 267.
99	15	FDRL Box 30, FDR to Daniels, September 8, 1914.
99	23	Quoted in Freidel, II, p. 260.
99	28	Freidel, II, p. 261.
99	36	Roosevelt and Daniels, pp. 34–35.
100	16	Ibid., p. 25.
101	12	*The Wilson Papers,* Vol. 41, A. S. Link ed. (Princeton, 1983), p. 403.
101	22	Ibid., pp. 189–90.
102	9	Quoted in Freidel, II, p. 274.
102	26	Ibid., p. 287.
102	31	Ibid.
103	11	Ibid., p. 288.
103	15	Daniels to FDR, Daniels mss., quoted in Freidel, pp. 288–89.
103	36	Robbie Burns, *Scots Wha Hae.*
103	38	Freidel, II, p. 301.
104	13	Ibid., p. 302.
105	9	FDR to Frothingham, quoted in Freidel, p. 311.
105	20	Daniels diary, quoted in Freidel, p. 312.
105	26	Freidel, II, 310.
105	38	FDR to Daniels, February 25, 1921, quoted in Freidel, II, p. 313.
106	24	Wilson papers, Vol. 42, p. 457.
107	9	Quoted in Freidel, II, p. 363.
107	33	Ralph Block, *New York Tribune,* quoted in E. K. Lindley, *Franklin D. Roosevelt* (1931), p. 147.
108	11	FDRL HPP, RGIO, Box 14, May 31, 1917.
108	33	To Eleanor Roosevelt, July 19, 1918, quoted in Freidel, II, p. 344.
109	3	Diary, quoted letters, II, p. 303.
109	12	FDRL HPP, PSF83,m John L. McCrea file.
110	17	FDR private letters, pp. 427–28.
110	31	Ibid., p. 429.
111	13	FDR *Letters,* II, p. 312.
111	32	Ibid., p. 389.

SOURCE REFERENCES

Page	Line	
111	39	London *Times,* July 30, 1918.
112	19	FDR private letters, p. 355.
113	4	Burns, p. 66.
113	23	FDRL HPP, Box 93.
113	28	FDR *Letters,* II, p. 445.
113	30	B. Maine, *Franklin Roosevelt: His Life and Achievement* (1938), p. 99.
114	32	Speech at Atlantic City; letters, p. 477.
115	10	Maine, p. 105.
115	27	FDRL HPP, Box 93.
117	9	*Churchill,* III, p. 658.
118	21	Hankey diary, June 5, 1916, Hankey papers.
118	27	*Churchill,* IV, p. 13.
119	34	Ibid., pp. 179–80.
121	4	Quoted in S. Roskill, *Churchill and the Admirals* (1977), p. 74.
122	10	*Churchill,* V, pp. 75–76.
122	23	Peter Kemp to author, September 17, 1984.
122	33	*Churchill,* V, *Companion,* I, p. 243.
123	5	*Churchill,* V, p. 104.
123	17	Beatty papers, quoted in Roskill, p. 78.
125	26	Conversation with Admiral Sir Guy Grantham, July 11, 1984.
125	29	Conversation with Kemp, April 11, 1984.
125	36	Conversation with Sir Clifford Jarrett, June 25, 1984.
126	26	W. S. Churchill, *The Second World War,* Vol. I (1949), p. 325.
127	29	S. King-Hall, *My Naval Life* (1952), pp. 97–98.
128	19	WSC, *Second World War,* I, p. 321.
129	26	Quoted in Roskill, *Churchill,* p. 95.
143	32	*Churchill,* VI, p. 188.
144	38	WSC, *Second World War,* I, p. 465.
145	31	*Churchill,* VI, p. 219.
145	36	Conversation with Jarrett, June 25, 1984.
147	10	*Hansard,* April 11, 1940.
147	21	*Churchill,* VI, p. 235.
147	29	WSC, *Second World War,* I, p. 474.

Page	Line	
148	1	*Hansard,* April 11, 1940.
148	24	Conversation with Martin Gilbert, August 1, 1984.
148	28	*Churchill,* VI, p. 257.
150	32	WSC, *Second World War,* I, p. 460.
151	30	H. Macmillan, *The Blast of War* (1967), p. 72.
151	35	Leo Amery, *Hansard,* May 7, 1940.
153	20	Morison, I, p. xxxiv.
154	22	Ibid., p. xlviii.
155	25	J. MacGregor Burns, *Roosevelt: The Soldier of Freedom* (1971), p. 149.
155	29	FDRL, PPF166, March 2, 1933.
155	38	Ibid., June 22, 1933.
156	31	FDRL, PSF83, Swanson to Roosevelt, June 11, 1934.
156	35	FDRL Swanson papers, June 30, 1937.
157	1	FDRL Roosevelt to Captain Daniel Callaghan, May 10, 1939.
157	33	FDRL Swanson papers.
162	9	WSC, *Second World War,* I, p. 435.
162	13	FDRL HPP Raeder war diary, September 11, 1939.
162	37	J.R.M. Butler, *Lord Lothian* (1960), p. 271.
163	16	Lash, p. 97.
163	22	Henry Morgenthau, quoted in Lash, p. 265.
165	26	*Lord Lothian,* p. 265.
165	29	Ibid., p. 287.
166	7	FDRL HPP U.S. naval attaché's diary, September 24, 1939.
166	10	Roskill, *Churchill,* p. 108.
166	14	*Churchill,* VI, p. 410.
167	29	*Churchill & Roosevelt: The Complete Correspondence,* Vol I, W. F. Kimball ed. (1984), p. 139.
167	30	Lash, p. 130.
168	37	Ibid., p. 156.
169	8	FDRL HPP Frank Knox, PSF 82.
169	22	WSC, *Second World War,* II, p. 357.
169	35	Lash, p. 209.
170	33	*Churchill,* VI, p. 733.
170	38	Lash, p. 134.

SOURCE REFERENCES

Page Line

171   7   London *Times,* October 14, 1940.

173   37   WSC, *Second World War,* II, p. 211.

178   14   Morison, I, p. 27.

178   33   *Churchill,* VI, p. 691.

179   15   Roosevelt to Leahy, June 26, 1941, FDR *Letters,* III, p. 377.

181   2   *Churchill,* VI, pp. 999–1000.

182   19   W. A. Harriman and E. Abel, *Special Envoy to Churchill and Stalin 1941–1946* (1975), pp. 33–34.

182   39   *Churchill,* VI, pp. 1095.

186   15   *The Memoirs of Lord Ismay* (1960), pp. 269–70.

187   30   *Churchill,* VI, pp. 972–73.

189   2   Sherwood, I, p. 435.

191   2   WSC, *Second World War,* III, p. 539.

191   27   Frances Perkins, Oral History Project, Columbia University, quoted in Lash, p. 488.

192   14   FDRL PPF 166, Stark to Roosevelt, October 23, 1941.

193   23   D. Macintyre, *The Battle for the Pacific* (1966), p. 30.

193   38   Sherwood, I, p. 165.

194   5   Ibid., p. 365.

194   20   *The Times,* June 26, 1956.

194   30   *Daily Telegraph,* May 28, 1981.

195   12   *The Alanbrooke War Diaries 1939–1943,* Vol. I, A. Bryant ed. (1957), p. 289.

195   31   *The Times,* February 22, 1966.

196   2   S. E. Morison, *The Two-Ocean War* (1963), p. 581.

196   11   FDRL PPF 8541.

197   2   *Two-Ocean War,* p. 581.

197   14   S. E. Morison, *History of U.S. Naval Operations in World War II,* Vol. IV (1953), p. 82.

197   19   *The Times,* December 16, 1969.

197   32   *Two-Ocean War,* p. 582.

198   36   Kimball, III, p. 118.

199   7   R. G. Albion and R. H. Connery, *Forrestal & the Navy* (1962), p. 127.

199   37   FDRL John L. McCrea file, February 24, 1942.

200   3   Samuel John Stone, *Lyra Fidelium* (1866).

Page	Line	
Page	*Line*	
209	16	J. MacGregor Burns, *Roosevelt,* p. 402.
209	22	FDR *Letters,* III, p. 484.
211	20	Conversation with Jarrett, June 25, 1984.
212	2	Conversation with Admiral Grantham, July 11, 1984.
212	12	*Churchill,* VI, p. 849.
213	34	A. J. Marder, " 'Winston Is Back': Churchill at the Admiralty 1939–40," *English Historical Review.*
214	36	Bryant, *Alanbrooke,* I, p. 215.
215	2	FDRL PPF 8552.
215	29	WSC, *Second World War,* III, p. 551.
216	38	*The Times,* December 27, 1945.
217	7	*Chips: The Diaries of Sir Henry Channon,* R. R. James ed. (1967), p. 190.
217	17	*Sunday Telegraph,* September 23, 1984.
217	23	Conversation with Captain John Litchfield, RN, June 21, 1984.
217	34	Conversation with Kemp, April 21, 1984.
218	19	Jarrett to Marder, September 9, 1973.
219	3	Kemp to author, December 9, 1984.
219	17	Ibid.
219	26	Ibid.
219	35	Ibid.
220	6	Bryant, *Alanbrooke,* Vol. II (1959), p. 56.
220	19	Admiral of the Fleet Viscount Cunningham of Hyndhope, *A Sailor's Odyssey* (1951), p. 641.
221	4	*The Times,* June 30, 1963.
221	14	Admiral Grantham to author, December 21, 1984.
222	8	WSC, *Second World War,* VI, p. 12.
222	38	R. Hough, *Mountbatten: Hero of Our Time* (1980), p. 165.
223	3	Kemp to author, December 9, 1984.
223	28	Conversation with Admiral Grantham, July 11, 1984.
223	32	P. Ziegler, *Mountbatten* (1985), p. 227.
224	17	*Action This Day,* J. Wheeler-Bennett ed. (1968), p. 160.
225	10	*Sailor's Odyssey,* p. 250.
225	20	WSC, *Second World War,* III, pp. 591–92.
225	25	Conversation with Martin Gilbert, August 1, 1984.

SOURCE REFERENCES

Page	Line	
227	15	Bryant, *Alanbrooke*, I, p. 282.
228	26	Kimball, I, p. 286.
228	33	WSC, *Second World War*, III, pp. 587–88.
229	9	Kimball, I, p. 304.
229	20	Ibid., p. 360.
229	27	Ibid., p. 363.
230	7	Ibid., p. 424.
230	27	Ibid., p. 477.
230	35	Ibid., p. 456.
231	6	Ibid., p. 478.
231	21	Ibid., p. 482.
233	19	Kimball, II, p. 167.
234	1	Conversation with Kemp, April 21, 1984.
234	25	Kimball, II, p. 501.
234	36	WSC, *Second World War*, VI, p. 212.
235	2	Ibid., p. 382.
236	31	Kimball, III, p. 38.
237	31	Ibid., p. 195.
237	36	Ibid., p. 376.
238	4	Ibid., p. 388.
238	15	WSC, *Second World War*, VI, p. 289.
238	35	Ibid., p. 297.
239	10	Sherwood, II, p. 41.
239	18	WSC, *Second World War*, VI, p. 299.
239	27	Ibid.
241	12	FDR *Letters*, III, p. 520.
241	18	WSC, *Second World War*, VI, p. 412.
241	35	Ibid., p. 413.
242	26	Bryant, *Alanbrooke*, II, p. 319.
243	7	Sherwood, II, p. 365.
244	4	Ismay, pp. 319–20.

Index

INDEX

INDEX

INDEX

INDEX